# ONCE IN A BLUE MOON ELECTION

## An Entertaining Narrative Guide to Running a Grassroots Campaign

# ONCE IN A
# BLUE MOON
# ELECTION

An Entertaining Narrative Guide to
Running a Grassroots Campaign

Gerry Bowles
and Andrea Bertole

Gerry Bowles
2017

Copyright © 2017 by Gerry Bowles and Andrea Bertole

All rights reserved. This book or any portion thereof may not be reproduced or used in any manner whatsoever without the express written permission of the publisher except for the use of brief quotations in a book review or scholarly journal.

The authors are the sole responsible entities for this work and bear all legal responsibility for the book. The stories, experiences, and the words are the authors' alone. Some identifying details may have been altered by memory or on purpose to protect the privacy of individuals.

First Printing: 2017

ISBN 978-0-692-86113-4

Gerry Bowles
405 Amelia Avenue
Raleigh, NC 27615

gerrybowles@yahoo.com

"It is not the critic who counts; not the man who points out how the strong man stumbles, or where the doer of deeds could have done them better. The credit belongs to the man who is actually in the arena, whose face is marred by dust and sweat and blood; who strives valiantly; who errs, who comes short again and again, because there is no effort without error and shortcoming; but who does actually strive to do the deeds; who knows great enthusiasms, the great devotions; who spends himself in a worthy cause; who at the best knows in the end the triumph of high achievement, and who at the worst, if he fails, at least fails while daring greatly, so that his place shall never be with those cold and timid souls who neither know victory nor defeat."

Theodore Roosevelt

# For those future candidates who plan to make people not special interests their priority.

# Table of Contents

**Section 1: In the Beginning** ................................................................ 1
  **Chapter One - Introduction: Deciding to Run for Office** ............... 1
    The "Call" ........................................................................................ 1
    Nature/Nurture ................................................................................ 1
    Work and Family Background ....................................................... 3
    North Carolina Legislature .............................................................. 3
    2000 North Carolina House Campaign ........................................... 7
    Wake County Citizens for Effective Government ......................... 9
    2006 North Carolina Senate Campaign ......................................... 12
    Motivation .................................................................................... 13
    Family Support ............................................................................. 14
    Favorable Conditions ................................................................... 15
    Reality Check ............................................................................... 16
    Answering the "Call" .................................................................... 16
  **Chapter Two – Getting Started** .................................................... 18
    Filing Requirements .................................................................... 18
    Structuring the Campaign ............................................................ 20
    Caucus Support? ........................................................................... 21
    Campaign Committee .................................................................. 22
    Enlisting Support ......................................................................... 27
    Misunderstandings/Clarifications ................................................ 30
    Listening Tour ............................................................................. 31
    Campaign Message: Education, Transportation, Representation .. 32
    Fundraising Letter ....................................................................... 38
    Campaign Kickoff Fundraiser ..................................................... 41
  **Chapter Three – Strategy** ............................................................. 45
    Choosing Imbalance .................................................................... 45
    The Numbers ............................................................................... 46
    Precinct Focus ............................................................................. 46
    Political Factors Favorable and Unfavorable .............................. 48

**Section 2: Implementing the Strategy** ............................................ 50
  **Chapter Four – Volunteers** ........................................................... 50
    Recruiting Volunteers ................................................................. 51
    Retaining Our Volunteers ............................................................ 59
    Challenges Encountered with Volunteers ................................... 75

**Chapter Five - Canvassing** ................................................................ 77
    2000 Experience ....................................................................... 77
    Improved Scenario for 2006 ..................................................... 78
    Schedule of Canvassing ........................................................... 78
    Walk Lists ................................................................................. 79
    Targeting All Doors .................................................................. 80
    Team Approach ......................................................................... 80
    Canvassing Approach ............................................................... 81
    Database .................................................................................... 86
    Including Event Information .................................................... 86
    Positive Response and Nuggets ............................................... 87
    Canvassing Etiquette ................................................................ 91
    Common Questions .................................................................. 91
    Political Educator ..................................................................... 93
    Combined Canvassing Efforts .................................................. 93
    Literature Drops ....................................................................... 95
    Phone Canvassing .................................................................... 97

**Chapter Six – Events** ........................................................................ 102
    Meet & Greets ........................................................................ 102
    Campaign Kickoff – August 8, 2006 ..................................... 125
    Community Events ................................................................. 129
    Political Forums ..................................................................... 136
    Democratic Party .................................................................... 141
    Conclusion .............................................................................. 153

**Chapter Seven – Special Projects: IACs & Point People** ............ 154
    Issue Advisory Committees (IACs) ....................................... 154
    Point People/Precinct Organization ....................................... 165

**Chapter Eight – Communication** .................................................. 173
    Questionnaires ........................................................................ 173
    Media ...................................................................................... 177
    Internet ................................................................................... 191
    Political Campaign Products .................................................. 212
    Mailings .................................................................................. 221
    Yard Signs .............................................................................. 228

**Chapter Nine – Financial** ............................................................... 236
    Money Matters ....................................................................... 236
    Trying to Play Fund Raising Ball with the Senate Caucus .......... 236
    Consequences of Not Playing Ball ......................................... 243
    Managing the Money ............................................................. 245

    Expenses ............................................................................. 250
    "Certification to Close Committee" ................................... 253
    Wrap Up ............................................................................ 254
**Chapter Ten - Special Interest/Endorsements ........................ 255**
    Explosion of Interest – Questionnaires and Interviews ............. 255
    Endorsements ................................................................... 256
    Newspaper Endorsements ................................................. 260
    Further Disappointments –Expected and Not ........................ 262
    Conclusion ....................................................................... 264

**Section 3: The Election ............................................................... 265**
  **Chapter Eleven – Early Voting ........................................... 265**
  **Chapter Twelve – Election Day ........................................... 271**
  **Chapter Thirteen - Post Election ......................................... 278**

**Section 4 – Conclusion: Post Mortem ........................................ 286**
  **Elections Have Consequences .............................................. 286**
  **Unintended Consequences .................................................... 286**
    Live a More Public Life ..................................................... 286
    Become a Graduate of the School of Politics ......................... 287
    Identified as a Political Expert ............................................ 288
    Effects on the Family ........................................................ 288
    Effects on Friendships ....................................................... 289
  **The Numbers: ..................................................................... 290**
    Voter Turnout .................................................................. 290
    Precinct Strategy Evaluated - Was This the Right Approach? .... 290
    People Raising .................................................................. 294
    Funds Raised & Expenses .................................................. 295
  **What Next? ......................................................................... 298**

# Section 1: In the Beginning

## Chapter One - Introduction: Deciding to Run for Office

### *The "Call"*

I noticed the red light blinking as I came into the house. I was taking a break from raking the last leaves of winter. I listened to the message with interest, a smile, and not too much of a surprise. It was late afternoon on February 27$^{th}$ 2006. Being a keen follower of all things political, I knew that noon of the following day was the filing deadline for public office in the state of North Carolina and thought well you can't get too much closer to that deadline than today. The message from Perry Woods was to please call him as soon as possible. I had an inkling of what he wanted to talk with me about. I had met Perry when I volunteered to help Charles Meeker in what would prove to be his first successful quest to become Raleigh's Mayor in 2001. Perry served as his campaign manager and I was the volunteer coordinator. We had formed a comfortable working relationship during that time and shared a love of history and the political process. We are both admitted political junkies. In returning Perry's call, I reflected that he might be calling in response to an earlier conversation we had had in January.

Some people love the numbers – the data pertaining to voters, party affiliation, and polling information – others, the issues surrounding politics. I have always had an interest in the human angle of the people who hold office. Who *are* these people? What drives them? What shaped them? What are their passions? What in their background led them to be the kind of leader they became? Why have some been embraced by the public while others were not so fortunate? My own road to politics had many influences.

### *Nature/Nurture*

I have a love of history that may well be attributed to a combination of nature and nurture. The genes came from my father. My dad shared my love of history, his passion revolving more around the Civil War, an outgrowth of his childhood exposure to hearing first-hand accounts of Civil War veterans. The environmental influence was multifaceted. I grew up in Williamsburg, Virginia which had been the state's colonial capital. My public school education was steeped in Virginia history (which was pretty much early American history). In addition, I daily walked the same streets that George Washington, Thomas Jefferson and Patrick Henry had traveled. I was also fortunate to have as my 11$^{th}$ grade American history teacher, Raymond Freed. Mr. Freed was a legend in his own time. He imparted the love and appreciation of our American heritage to countless hundreds of students at James Blair High School. After graduation, I nurtured this passion further and went on to attend the College of William and Mary, receiving an AB degree in History and a certificate to teach at the high school level.

In hindsight, I have come to realize that my decision to identify myself as a Democrat can be traced to those early lessons in junior and high school. My first political exposure was as an eighth grader in 1960. Our social studies assignment was to create a bulletin board for each of the presidential candidates. Our team was assigned John F. Kennedy. I still can envision our "Meet Mr. Kennedy" complete with pictures of the future president in his PT 109 ("patrol torpedo" boat) and a picture of him receiving the Pulitzer Prize for his book "Profiles in Courage". I was smitten with his heroism and charisma. It would require a few more years of education and maturation to appreciate his support for policies I believed in.

A few years later while learning about America in the "Great Depression" I was introduced to Franklin Delano Roosevelt. I was captivated with FDR's style, passion and vision for America. I was enthralled with his address before Congress in which he shared that "the only thing we have to fear is fear itself." I loved that he was proactive in the face of the Great Depression recognizing that there was a role for government in providing a safety net for its citizens. I marveled at the alphabet of agencies that were begun to stimulate the economy and provide work and sustenance to our citizens; The CCC (Civilian Conservation Corp), the WPA (Works Progress Administration and the (TVA) Tennessee Valley Authority were ideas that delighted me. Roosevelt was criticized for his radical proposals and for abandoning his "class." My view was that he saved our nation from the voices of fascists and isolationists and more importantly brought people and their government closer together recognizing that people are important to the nation's strength rather than the nation's strength being necessary for the people. The examples of Kennedy's and FDR's leadership and beliefs led to my identifying myself as a Democrat and the idea that government exists to serve people. I never bought into the philosophy of Calvin Coolidge and Herbert Hoover that "the business of America was business" or what's good for General Motors is good for America." My philosophy of governance was inspired in the beliefs of Jefferson, Roosevelt and Kennedy. They all embraced the notion of an informed citizenry with unlimited opportunities. I have always felt that the Democratic Party has this belief as its ideal.

## *Work and Family Background*

I began teaching in the late1960s, a period associated with cultural change. My first three years of teaching American history in Hampton, Virginia coincided with the state's first years implementing an integrated school system. Prior to that, as in my public school experience, white and black children attended separate schools. I embraced this change as I did many of the other movements whose goals were for personal empowerment. This openness to societal transformation was in many ways at odds with my upbringing which followed a more *Leave It to Beaver* traditional 1950s lifestyle. My Dad worked and my Mom ran the house and took care of my sister and me. In like manner, when I met and married my husband, Harry Bowles, we agreed in jest that "he would make the living and I would make the living worthwhile." Harry's work brought us to Raleigh, North Carolina. We had three sons in fast fashion and I for the most part was a stay-at-home mom. The exception came when our youngest, Matthew, entered Kindergarten and all three of our sons were in school. I was hired at Millbrook High School to teach ELP (economics, law and politics) to 4 freshmen classes and an additional world civics course to sophomores. However, at the end of the school year, I found that what I wanted to give to teaching required more time than I could offer when balanced with my family needs.

## *North Carolina Legislature*

In subsequent years, when alternate job opportunities would arise, the passion I felt for teaching was always my litmus test. Unconsciously, I was seeking something that was as fulfilling. One late fall morning in the early

1990s, while sitting at the kitchen table reading the *News and Observer*, Raleigh's newspaper, I noticed that United States Representative Pat Schroeder from the state of Colorado was to be the keynote speaker at the North Raleigh Hilton that day. I decided, on the spur of the moment, to attend. Upon arrival, I discovered a large crowd and recognized only one person, a neighbor. I sought her out and inquired how it was that she came to be there. She explained that she worked at the North Carolina Legislature as an assistant to Representative Ruth Easterling. I was embarrassed at my lack of knowledge of our state legislature. I knew that Raleigh, being the capital city of North Carolina, was the seat of government; but I really didn't follow state politics. I was fascinated by the idea of working at the Legislature and wondered what being a Legislative Assistant entailed.

The following January, on Martin Luther King Jr.'s birthday, I noticed in the paper that Governor Jim Hunt was going to call for a special session of the General Assembly in February. I remember thinking that given the nature of this unscheduled session there might be the need for Legislative Assistants. Still a time when phone books were your go-to guides, I looked up North Carolina State Government in the blue pages to find the number for the Legislature. In my haste to take action, I forgot that it was a state holiday. Nevertheless, I called and someone actually answered. I inquired about the availability of assistant jobs and was asked "House or Senate?" I didn't really have a preference but thought why not the Senate? The information officer gave me the contact name of Janet Pruitt, the Clerk of the North Carolina Senate, and indicated that she would call me.

Indeed, Janet called and we set up an interview. During the interview, I found that the individual Senate and House members selected their own assistants. If the member had no one in mind, then there was a pool of candidates that the General Assembly would supply. In our discussion, we discovered that our sons were in the same high school class. I shared that my background was in education and that I had no legislative experience although I had completed two and a half years of law school. She asked if I knew any senators in the General Assembly. While Janet did not mean this as a test, I felt like a deer in the headlights and drew a blank. Suddenly the light bulb turned on and I thought of Senator Linda Gunter. I didn't know her, but I had followed her race the previous election cycle because she taught American history as I had. Janet didn't know if Linda Gunter's aide was returning for the special session, but she promised to check. Within the week she called and said Senator Gunter wanted to interview me.

When I met with Senator Gunter we connected immediately because of our shared teaching background. She confided that she still found it hard to see herself as a senator. At that time, she didn't fit the stereotypical white male, over 50 profile. She asked me to take a typing time test on a word processor on which I had precious little experience. I sweated bullets – I didn't know how to "save", to "insert," to "delete" or operate the word processor efficiently in other ways (hard to believe now). I was afraid that I had lost my entire test having accidentally hit a button that caused it to disappear. I felt so out of sync. When Senator Gunter returned to the room, she was very encouraging and kind, saying that these computer skills were easily mastered. She offered me the job. Her confidence in my ability to learn was not misplaced. She would later compliment that I was one of the few people who could keep up with her. I would come to discover that she was resented for being hard working. She was a woman, she was assertive, she was passionate, and was not always well received.

I loved the multifaceted nature of the job. I was the face of the office. I interacted with constituents who visited, called or wrote our office. I dealt with the media, handled the Senator's correspondence and her schedule. I served out this six- week special session with enthusiasm and ended up serving with Senator Gunter through the "short session," May through July. Over the summer I helped with her reelection campaign. Little did we know national historical forces – the Republican Revolution of 1994 - would shape the outcomes of many state elections. It was America's introduction to Congressman Newt Gingrich from Georgia. His blueprint for change, which would come to be popularly known as the "Contract with America," catapulted him to national prominence and the Republicans to control of the United States Congress for the first time in 40 years. All the NC Democrats on the November ballot, including Senator Gunter, were swept out of public office in this electoral tidal wave. Even long serving, well respected incumbents were casualties. The North Carolina canary in the coal mine was Congressman David Price who lost to his lesser known opponent, Fred Heiniman. This election had a personal impact on me as well. I was out of a job.

The next legislative session began in January. In February, Janet Pruitt called to ask if I would like to be a "floater," which I came to learn was similar to being a substitute teacher. I accepted. I came to value this position as both enriching and instructive. I was able to experience the diversity in the different offices and appreciate the personal flavor each one had. This opportunity offered an exposure to a broader range of legislative life. During the session, Janet approached me to see if I was interested in taking on another full-time position for a newly elected female Senator, Virginia Foxx, from Banner Elk. I knew that no Democrats had been elected so I questioned whether my political affiliation would present a problem to this Senator. Janet assured me it would not. I was selected because I had demonstrated an ability to work successfully with a proactive, energetic, hard charging, freshman woman. I was hired to work for Senator Foxx for a week so we could both decide whether there would be a comfortable working relationship.

On my first Monday morning, I arrived before Senator Foxx as she had a long commute from western North Carolina. I didn't arrive with any agenda as we had not yet had a conversation so I just proceeded as I had done for Senator Gunter. When I was retrieving the weekend messages from the answering machine, I listened to one of the most bigoted, hateful calls from a constituent that I had encountered heretofore. I was concerned what Senator Foxx's reaction would be. What if this was her cousin – did she agree with these views? Upon relaying the message, I was relieved at her comment "that little Nazi called again." She explained "I'm conservative, but I am not crazy." This response sealed the deal – I felt certain we could work together. I stayed with her for the remainder of the session. In considering her current extreme right wing positions as Congresswoman representing North Carolina's $5^{th}$ District, I doubt this would be the case now.

This experience was my first taste of partisan politics. While Senator Foxx and I worked well, the atmosphere in the Legislature itself was different. Unlike my last experience, I was aware of being surrounded entirely by Republican members and staff, particularly being located in a Republican wing of the Legislative building. While everyone was very polite and nice, cordial and welcoming, because of my party affiliation I still felt a sense of awkwardness amongst some members of the Republican Caucus. I believe Senator Foxx was aware of this situation and suspect she was receiving some grief from her colleagues. She kept me on for the rest of the session but with the next election she brought in a registered Republican to assist her.

Once more I was out of a job. The good news for me was this election produced new employment opportunities in that many Democrats were elected to office. Janet Pruitt called to ask if I would like to work for a freshman Democrat, Senator Jim Phillips. He was a freshman in name only. He had served as a congressional staffer to North Carolina Representative Steve Neal. When Neal retired from Congress, Jim Phillips retired as well. By his own admission he didn't play golf and wasn't ready to sit around, and after painting his entire house he offered himself as a candidate for the Senate to represent Davidson County. During my job interview, he posed a practical question – how long would you take to respond to a letter from a constituent? I thought to myself, is this a trick question? My answer was that I would respond as soon as I got the letter. He nodded and said I was hired. Once I was on board, my curiosity got the better of me and I asked what the other applicants had replied. An experienced candidate had indicated she would probably take 2-3 days if she got to it. It was an inspiration to work for Senator Phillips. His election in a Republican dominated area was a testament to his integrity and character. One of the comments Senator Phillips shared with me that has had a lasting impact revolved around his approach to office. He noted that he was in his 60's and that the Legislature was not a career move. He was not interested in starting a dynasty, which freed him to vote his heart and to vote for what in his mind was the right thing to do.

## *2000 North Carolina House Campaign*

Working in Senator Phillips' office, I was back again in the Democratic wing of the Legislative building and interacting with like-minded colleagues. I was invited to join a fellow Legislative Assistant as a guest at the monthly Democratic Women of Wake County luncheon. In becoming more involved with this group, I became aware of the distinct localities within Raleigh. Many members had not been to North Raleigh at that time. I was one of the few people at these luncheons who worked downtown, but lived outside the city limits. I was astounded to think there were people making laws about an area they knew little about. One case in point involved a piece of legislation that would have direct impact on my North Raleigh community. There were three legislators crafting policy for an area that they had never visited. They kept speaking of North Raleigh as though it was a foreign country. I was amazed and angered by their dismissive attitude. There was an arrogance among a significant number of legislators who seemingly felt no compulsion to understand the variety of needs within all the areas they represented.

There was no identified Democratic leader who represented the northern area of Wake County at that time. Folks would come up to me in the halls of the Legislature and ask "aren't you a Democrat and don't you live in North Raleigh - why don't you run for the House? Someone needs to raise the flag." One of the results of the 1994 Republican landslide was the election of Russell Capps to represent this area. Even though he had been successfully reelected, it was my belief that he didn't represent the viewpoint of most of my neighbors and was one further example of the disconnect between the Legislature and the people living in this community. I found myself always having to defend my neighbors, who more closely identified themselves as business Republicans rather than social conservatives.

To my thinking, Capps' viewpoints on social issues were extreme and the national acclaim he had received for his stands on evolution were truly concerning. I was troubled also by his trumpeting the importance of family values when his own family track record was flawed to say the least. Capps' name was also synonymous with the Wake County Taxpayers Association and much of his focus was about cutting taxes. Furthermore, he was instrumental in the defeat of the 1999 Wake County Schools bond. An independent group had done a survey in which Capps had been voted the least effective North Carolina legislator during the previous session of the General Assembly. To his favor was his deep baritone voice which sounded reassuring to the voters and the support of the "Religious Right" and those who favored reduced government spending.

Up to this point, I had not really seen myself as a player in the political arena but merely as an interested spectator. I followed politics like others followed sports. The result of these numerous discussions about the mindset of my community was the decision to throw my hat into the political ring. In the summer of 1999, sixteen months out from the November 2000 election, I laid the foundation of my first, albeit unsuccessful, campaign for election to state office. While I had run for the

Wake County School Board in 1996, I hadn't run at the state level of government before and my 2000 campaign informed much of my thinking when running for the Senate 6 years later. In between I did take an initial, quick swing at the NC Senate seat in 2002, but I did so just 2-3 months before Election Day due to the loss of my mother and care for my father over the summer. My heart and soul were not truly committed to seeking office on that occasion.

## *Wake County Citizens for Effective Government*

One of the things that is hard when you develop a community around an election, as I did with the House race in 2000, is the aftermath to a losing effort. If you haven't won, you and your supporters are left saying "what will we do now?" In some respect part of the "lost" feelings is a result of not being part of a group with a common purpose. People say "we will carry this forward" but there isn't the same magnetic pull that a campaign provides to keep everyone moving in the same direction. After my November loss, a friend hosted a December "Thanks for the Memories" party to gather together those who had been supportive in the campaign and to thank them for their help. All who had given time and/or money were invited. In addition to offering people a chance to see one another again (friendships were made during the campaign) this get together also provided a chance to share reflections on what could be done to take the energy and interest from the campaign and keep people engaged. In my 2000 campaign, I had identified one of my goals as being for effective government and I decided that if folks still felt strongly enough, I would find a way to get them together again in the New Year. This motivation combined with the thank you party discussions planted the seed for the start of the *Wake County Citizens for Effective Government*.

In mid-January of 2001, I followed up with the folks who had indicated an interest in continuing an involvement in the political process in some capacity. I invited folks to my home on January 30$^{th}$ for a brainstorming session to see what form such an undertaking could take. From this meeting of approximately 18-20 attendees, the *Wake County Citizens for Effective Government* (WCCEG) was formed. In choosing this name, we wanted something encompassing. Our experience from the campaign was that people do care about a variety of issues, but it was difficult for them to find nonpartisan settings in which to educate themselves. We wanted to provide a venue where people could just come and listen about different topics, be anonymous, or ask questions, and in all cases feel engaged. The stated vision for the group was as follows:

> *"The purpose of the organization is to advance the cause of progressive government, which has as its mission the improvement of quality of life for all Wake County citizens. A nonprofit, nonpartisan organization, Wake County Citizens for Effective Government provides information and an opportunity for dialogue on issues that impact Wake County citizens, through monthly forums held on the third Thursday of the month. 7:30-9:00pm at Borders Books (Strickland & Six Forks). Membership dues are $10 annually* [no one had to be a member to come, but money raised was to be used for our mailings]"

At the heart of our group was a Margaret Mead quote "never doubt that a small group of thoughtful, committed citizens can change the world, indeed it's the only thing that ever has."

At this first meeting several of us volunteered to take on roles to help the operation of the group:

Gerry Bowles, president
Officers: Bill Robinson, VP
Charles Keeling, Secretary/Treasurer
Susan Grigg, Membership
Diana Zandt & Nancy Gentry, Program Development
Nell Whitlock, Publicity and Media Relations

The first program of the WCCEG was held in March 2001. We had selected a bookstore, *Borders,* now closed, which was located in "North Raleigh" as we felt it was important to start this venue in the NC house district in which I had run. We also wanted something with the feel of a "community center," like the country store of past days. Furthermore, we wanted a setting where we might be able to get local news coverage, where folks could drop in without discomfort, and that wasn't identified as Republican or Democrat. Sadly, the nonpartisan nature of this group was not well received by some of the Democratic Party officials. The bookstore had the perk of containing a café and the definite advantage of not costing us anything to use the space. With the blessing of the store manager, we were included in *Borders'* regular calendar of events for the 3rd Thursday of the month.

In deciding on the program for our first meeting, we wanted something interesting and timely. In early January, I had attended a breakfast sponsored by the Common Sense Foundation - "an activist think-tank that works closely with grassroots groups in North Carolina to help make their voices heard" - and met the founder, Chris Fitzsimon. I invited him to be our first guest speaker and to give us an overview of the challenges facing the newly elected General Assembly and to be available to take questions from those attending. He immediately answered yes. We had a place, a time, a speaker, and a topic. We found that a great headline could go far in generating interest so we titled the first program, *"Show Me the Money: Budget, Taxes, and the Lottery"* à la the movie *Jerry McGuire*.

Given that our group had very little money, we started trying to think of ways to inexpensively publicize our organization and its programs. Nell Whitlock, who had been my media volunteer for the 2000 campaign and who had segued on to handle this role for the WCCEG, was key to publicizing the meetings. She sent out press releases to the media contacts she had created during the campaign; all the local TV stations and newspapers, emphasizing the citizen involvement nature of the group. As mentioned, we also were included in the monthly *Borders* newsletter, which was printed 6 weeks in advance thus necessitating our juggling a couple programs at a time. We also photocopied fliers of upcoming events to leave at the information/checkout counter in *Borders*. For this first meeting, I sent out letters to my campaign contacts about the formation of WCCEG and the details of our March program.

In terms of preparing for this kickoff and subsequent programs, the WCCEG decided to have a banner made for the group – it was huge, blue and red with white type. We were fortunate to be given the banner as a gift from a former member of my campaign committee. Prior to the start of each program at *Borders* we hung the banner, set up, and I wiped down the tables upon which we placed our fliers and agendas which included the WCCEG's mission statement, a membership and topics of interest form, and a flier announcing the following month's program. I arranged the tables and chairs in a semi-circle around the microphone. For each program, we had no idea who or how many people would come and at some of the future events we had to have folding chairs for the overflow of attendees. We had a sign-in sheet for attendees and at our first program we had about 25 people. Though late due to confusion as to which *Borders* the meeting was to be held in (there were two *Borders Books* on Six Forks Road), Chris Fitzsimon was well received and lively discussion ensued. This first program started a 4 year run by the WCCEG with subject matters including education, the media, triangle transit, The Patriot Act, the Second Amendment and candidate forums for the City of Raleigh, the NC Legislature and the Wake County School Board

During the early years I had help with setting up and conducting our monthly meetings. As time passed and others were less engaged in the leadership of the group, responsibility for the monthly forums began to rest solely on my shoulders. In early June of 2005, Gail Christensen, who was serving on our board, emailed an SOS to our membership indicating that I needed help with our meetings if we wanted to keep the organization functioning. Although there was positive support to keeping the group together there were not enough volunteers to take on the assignments necessary to maintain our monthly forums.

Many viewed my involvement in the WCCEG as a way to get back into the political game. They thought I had created this "baby" not because it had merit on its own accord, but rather to serve as a vehicle to get elected down the road and to keep my name before the public. While my experiences in running this group undoubtedly benefited me in my 2006 campaign in terms of building relationships with people in North Raleigh and honing key organizational skills, I viewed it for the lovely child it was and not as a front for political ambition.

## *2006 North Carolina Senate Campaign*

In February of 2006, listening to Perry's message, I reflected on these past experiences. The month before, I had called Perry to see if he knew of a Democrat planning to run to represent North Raleigh in the State Senate. Perry had witnessed my organizational abilities during Charles Meeker's mayoral run. In addition, I knew he understood and shared my belief in the value of grassroots campaigns through our conversations while canvassing together in South Carolina for John Edwards for President in 2004.

Furthermore, Perry had mentioned having a friend in Washington who worked with the Democratic National Committee who could access the numbers which are used to assess electoral viability. I had a strong sense Perry would be honest with me and that any conversation we had would be confidential. What I didn't know when I called him was that he had just started a new job. He had been a freelance "political operative" in our previous encounters and I assumed that he still was. However, he was now employed by the North Carolina Democratic Senate Caucus as a Deputy Director. Part of his current job description was to recruit candidates to run for the Senate from across the state.

## *Motivation*

This call to Perry was the result of ruminations and reflections about where I wanted to place my energies in the coming New Year. One of the possibilities, that repeatedly captured my imagination, was a further attempt to seek elected office. I felt disturbed by the proliferation of groups whose definition of "family values" were narrow and non-inclusive. This "movement" by the "Religious Right" (which I felt to be neither religious nor right) was potentially dangerous to civil public discourse and the political process and was an affront to my belief system. It was a force to be reckoned with and one in which there was little allowance for negotiation or compromise. I consider myself a Christian but I prefer to take direction from the prophet Micah whose response to the question, "what does the Lord require of you" is to "do justice, love mercy and walk humbly with the Lord your God." Religion was not to be used as a wedge to divide people, nor as a club to bludgeon them.

Furthermore, contrary to my understanding of the constitution and the separation of church and state, the behaviors of these groups led me to worry that people of good faith might be marginalized if they didn't share the opinions of these groups. I have my own strong personal beliefs but recognize that others of equally strong faith may hold divergent views. My fears were born out in a personal way through an incident at the Y.M.C.A. In updating its definition of "family" for membership requirements, the Y had incurred the wrath of a newly formed group, *Called 2 Action*. My husband, Harry, was a member of the Y's board that created this new policy. Members of *Called 2 Action* wrote scathing letters to the *News and Observer* filled with half- truths and innuendos about this policy. Consequently, some members of the Y withdrew their financial support. I reasoned that if *Called 2 Action* could take on and harm a fellow Christian organization, what might they do to other groups? I had observed the growth and the influence that this group had in our community. Opinions once viewed as "kooky" came to be acceptable. Ironically enough during this attack on the Y's policy, Harry received an invitation to join this group. The names of board members were printed on the letterhead and included the name of my representative for the State Senate. A favorite quote of mine that I found applicable was "evil flourishes when good men do nothing." In view of the potential harm that might affect the body politic and our community, I felt "called to action." I had the time and the wherewithal to pull together a campaign and a network of supporters to speak to these issues.

## *Family Support*

Before I made the decision to run, I needed to speak with my family. The timing of such a conversation may vary amongst individual candidates, but for me, it worked best to check out the political scene first to see the viability of being elected to office. Whatever the timing, you want to be sure you have family support which doesn't mean all members are necessarily politically inclined or active, but if they have any reservations about the prospect of a campaign, those concerns need to be addressed early on because family support is invaluable. I knew firsthand one of the consequences of losing an election is its impact on the family. In my case, Harry seemed to take my loss in 2000 more to heart than I did. We had agreed, if there was to be a further race, certain criteria would have to be different. One of his favorite adages pertains to the definition of insanity, "doing the same thing over and over and expecting a different result." Having assessed that many factors significant to the district were more favorable this time, I broached the possibility of my throwing my hat in the ring once again. He was initially quiet and left the room. When he returned he asked me if I was not bothered that people might think of me as a loser based on the results of the 2000 election. I looked at him and said "Harry, just because you lose doesn't make you a loser." I continued "I am not a sacrificial lamb on this though I know it will be a challenge." After a bit of reflection, Harry acknowledged that just as fishing was his bliss, politics was mine. He recognized that I needed to pursue the challenge in the same way that he continued to go fishing despite the many times he returned home empty handed.

## *Favorable Conditions*

In 2000, as a part of the 10- year redistricting mandated by the state constitution, the district in which I lived was redrawn to include more precincts with a Democratic voting history. In addition, a large portion of the growth impacting Wake County had taken place in my community and many of the new residents had registered as Unaffiliated (neither Democrat nor Republican). The statistics showed for my district 22% of the voters registered as Unaffiliated, 42% registered as Republican, and 37% registered as Democrat. As such, it was viewed as being on a bubble (not easily predictable), which is very similar to being a swing district. Such voters are not tied to either party, but can be reached by an effective campaign. In other words, though favorable to Republicans, the race could be won by a Democrat given the right issues.

Having been a casualty six years earlier of "straight ticket" voting by Republicans in my area when President George W. Bush topped the ballot for reelection, I was mindful of current national events creating a different voting atmosphere. As a result of the situation on the ground in Iraq, President Bush was losing popularity. In addition, the upcoming election in North Carolina was to be, in political parlance, a "blue moon election" in that there was neither a president nor a governor at the top of the ballot. Indeed, the Senate position I was considering would get top state billing on the ballot. Furthermore, it seemed that the incumbent, Neal Hunt, was not yet entrenched as he had only served one year of a two-year term.

Having these favorable factors for running in mind, I wanted to bounce my interest in elected office off someone involved in politics but without an agenda, whom I trusted, respected and with whom I had a personal relationship. In addition to Perry Woods, I decided to consult with Bill Robinson. I had met Bill when I was running for the State House in 2000. He was new to the area and lived in my neighborhood. He previously had worked in Washington, D.C. with Teddy Kennedy and within the Carter administration. His political activism was long standing from his early days as a volunteer in the first Peace Corps. We shared a love of "retail politics" where everyone met is a potential voter. Bill talked politics with everyone and to him, indeed, life is a campaign. Bill's response to my query was "knowing the district like you do, go for it."

## *Reality Check*

In early January, I contacted Perry to get his thoughts about my desire to stand for election. Perry was less enthusiastic about my running in this race. The State Senate was securely in the hands of Democrats so there was less urgency to turn the seat for my district from Republican to Democrat. The Caucus' focus was on the vulnerable Senate seats held by incumbent Democrats. He was candid in explaining that the numbers of registered voters –Democrat versus Republican - were improving but it was still not the most favorable district for a Democrat to be elected. These numbers would be one of the determining factors in assessing where the Caucus would provide monetary support. While some districts within the state would certainly receive support and others would most definitely not, my prospective district was borderline because the make-up of registered voters was constantly changing due to continued high growth. Perry knew I was not a person with "deep pockets" nor one who had strong ties to those in the area whose pockets were. He knew that my prospective opponent had already lent his campaign $100,000. In addition, Perry explained that the Senate Caucus was looking for younger candidates with financial connections who had paid their dues.

I had asked for honesty, and I received it. On the bright side, Perry admitted that it would bring him great joy to see me run if the district was more favorable. With my profile – unblemished record, honest woman, wife, mother, community activist – he saw the potential to run a strong campaign against the incumbent. I asked if he knew of anyone else interested in running for this office and he said no. In the end, he offered the possibility that if no one else was available to take on this challenge, then we might be able to do business focusing on a small budget campaign with a large focus on grassroots support. He said the Caucus was trying to recruit for this district but if in February, on the last day of filing, no one else had come forward, then he could see me taking this campaign on.

## *Answering the "Call"*

Six weeks later, with Perry's call at the $11^{th}$ hour, I anticipated that I might need to make a quick decision about running. I knew my experience in campaigning for state office would serve me well by having an established network of supporters to call upon. From the time of Perry's call to

Election Day was approximately 8 months, half the time I had available for my first campaign for state office. As I pictured this campaign, the image that came to mind was of being invited to go to the prom with the quarterback, knowing you are not his first choice, but at least you get to go and you have the expectation you will be treated well. With one call, my scenario proved true. I couldn't resist having some fun with this situation. My first question to Perry was "how many people have turned you down?" He acknowledged "there have been a couple." I pressed further for the names and their rationale for declining. I was satisfied with his explanation that their reasons were personal and tied to family concerns rather than potential electability. Unlike how I usually operate, I decided to take advantage of the potential leverage the circumstances presented. Teasingly, I inquired "so what's in it for me?" After all, I thought, I am dealing with the quarterback here. In the past I hadn't had an escort, so there was some status to being invited this time by the quarterback. I thought, even though we both know we are not a couple, "Am I going to get a corsage? Will he dance with me all night?" Though Perry did not promise monetary support from the Caucus, he established the parameters for receiving such. He did promise to pay my filing fee – I assume the check is still in the mail. The reality became that I went to the prom but I paid for my flower and was left on my own for much of the evening. Still, I came close to becoming the prom queen on my own merit.

# Chapter Two – Getting Started

## *Filing Requirements*

I planned to meet Perry at the Wake County Board of Elections the morning of the following day, as noon that day was the deadline for filing. I had some concerns that someone not known to the Caucus had planned to file, but was assured that was not the case. It being the final chance for candidates to declare their intention to run for office, I was mindful that the local paper, the *News and Observer*, might have a reporter on site and as such was prepared with my reasons for running if asked, knowing that as soon as you file you are part of the public domain. With the late nature of my decision, I felt uncomfortable that I hadn't been able to give a heads up to friends.

My first order of business was to take care of the two requirements the state has established to have your name on a ballot: paying a filing fee and determining if you will need a treasurer. You can opt out of having a treasurer and filing reports if you promise to limit your campaign spending to not more than $4000 for a primary or $10,000 in a general election. I had the fee ($218) and I decided my anticipated budget would require a treasurer. Fortunately, within weeks this position was filled. After meeting that morning with the very helpful and professional folks at the Wake County Board of Elections, who walked me step-by-step through the further requirements for larger budget campaigns, it became obvious that the job of treasurer would be complex and time consuming, a challenging job for a professional, let alone a volunteer, as I would be seeking. I left that day with reams of paperwork to complete, including the need to name the campaign committee and establish a checking account.

The second order of business was to announce my candidacy in a more personal manner. The timing of this announcement can be a strategic decision for many candidates. There is a school of thought that it shows strength and commitment to be the first to file with the added benefit of potentially deterring others from doing so. Of course, given the last minute circumstances of this campaign, I was last to the gate. Back in 1999, when I was considering running for the House, I was concerned there might not be enough interest in my campaign. I received some helpful advice from Senator Phillips in answer to my question "how do you start?" He suggested first sending a letter to *everyone* I knew (not just close friends and family) telling them of my intent to run for office, my reasons for doing so, and a request for their monetary and volunteer support. If I received monetary response from at least 5% of those I notified, then I would be in a good place. I felt this approach would offer a fair gauge. If my friends and family didn't respond in a positive fashion, then what would the chances be that people who didn't know me would respond any better. In July of 1999, I sent out my letter and I came home to find my mailbox filled with response cards sharing enthusiastic replies and offering help. The financial support received far exceeded the 5% litmus test.

This time around, I was less concerned about having enough support to run because I had been asked to file. However, following in the spirit of prior campaigns, I wished to gauge interest and enthusiasm for my candidacy. I proceeded to send out an e-mail notice to friends and acquaintances I had worked with on past campaigns and on other volunteer undertakings. I reported I would be forming a committee to help in this new campaign and I would be grateful for their involvement. One of the first replies came from Gail Christensen who had been involved most recently with me in the Wake County Citizens for Effective Government and who indicated she would be happy to serve as my treasurer. I was hugely relieved!

With Gail by my side, I tackled satisfying the remaining state requirements for running a campaign. As relative novices, we arranged to meet with a staff member of the State Board of Elections. New to the role of treasurer, Gail had concerns about proper accounting procedures. Ever fresh in both of our minds was the specter of former North Carolina State Agriculture Commissioner, Democrat Meg Scott Phipps. She was serving several years in Federal prison for extortion, mail fraud, and conspiracy in relation to improper fund raising methods. She had financed part of her campaign by promising a vendor success with their State Fair bid, in return for a donation. One of the ramifications of this crime was the passage of stricter campaign finance regulations that required more complex accounting and more details in identifying individual contributors.

I was delighted to discover our contact at the State Board was Jason Schraeder, someone with whom I had a personal connection as he had volunteered in my 2000 House campaign. I was particularly grateful to have someone to whom I could safely ask "stupid" questions. As this Board of Elections was short staffed, we couldn't count on an immediate response to clarifications we might need. Many employees were involved in providing information about Jim Black, North Carolina's Speaker of the House, who was under investigation for a variety of offenses which included fund raising improprieties. One such allegation involved the transfer of money stuffed in a paper bag to the speaker from a campaign lobbyist in the restroom of a Charlotte IHOP. Cognizant of this ongoing investigation and worried about any innocent bookkeeping errors that we might make, Gail and I used humor to convey our concerns. Our running joke with Jason was to put our hands out in the handcuff position and explain that as "orange was not our color," we would not look good in prison clothing! Jason reassured us that we would not be hauled off for a minor mistake. The question would be one of intent. As with the IRS, we might be fined for making an error but not be sent to jail. We didn't even want a fine as we knew our campaign would be operating on a shoestring. While there was an added comfort in knowing Jason previously, being able to identify someone at the State Board of Elections to contact any time we had questions was invaluable.

We left the meeting with Jason with a "to do" list in hand. Our next appointment was to open a campaign account at the bank. Keeping in mind campaign regulations, we wanted to choose a name for the account that would be simple, knowing this name would be used with each contribution. When supporters wrote a check, would "Campaign to Elect Gerry Bowles" or "Gerry Bowles for NC Senate" be better? We opted for the latter as it seemed more specific. I chose to use my personal bank even though I had concerns at the possibility of confusion between my personal and campaign accounts. I would always take care when making deposits that the proper account was used. Having a relationship with your banker is helpful in keeping things straight.

## *Structuring the Campaign*

Within days, in early March, Gail and I met with Perry, serving in his new role as the liaison with the North Carolina Senate Caucus, to strategize about the campaign. At the meeting, I had my first inkling of how valuable Gail would become to my campaign. I recognized in Gail a fire for politics similar to my own. Both she and I were making notes, and I sensed that she, like me, was loving the whole learning process. It's so seldom that one can talk politics and everyone at the table knows the same references, just as some people might talk sports. Perry, Gail and I were all political junkies.

We asked Perry to describe the steps needed to structure the campaign. In a straightforward manner, he outlined that we needed to:

- get a campaign committee together;
- find a campaign manager;
- decide on the message that would answer who I was and why I was running;
- send out a fund raising letter to potential supporters to acquire funds to move things forward;
- and to begin planning my campaign kickoff fundraiser.

I was familiar with these steps from my previous run for state office, but it was helpful to have the process refreshed.

## *Caucus Support?*

Perry described that all campaigns are driven by three variables:

*money, time, and people*

Ideally you have a balance between each. Perry reiterated the steps needed for my campaign to receive monetary support from the Caucus. The first step would be to raise $30,000 by June. Next I would need to give the Caucus $8,000 of this amount to conduct a poll which would be used to determine the issues that were important in my district and to assess my name recognition among constituents. At this point the Caucus would weigh the viability of my electability. So, even if I completed these steps, I was not assured of their support. Perry further indicated that I needed to have a campaign manager who would provide a plan of action for the campaign and who would provide weekly reports to the Caucus. Caucus support, in other words, did not come without strings. My reaction was "there goes my control." I knew that money was not going to be my strength. I was mindful that my opponent had already invested $100,000 of his own money and could easily tap into more and that any big move to raise money on my part would "escalate the war."

I never went into a race thinking that I could not win. I always knew I had challenges. I am not a masochist, but I prefer to look at the "what ifs." What if all registered Democrats voted! I was cognizant of the numbers but allowed for the possibility of getting votes from those who had become disengaged, for example, those who hadn't voted in the past because no one spoke to their heart, disenchanted Republicans, and business Republicans alarmed by the evangelical influence in the party. I was not uninformed, just hopeful and certainly not cynical. I told Perry that I was not naïve about money and numbers being a focus of campaigns but I was choosing to do things a different way, with a greater focus on people and time. I just wanted assurance from Perry that even if my campaign did not receive monetary support from the Caucus that he not be dismissive of us because of this choice. I knew my time would be better spent in making contact with people, raising numbers of supporters, rather than on the phone raising money. In my experience, those with the funds to offer a large contribution to my campaign were cautious in doing so due to the relatively unfavorable demographics of registered Democratic voters in the area. Perry's advice was more conventional. He wanted me to spend the time raising money upfront so that I would have the funds to do targeted mailings to get the people's vote. My thought was that in this money contest, I was the David and my opponent the Goliath. I only had an eight-month window of time and I needed to mobilize my network and go door-to-door to get votes, not money. It was not to trivialize the need for money, but to recognize my campaign's relative strengths.

## *Campaign Committee*

My hopes for a people focused campaign seemed affirmed by the great response I had to my initial email announcement. In addition to Gail, I had favorable response from a wide variety of friends from near and far. In the follow-up to their interest in joining my team, I organized the campaign using the same principles I had learned from my work with a variety of groups including my church, Parent Teacher Associations at three different schools, and the YMCA. Uppermost in my thinking, was the notion to involve and include people in the political process who had felt excluded in the past. Membership on the committee was never limited to those who first responded. With each step along the way, I welcomed supporters to take a role in the campaign if interested.

My definition of Committee may have been different from many of the more traditional campaigns. Whereas I had a core group of about 19 members, my committee was ever growing and evolving. It included folks met while campaigning door-to-door, while in the grocery store, while pumping gas, and while eating baklava at one of my regular eating spots. Subsequently, I added folks from book clubs, my dance group, my neighborhood, the Democratic Women and Men of Wake County, and Wake County Citizens for Effective Government. While there were specific roles I asked members to fill, I was more interested in obtaining their ideas and feedback about the campaign and its direction on an ongoing basis. I was building a team. As the candidate I was the captain and just one member of a larger team. Victory required that other teammates carry the ball forward as well.

Many books have been written about the how to's of structuring a campaign and the responsibilities of roles like the campaign manager, volunteer coordinator, fundraiser, and treasurer. The book I consulted that fit best with my approach and which offered the most straightforward practical guidelines was *How To Win A Local Election, Revised: A Complete Step-by-Step Guide* by Judge Lawrence Grey (1999). While many may be fortunate enough to have people in mind to fill these positions before starting their campaign, I began this race, as I had with my others, with only the commitment of a treasurer. The other positions were filled, many by novices to the political process, as the campaign evolved. I found these individuals often had a more realistic view of what the average person was thinking in contrast to those folks who lived and breathed politics. As I involved people in my committee, I considered their strengths and tried to determine their interest in taking on specific roles. Uppermost in my mind, when building the team, was to seek out people with high emotional IQ. As the captain and candidate, I knew I was going to encounter many challenges during the campaign and that my team would be my main support network. I wanted a group to share the journey who could appreciate the foibles of human nature and idiosyncrasies of the personalities we would meet on the campaign trail. I valued a positive attitude knowing that negative energy can be deadly to a campaign. At the end of the day, I was potentially going to be spending more time with this group of individuals than with my own family and I wanted to feel comfortable with them all. The specific roles staffed in this campaign were treasurer, campaign manager, volunteer coordinator, and events coordinator. What proved to be elusive were volunteers to fill the roles of media relations coordinator and fundraiser.

## *Treasurer - Reprise*

As I mentioned earlier, I was so fortunate to have Gail Christensen as my treasurer. In addition to being ethical, organized and detail oriented, she was good humored about the increasingly demanding quarterly report requirements. Our system of recording funds was somewhat tedious. I made a photocopy of every contribution the campaign received, no matter how small, so I would have a sense of funds on hand, so I could make judgments about expenditures, and have a record of the person who had donated the money. For "in kind" donations, such as food, beverage, and entertainment provided at events, Gail and I would estimate the monetary value and note this amount for our records. In addition to providing a paper trail for the Board of Elections, if ever it was required, I used this information to send thank you notes, to update my database of people involved in the campaign, and to remind myself of recent contributors so I would not seek funds from the same person too soon. I would then pass this information along to Gail to include in her treasurer's reports.

Not only was Gail invaluable in the more traditional duties ascribed to a treasurer, she was also a huge asset as a liaison with the State Board of Elections in ensuring we adhered to various regulations. Something as simple as interpreting the "paid for by" intentions of the regulations for yard signs required a phone call or two as we were unsure if we needed to cite Dorothy (Gerry) Bowles, NC Senate Campaign, or some other designation. The last thing we wanted was to expend the funds for signs that failed to comply to the rules. The minutia was overwhelming as illustrated by the following phone reply from a Board staff member to Gail:

> April 10,
> *You are NOT required to put any "paid for by...." on any MAILINGS under 500. You are NOT required to put any "paid for by..." on the regular size yard signs (smaller than about 3' x 4'). You ARE required to put "paid for by..." on fliers, palm cards, and even your business card (the staff member suggested that if you have these already printed, buy a stamp with the phrase on it and stamp the back of your business cards). The phrase must*

> contain the COMMITTEE NAME that is used in your statement of organization. Not just Gerry Bowles. Please look at your statement and that is exactly what you may use. Is it Dorothy (Gerry) Bowles NC Senate? Is it Committee to Elect Dorothy (Gerry) Bowles? The size is important. The "paid for by..." phrase must take up 5% of the size of the item (palm card, business card, etc.) or be in 12 point type - whichever is larger.

The job required advanced computer skills. Thankfully, in addition to her own expertise, Gail had the help of her husband Alfred, an IBM computer guru! In preparing the monthly financial report, Gail and Alfred spent considerable time working out glitches in the Board of Elections' provided software. We were fortunate that our Board of Elections was close by so that Gail could drop in for assistance.

Gail affirmed that she received good training from the Board, though she was surprised to be instructed to get all reports in on time, even if they were wrong! In addition to technical expertise, Gail's passion and enthusiasm were huge assets to the campaign and to me personally. It was important for me to have a personal relationship with my treasurer, rather than having a "hired gun."

### *Campaign Manager*

The proverbial wisdom shared at the campaign workshops I had previously attended was that each campaign needed a campaign manager and that a candidate who managed his or her own campaign was like an attorney who represented himself in court; he had a fool for a client. I acknowledged the wisdom, but I never had the good fortune to have an identified manager in my earlier campaigns. Different aspects of that role were filled by a number of people, but, in reality, I was the manager. I could have hired a campaign manager through the North Carolina State Senate Caucus, but in addition to conserving my funds, I felt that these individuals would not be the best fit for my style of campaign. From what I had observed, they had to adhere to certain Caucus requirements, with a strong focus on numbers whether they were contributions, phone calls, contacts etc. What seemed to be less important was the human interaction of a campaign.

Happily, this election afforded an opportunity to have a volunteer, Dan

Williams, fill the role of campaign manager. Dan came to my attention through one of my committee members, Bill Robinson, who served as Dan's precinct chair and was also his neighbor. His credentials were noteworthy. He was just completing his first year of law school, had volunteered with John Edwards' presidential campaign in New Hampshire in 2004, and had served on several boards of the Wake County Democratic Party. Most recently, he had co-managed the successful campaign of a North Carolina House Representative. I was delighted to welcome an experienced campaigner to share the responsibilities of day-to-day operations. He proved to be particularly valuable in acting as the liaison between my campaign and the party hierarchy. While Dan's role as campaign manager was primarily limited to the summer months due to his school obligations out of state, he provided valuable insight and help. Significantly, he drafted two plans for the campaign, which he laughingly distinguished as the Cadillac and the Pinto versions. The first was geared to a scenario where the campaign had raised at least $100,000 while the second was our budget model for $35,000. What he didn't plan for was the reality of our riding in on a horse, "pinto" or otherwise.

**Volunteer Coordinator**

An important role particularly in a grassroots campaign is that of the volunteer coordinator. In my previous campaigns I had performed this role myself but for this one I was happy to have Andrea Bertole take on the challenge. We shared the thrill of a whodunit, were both members of the same mystery book club, and often joked that murder had brought us together. Prior to my running for office, we hadn't had a personal relationship. Andrea is Canadian and had not previously been involved in politics. The day after I filed to run, we had our monthly book club meeting and I announced my candidacy to the group and welcomed all to participate. Most members had no idea of my political interest as we largely tried to keep our discussions on the mystery book at hand. Andrea contacted me after the book club meeting and her March 9th phone message provided me with an emotional boost:

*Hi Gerry,*

*This is Andrea Bertole...I believe you mentioned you are out of town until Sunday but I just wanted to thank you for your call yesterday and let you know I would be delighted to join your* campaign team (though let me admit upfront, I have not helped with a campaign before, but am eager to learn and be of assistance in whatever ways possible.) I will look forward to seeing you at your meeting at 6:30 on March 16$^{th}$ at 405 Amelia Avenue. If you need to reach me feel free to call at 919-793-0160. Thanks.

### Events Coordinator

Events offer another great way in a grassroots campaign to involve people in the political process. To have two Events Coordinators in this run for office was a plus. Diana Zandt and Sharon Norton accepted this responsibility. Diana had been a valuable addition to my earlier endeavors in seeking election, though not in an events coordinator capacity. The flexibility of this role appealed to her as she was providing care for her terminally ill mother. I knew Sharon through a senior dance troupe, The Sassy Classics, which she had started. She had agreed to take on this role at the first campaign meeting. While she shared that she did not know much about politics, she had great energy and a talent for putting people at their ease, a great fit for this role. While Diana and Sharon each helped with various events, circumstances in their personal lives did not end up allowing either to take this role on in a more systematic fashion. In establishing my team, I noticed the multiple demands on people's time. "Life is happening" to them all the time. In considering those closest to me, those who were on my committee, some were challenged by deaths in the family, divorces, children going to war, and illness. I always tried to be aware of how busy others were and show understanding of and flexibility towards what contributions people could make to the campaign. As I was relying on volunteer help, I knew that the responsibilities tied to a particular role might not be carried out in textbook fashion.

## *Enlisting Support*

In each of my campaigns, a key approach to enlisting help and increasing name recognition, passed onto me by Senator Gunter, was to take advantage of every opportunity to interact with people.

### Name Tag

One suggestion was to always wear a name tag. My doing so often served as a conversation starter. I went to *Mort's Trophies* to have a name badge designed with my name and the position I was running for. I selected a color that matched my campaign colors to reinforce my branding. I never left home without my "Gerry Bowles, NC State Senate" name tag. I wore it everywhere, apart from church and to bed, and welcomed the inquiries that it elicited. In true grass roots fashion, it offered folks a way to approach me, then with this entrée into a conversation, it gave them a comfortable way to follow-up with personal and political questions. In meeting people at the grocery store or gas pump the unspoken message was "I am one of you." It also allowed others who were nearby to hear the conversation and to be potentially drawn in. It seemed likely that these people would leave and tell someone about the encounter. After all, it is not every day that one meets a candidate for public office so our conversation might provide material for a response to the question, "how was your day"? While admittedly, I am a very social animal, there were times when I had to go outside my own comfort level to engage people. My technique in these instances was to don my "candidate" role as I would a hat. I had to make a conscious decision to be the candidate and to be prepared to risk the possibility of rejection.

## *Engaging All*

I was always encouraged by the interest expressed in politics by someone pumping gas next to me or searching for produce at the grocery store. Too often we limit ourselves to thinking of only the more traditional sources of support in campaigns such as those involved in political groups and organizations. But I was always interested in broadening out to involve those who hadn't connected with politics in a systematic way before. Of course, as much as I would attempt to connect with everyone, I would try to read body language to recognize who might prefer not to be approached. While I would wear my name tag to a restaurant, I would not actively canvass the patrons, although if they asked I would happily introduce myself. Even so there were occasions when I misread a situation. For example, one morning while preparing materials for canvassing in the BP, my neighborhood gas station/convenience store, I observed a woman obviously distraught who was making a call at the pay phone just a couple of feet away. After she got off the phone, mindful of her condition, I chose to forgo my usual introduction. A couple of days later she aggressively approached me and my volunteers at the BP and asked what we were doing. When I explained that I was a candidate for the State Senate she confessed that she had felt excluded on the previous occasion by my not engaging her in conversation. I apologized and explained that I had noticed her previously but had chosen not to intrude on what seemed to be a private moment. By the end of our discussion, I had managed to rectify the situation and add her to my list of supporters.

On another occasion, I was encouraged by an email I received July 15$^{th}$ after canvassing with Andrea one summer day. As part of our routine we would reward ourselves with lunch while we assessed the morning and compared notes with our experiences at the doors. We made no attempt to disguise who we were and were always open to folks who shared our space. There were benefits to our silent speech as evidenced by the following:

> *Gerry,*
>
> *I sat next to [you] yesterday in Bojangles. You were busy, & I didn't want to interrupt.*
>
> *I wanted to write to mention a public transportation system that is working extremely well. My wife is from Colombia, & I visited Bogota for the 1$^{st}$ time last Christmas.*
>
> *Bogata has a dedicated bus line called Trans Millenio, a High Capacity Bus System. It's cost-effective & is hugely popular in ridership. It operates with elevated terminals, curb-contained double lanes, and credit card style bus passes.*
>
> *I believe Charlotte has a small version of a High Capacity Bus System.*
>
> *I hope that you are elected & will consider as a sound alternative to the much over-priced TTA regional rail plan.*
>
> *If you'd like to hear more, I'd be happy to share all that I can with you.*
>
> *Sincerely,*
> *Matt [last name removed for privacy]*

### Volunteer/Contribution Cards

An important follow-up to conversations such as these was to ask the person I was speaking with to join my campaign and to offer my palm or business card and website information. I never wanted to seem threatening to people, but I did want to give them the chance, upon leaving, to reconnect if their interest had been peaked. I would often ask if they were comfortable sharing their contact information with me, keeping in mind the setting we were meeting in. After all, their intent hadn't been to attend a political meeting, they had just stopped to put gas in their car. When there was a positive response, I would offer them a "Contribution Card" (see sample under "Fundraising Letter" below) to get their contact information and determine their interest in giving monetary and/or volunteer support. At the end of each day I would collect any information I had received that day and pass it on to Andrea to add to our database so that I could connect with these folks again. In addition to a contact's personal information, she would add where I had met them as well as any political concerns they noted. At the end of the campaign, I had met so many people that this database proved to be a great resource in helping me remember where I had encountered someone. I was sowing seeds, building a campaign organization, and polling my constituency.

## Misunderstandings/Clarifications

Uppermost in my mind was the notion of community. When the election was over, I was still going to live, work and worship with people who might not share my political persuasion. In all conversations, informal and otherwise, it was my intent to speak honestly without being hurtful or judgmental and to keep the door open to those with different opinions.

Wearing my name tag led to many amusing situations. I was continually having to distinguish my candidacy from that of Erskine Bowles, former White House Chief of Staff to President Bill Clinton and candidate for the U.S. Senate from North Carolina in 2000 and 2002. In my earlier campaigns, I was asked if I was his wife and even in this current undertaking I was often asked if we were related. This question came up so frequently that, at the first opportunity I had to introduce myself to him, I couldn't resist sharing with him the confusion generated by our shared name. I indicated that I doubted we were related since my husband had grown up in West Virginia. He responded, "our people are from West

Virginia" and we simultaneously declared "cousin!" and embraced one another. From then on, "cousin" became our greeting for one another. Bowles was not the only part of my name to lead to confusion. Gerry posed its own challenges. Any number of people asked me "who is Gerry Bowles," some even asking if Gerry Bowles was my husband. The assumption was that "Gerry" was a man's name, though I had always used it instead of my given name of Dorothy Geraldine.

The clarification of names did place me in the role of teacher again, in explaining the role of State Senator as compared to U.S. Senator. This misunderstanding around names also reflected uncertainty about the different levels of government. Contrary to Tip O'Neill's, Speaker of the US House under President Reagan, belief that, "all politics is local," it was my experience that most folks I encountered were more familiar with the goings on in Washington than in Raleigh.

## *Listening Tour*

A further helpful suggestion from Senator Gunter was to conduct my very own "listening tour." Seven months before filing for the 2000 election, with notebook in hand, I contacted a variety of veteran politicians and community leaders including the President of the Chamber of Commerce, the Chair of the Wake County School Board, members of the City Council, Wake County Commissioners, members of the General Assembly, and my minister. Some of these offices were non-partisan while others were not. I did not let party affiliation prevent me from asking for people's thoughts on what the important issues were for their organization. Starting from my initial list of leaders to contact, I followed-up with others that were mentioned within my interviews. Most people were happy to talk with me. Some had been contacted in the past but a number had not and were unsure how they could help me. I wasn't asking for a monetary contribution or for their vote but just wanted the benefit of their experience and knowledge. I figured that at each step along the way, if a conversation did not generate new perspectives, then all I had lost was time. That said, I always found my investment in time was rewarded.

I kept a journal with input from these discussions. I followed a general questionnaire which I tailored to the specific person. I assured the individual I was speaking with that our conversation would be kept confidential. The questions ranged from asking about her opinion on my running for office, to my opponent's strengths and weaknesses and any issues she felt needed addressing. I trusted that these folks were candid with their answers. One of the side effects in consulting with others was to involve them in the process in addition to gaining their insights. In total, I interviewed close to a dozen individuals from varying backgrounds. Keeping in mind that the whole is greater than the sum of its parts, I was less concerned with the perspective of any single person, than I was in the overall sense I discerned from all the conversations put together. My goal in collecting this wealth of information was to distill and reflect on it to see how it related to my campaign and try to identify any potential pitfalls. In 2006, with only 8 months until Election Day, my flexibility in following this same approach was limited. I took my insights from 2000 and added to them from conversations along the campaign trail with voters and community leaders alike.

## *Campaign Message: Education, Transportation, Representation*

One of the challenges in crafting a campaign message for the district I hoped to represent was its varied make up. It included rural, urban, and limited agrarian areas as well as established neighborhoods and new developments. What issues would resonate for these different communities? Early on I asked members of our campaign team for their suggestions as to the issues that they felt needed to be addressed.

I had plenty of help from all walks of life: friends, family (near and far) and the person on the street. Humor was never in short supply as demonstrated by this play on words from one of my most ardent supporters.

> *"If I've said it once, I've said it once: the real issue is the right to arm bears. Until we get this message across to the general public, we're doomed."*

A more serious response came via email in early May:

> *"Gerry's site looks good. But what I'm surprised that I don't see are the issues like Gasoline prices and ILLEGAL immigrants (not to be confused with LEGAL immigrants as the press has done consistently), and Healthcare (as it would relate to NC's portion*

32

of Medicaid).*" POCKETBOOK ISSUES *are going to get votes and hopefully get some changes made.*

Later in May, a letter of support arrived from my sister-in law's mother!

> *Gerry: Patty forwarded your Key Issues article to me. I was very impressed with your ideas. Wish I lived in NC so I could vote for you! At least I can say, "You go, girl."*

The following email proved prescient to where a sizable portion of my district "lived"

> *Monday, June 5, 2006*
> *Subject: Weapon of Mass Distraction-Round 2*
>
> *Gerry Don't look now but Bush administration has started a new offensive on diverting the attention of the government and the public on critical issues by suddenly resurrecting **the idea of a constitutional amendment to ban gay marriage**. Why did they bring this issues up now? To raise the conservative attention and get them hyped up so that they will vote in the up-coming elections.*
>
> *Yesterday on Meet the Press (I didn't see it but heard this clip) Sen. Biden said this, "the world is going to Hades in a Handbasket and all the focus is being diverted"...He's dead on accurate.*
>
> *Bush fooled us once with the WMD scam. Now he's trying to do it again.*
>
> *And as The Who sang- "We Won't be Fooled Again!!"*

This suggestion arrived in my in-box on the same day:

> *Gerry- By the way -I think you should incorporate the key word "progressive" in your campaign rhetoric- it is a signal that you are not stuck in the mire of old labels, and are appealing to independents as well as dems, etc and repub moderates- you may have already thought about this, but if not, I hope you do. It also has the sense of forwardness and future about it.*

*It is an important buzzword these days.*

During my previous run for office, I found workshops offered by various groups (e.g. Wake County Democratic Party, North Carolina Association of Educators, Emily's List) to be invaluable in offering advice on how to focus my issues, frame a message, and manage a campaign. One of the rules of the road was to distill the dozens of issues you care about down to just three main topics. This approach offers an easy number for folks to remember and yet gives your message substance. Another piece of advice was to fine tune an "elevator speech," a three-minute talk in which you would introduce yourself to voters and explain why you were running for office. The workshops provided a variety of suggestions for capturing the attention of the electorate. For this campaign I chose to focus on education, transportation, and representation.

## *Education*

To frame my 2006 campaign message, I gathered my campaign committee to help me learn which issues were of greatest interest to the community. Living in North Raleigh for thirty years gave me first-hand knowledge of the concerns of many of my neighbors. The group offered additional insights and reflected genuine concerns for the area, as opposed to being agenda driven. In both my 2000 and 2006 campaigns, education represented a key concern for my community and it also represented my passion. North Raleigh had experienced high growth for many years and the pressure on schools and teachers was high. I was worried about the area being able to provide sufficient facilities for students. In addition, North Carolina had a large high school dropout rate. Only sixty percent of the young people in NC who started their freshmen year of high school graduated in four years. As a former teacher, I felt that the state needed to focus more attention on solving these problems. Thus, education provided the first of the three issues in my slogan.

## *Transportation*

In 2000, one topic of concern on the minds of customers at my local convenience store was potential residential development in the Falls Lake watershed, the major source of water for the city Raleigh. The Army Corp of Engineers had conducted an extensive study. It concluded that dense residential development in this area would jeopardize water quality. In response, the city council had limited development. Despite this assessment and ruling, developers were pushing council members to revisit the issue. For the people at the store, this was an example of government answering to special interests at the expense of the residents. I incorporated this important North Raleigh issue into my 2000 message. In 2006 the issue that reflected poor state governance and had people talking was the need for new roads. North Carolina did not have toll roads and had established a precedent of being a state that opposed them. A Highway Trust fund had been established to finance highway projects. However, when money was needed to complete the 540 Expressway, a highway that went through much of North Raleigh, the fund was found to be wanting. It had been raided to offset deficits in the State budget. Toll roads were being considered to pay for the needed work, going against the previous stance that tolls would not be used as a source of funding. I incorporated this concern into the second issue: transportation.

## *Representation*

In recalling my experience at the Legislature and in daily conversations at the local convenience store, I saw the seeming disconnect between citizens and their government as another area of focus. I hoped to make government more responsive to the people. In addition, I tried to model how I would govern through my approach to the campaign: as a partnership between the candidate and the community. I had observed the growing cynicism of many of the electorate and worried that this cynicism would lead to their eventual disengagement from the electoral process. I hoped to make politics more accessible by offering myself as a leader who encouraged citizens to become more involved and invested in their government. With this focus, I identified my third and final issue: representation.

## *Message Summarized*

With the help of my son, Hal, whose business *Hardin-Bowles* focused on brand identification, I summarized my message in a palm card as follows:

> **KEY ISSUES**
> **EDUCATION**
> *How do we best fund the construction of new schools? How do we attract and retain exceptional teachers with the ability to educate and inspire greatness in our children? How do we reduce our*

*dropout rate and negate the drastic consequences to us and to those left behind?*

*First Step: Don't Let The Lottery Play Us.*
*Whether you support it or not, the North Carolina Lottery is a reality. Gerry will make sure that funds dedicated to school construction will not simply supplant money already being spent on our schools and early childhood programs. Equally important, she will fight for our share of the education pie. Already, Wake County is receiving half the lottery share of Mecklenburg County.*

*Before becoming involved in local government, Gerry Bowles was a Wake County public educator and the founding director of a downtown Raleigh after school tutorial center. She will bring a welcomed voice to these and other pressing educational issues and will be a passionate advocate for progress on this crucially important front that touches us all.*

**TRANSPORTATION**
*How do we pay for new roads? How do we fund unprecedented local growth without burdening property owners? Are toll roads the answer or another financial burden?*

*First Step: Be A Road Worrier.*
*In recent months, the prospect of Triangle toll roads has become front-page news. While there are strong arguments on both sides of the issue, the real question has to be raised: Why are we in this mess in the first place? The answer is ineffective government. The need to balance the state budget has gutted the Highway Trust Fund. Instead of using our transportation tax dollars to adequately fund our roadside needs, they have been expropriated to make up for mismanaged revenues in other areas. This, along with the proposed toll road solution, is unacceptable.*

*Gerry will fight any toll road that unduly burdens selected citizens or does not completely cover the cost of its own construction. Typically, 30 percent of a toll road's construction costs are never recouped from the tolls. These funding shortfalls are often made up from local sources. As a result, toll roads do not reduce taxes*

36

*and often lead to increases.*

*As a resident of this district for over three decades, Gerry Bowles has experienced the disappointment that we all feel from our local transportation shortfalls. Many of the so-called solutions seem tantamount to putting band-aids on broken limbs. With Gerry as your senator, you can rest assured that when the road tolls, it won't be for thee.*

**REPRESENTATION**
*How can we have our voices heard? How can we make people the special interest? How can we work together to make things work?*

*First Step: Make People The Priority.*
*As many have become increasingly aware, government at all levels is becoming dangerously beholden to special interest groups. While there is nothing wrong with these groups having their voices heard and their concerns addressed, Gerry feels that the needs of the common citizen have taken a backseat to many of these groups. The only way to combat this growing problem is to make the citizens the special interest. By being beholden to no financial interest, Gerry will make people the priority.*

*As the founder and president of Wake County Citizens For Effective Government, Gerry Bowles has put words into action by addressing and seeking solutions to issues that remain important to our citizens. She truly cares about the concerns of the people and understands that our society cannot long stand without adequate representation for all.*

## *Consultants*

While I chose to hone my campaign message relying on input from my committee and community interaction, I was aware that there were consultants available to the campaign who I could pay to do this. It does take a tremendous amount of time to determine and then distill your message. If you are unsure whether your concerns match those of your community and when weighing your time, people, and money variables, it may be preferable to use consultants who will identify the issues through polling. In 2000, one of the first appointments I made on my "listening tour" was with a noted consultant. He had successfully managed the campaigns of many North Carolina State Senators and judges. After introducing myself, I was dumbstruck that the first question out of his mouth was "do you have money?" I remember being dismayed and disheartened that this was the question he considered most important. It was like a defense attorney asking how much you can pay before inquiring about any elements of the case. Going into this meeting, I had expected we would discuss my background and interests. But I quickly realized that it didn't matter what was in my heart or whether my goal was to save mankind, it all came down to "show me the money." His second question was "do you know people with money?" I was feeling intimidated by his brusque manner and couldn't shake the need for approval so while the answer was "no," I didn't want to answer "no" twice in a row. As is usual for me, I used humor as a defensive mechanism and replied, "well yes I do but they don't know me." From the start of the conversation I recognized that using this consultant wasn't going to work. I just wanted to leave, but we continued. The consultant explained that his fee for services would be $10,000 which would cover framing the message, determining the campaign colors, creating logos and slogans, and managing the mailings. My thought was that with the help of volunteers, I could do everything he had proposed. I had the gift of time (I wasn't employed at the time) and people so I could get by with less money.

Another consideration for me was the need to be in charge. I had felt like a pawn in my own campaign through this conversation rather than the leader of it. I wanted the consultant to be interested and concerned in the success of my campaign and not just in receiving a fee. While I am sure the consultant would have been competent, I wanted more than a hired gun, I wanted an emotional partnership. Upon leaving the consultant's office I returned home and took a shower; I felt dirty. My soul had been bruised by this experience. Needless to say, I took a pass again at using a consultant for the 2006 election.

## *Fundraising Letter*

Keeping in mind the list of campaign needs outlined by Perry to Gail and myself at our earlier meeting (filing, campaign committee, campaign manager, message, fund raising letter, and campaign kickoff), I focused my attention on generating funds. I drafted and sent a letter to those I hoped would be supporters asking for financial contributions, while at the same time started formulating my plans for the kickoff. As I had done with my approach to forming my campaign committee and identifying contacts for my "listening tour," I pulled together a list of contacts from my circles of friends, family, and various groups I had been involved with. In developing this list, I had my own litmus test that I followed. Not only did I need to know the person I was sending the letter to, but I also wanted them to have a sense of who I was, in other words, that we would recognize each other if we saw one another on the street. In terms of the content of the letter, I announced my candidacy, stated my issues, asked for the recipient's financial support, and offered a way to volunteer in the campaign. The letter had to cover a lot in a small amount of space. I kept it to one page and kept the message concise. Even though the letter was being sent to people I was acquainted with, many knew me in different capacities, and I therefore included biographical information blended with my reasons for running - a short resume presented in a personal way. I enclosed within the mailing a contribution card and a return envelope.

---

## *Yes!* I want to help elect Gerry Bowles to the NC Senate

**Name**

**Address - Street**

**Address – city, zip**

**Occupation**

**Phone**

**E-mail**

Contributions may be made online at
www.GerryBowles06.com

**I would like to volunteer to:**
☐ Help with phoning
☐ Campaign door to door
☐ Coordinate volunteers in my neighborhood
☐ Display a yard sign
☐ Work the polls
☐ Help with mailings/ newsletters

**Enclosed is my contribution of**

☐ $25   ☐ $50   ☐ $100   ☐ Other

Checks payable to
"Gerry Bowles NC Senate"
No corporate contributions please.

GERRY BOWLES NC SENATE ♦ 405 Amelia Avenue. Raleigh. NC 27615 ♦ 919-847-9901

The card not only offered various suggested monetary contribution amounts, but also ways in which the recipient could contribute his or her time and energy such as helping with phoning, campaigning door-to-door, coordinating volunteers, displaying a yard sign, helping with mailings and newsletters, and/or working the polls on election day. The letter read:

*May, 2006*

*Dear Friend,*

**Had Enough?** *I know that I have!*

*Enough of elected officials who spend their time running for reelection instead of making government work.*

*Enough of partisanship at the expense of people and policy.*

*Enough of elected officials who would rather polarize our community than work together to find solutions to our growing concerns.*

*Enough of elected officials catering to special interest at the expense of the People's interest...*

*That is why I am running to represent you in the NC Senate. It is time to restore fiscal sanity to managing our budget. I promise to be a good steward of our resources.*

*My campaign slogan is* **effective. government. now.**

*I am a democrat but the issues that I will advocate for, Education, Transportation and Representation transcend party.*

*As a former Wake County public educator and founding director of an after school tutorial center in downtown Raleigh, I will apply my expertise and passion to finding solutions to the questions of how we best fund new school construction; how we attract and retain exceptional teachers and how we reduce our dropout rate.*

*As a taxpayer, I am uneasy about talk of toll roads in our area when we have paid taxes into a Highway Trust Fund that has been gutted to balance the state budget instead of funding our roadway needs.*

*As one of the founding members of the Wake County Citizens for Effective Government, it alarms me when our Wake County Commissioners vote to hire a former Wake County legislator to lobby the NC Legislature! HE will be paid $5,000 monthly to do the job that our legislators ought to be doing. We are being double taxed!*

***There is clear evidence we need change.***
*You know me as a mother, friend, neighbor and community volunteer who will find solutions to these problems instead of just pointing fingers.*

*Please help me with this challenge. An immediate contribution in the enclosed envelope will provide the necessary funds to finance the literature, mailings, and web support to get out my message.*

*Gerry*

Unlike my first race for state office in 2000, the response to my letter, while good, was less financially enthusiastic, though still meeting Senator Phillips' suggested litmus test. This circumstance may have been due in part to the likeability of my opponent. Also, the times had changed. A few of my friends who had donated in my first campaign had since become more allied with the religious right and did not contribute this time. On a personal note this response was difficult on a human level as it made me question myself; what about me no longer merited their support? In retrospect, like so many things in life, "it was not about me." I came to discover that many friends were struggling with their own challenges that did not include my campaign. While the campaign may have dominated my world, others were not eating, drinking, and sleeping the election.

## *Campaign Kickoff Fundraiser*

The next item on our agenda was to plan a fundraiser to kick off the campaign. Not being able to identify a specific volunteer to take on the responsibilities of fund raising, I appealed to the committee to help me fulfill the role. I viewed the kickoff, and all events, as an opportunity to accomplish a variety of goals. There was the money raising aim certainly, but there was also the chance to improve my visibility and my name recognition in the district and offer a location in which people could meet me in a more intimate setting. I hoped that the kickoff would be the venue to raise most of my funds and planned it to have a broader reach by inviting identified supporters, new folks I met on the trail, and others I hoped might become involved in the campaign. In terms of location, the wisdom is that the event should be held in your district, better still if it is in a central location. In addition, I considered the ease of getting to the event, the adequacy of parking, and the safety of the location. It was also important to me to use a home rather than a business as to provide a more relaxed atmosphere.

It goes without saying that I was the focus of this event, however, I was fortunate that Congressman David Price accepted my invitation to be my guest of honor. As our districts and interests overlapped, I felt that the people in my district would enjoy meeting and hearing him. As an elected official at the federal level, he was a draw to those who were familiar with the national scene. I had a personal relationship with him dating back to my first run for state office. In 1999, shortly after filing, I noticed in the paper that Congressman Price would be meeting the public the following Saturday morning at a local coffee shop. Realizing an opportunity to hear the concerns of the citizens I hoped to represent, I decided to attend. I arrived 15 minutes before his scheduled appearance and found, to my surprise, it was just me, the proprietor, and a couple who seemed to be there just for a caffeine fix. When Congressman Price and a couple of his staffers arrived, the crowd numbered perhaps eight. Without fanfare, he began to introduce himself to each of us at the coffee shop. I introduced myself to him as the Democratic candidate for the NC House representing the district we were in. As the coffee shop filled, his audience grew. I was impressed with the relaxed way he responded to people's questions. Much to my surprise, the Congressman took time from his presentation to introduce me to the group and gave me an opportunity to speak as well.

As a relative novice in running for office, I gleaned several insights from that morning. The success of an event is measured in different ways, not simply by the number of attendees but also by the quality of the interactions with those who have attended. That morning I saw people who had come in for coffee, not necessarily anticipating a political event, were nonetheless comfortably engaged in political discussion. Congressman Price's respectful and non-intrusive manner allowed people to simply purchase coffee and leave, sit and listen, and/or ask questions and join the discussion. The Congressman provided a model, too, for peer relations. I had the very real sense that I was a member of the same team. There was no sense of competition for the spotlight, resources, or supporters.

On this first occasion and subsequently, I always found Congressman Price to be down to earth and warm. He personifies my idea of what a representative of the people should be. He seems as equally comfortable in an intimate gathering as he is in speaking before large groups. In 2004, I was asked by the Congressman's staff to host a fundraiser for his re-election. I had reservations about hosting an event that my friends and neighbors would not be able to afford. I was uncomfortable with big ticket events and with politics viewed as a rich man's sport. Even though I had great respect for Congressman Price and wanted my neighbors to get to know him, I said I would feel more comfortable with something like a pig pickin' where people could attend for a minimum cost of $25, and give more if they wished. The Congressman's campaign enthusiastically supported this approach. The event was remarkably successful and well attended. For many this occasion was their first introduction to a political event.

Two years later, in planning the kickoff to my campaign, I applied the same principles of affordability and inclusiveness. I contacted Congressman Price's staff in early April to ask if he would be willing to support me in this event. The challenge was not in his saying "yes" but in coordinating our schedules. The kickoff to a campaign, by its nature, is usually early in the campaign, but in this case our official launch had to be August 8$^{th}$ so that the Congressman could participate. Admittedly, this timing was not ideal. Perry had discouraged me from holding a fundraiser in August worried that attendance would be low. Historically Labor Day has marked the start of the election season as it is thought that the public does not focus on the November election any earlier because they are so involved in summer activities and vacations. However, I never took a vacation from campaigning. We do not live in the agrarian society that existed for so much of the earlier twentieth century. Some Wake County schools are now operational year-round, and thus many of the parents and the society in general follow politics year round as well. I decided that the August date was the best choice for my campaign. While the kickoff is usually viewed as a main source of funds for the campaign, I was far from idle in trying to generate money in the interim. My campaign planned a meet and greet with special guest, Mayor Charles Meeker, which was hugely successful, as well as a variety of smaller neighborhood gatherings. One of the benefits of a kickoff is getting your name on the voters' radar. My campaign was active throughout the spring and summer with canvassing and participating in precinct gatherings and other community events. With all these activities, I could promote the kickoff in August and broaden the scope of possible attendees.

# Chapter Three – Strategy

A key variable in my decision to run was having a strategy for victory. There are multiple books about election strategy and any number of workshops that offer "how-to's," but in absorbing the guidelines presented, I chose an approach that fit my personality and comfort level. Just as you can consult fashion magazines to determine how to dress, if you are size 14 viewing the image of a size 2 model, you need to adjust your expectations of what will work for you. One size does not fit all. I found it important to adopt a strategy that was authentic to who I was. We all know of politicians who try to be someone they are not so that they are more electable. In reflecting on how I would run my campaign, I hoped to model the ways of those political figures I admired. Mayor Charles Meeker served as one role model. While some believed he needed to take on a more assertive, flashy style in order to win the election for Raleigh's Mayor in 2003, he was able to stay true to his unassuming nature, avoid personal attacks on his opponent and remain issue focused. A second role model was Franklin Delano Roosevelt who did not seem to cater simply to elite groups to get elected but kept true to his style that embodied an easiness with and genuine liking for people from diverse walks of life.

## *Choosing Imbalance*

While Perry Woods had set out the ideal of a *money-time-people* balanced approach to winning in my district, my uneasiness with fundraising combined with my joy in bringing people into the process, led me to choose a more people focused strategy. While only having 8 months until Election Day, I could devote all that time to the campaign. In addition to fitting my personal style, my imbalanced and purer grassroots approach also suited the realities of my district and the strengths and background of my opponent who was a Raleigh native, former Raleigh City Council member, and respected member of the development community. As I noted before, money alone was not going to make the difference. I needed to raise the awareness and support of potential voters. I did not discount the importance of raising money for the campaign, knowing that "money is the mother's milk of politics," I just placed greater emphasis on the people component, hopeful to fly under the radar and not alert my opponent and awaken this sleeping bear. As I stated earlier, my opponent had already donated $100,000 of his own money to his campaign treasury and had access to most of the big political donors in the district. As summarized by my campaign manager, Dan Williams, the only way I could beat my opponent's *money* was with more *people* and more effective use of my *time* in areas that could make more of a difference.

## The Numbers

Based on the lower expected turnout of a "blue moon election" (as was defined in Chapter One) of between 35 and 41% of registered voters, Dan used an anticipated turnout of 38.5% in Senate District 15 to calculate the number of votes I needed to win. With a total number of 126,776 registered voters, and a turnout of 48,809, I would need 24,405 votes to reach 50% plus 1 and victory. For a sure victory of 52%, he calculated I would need 25,381 votes. There were 45,589 registered Democrats in my district. With the projected 38.5% turnout, I could hope for 17,552 votes. As the numbers were not large enough with just registered Democrats (short 6,853 votes), I knew I had to target moderate Republicans who knew me personally and Republican women who were mothers of school age children who might identify with my background and appreciate my stance on public education. I further needed to capture some Unaffiliated voters.

## Precinct Focus

In implementing a grassroots campaign, I was informed both by my previous experience running for office and by the afore mentioned "How to Win a Local Election, Revised: A Complete Step-by-Step Guide." As part of my strategy, I adopted a precinct focus, identifying specific electoral areas within my district. In my largely rural and suburban district most voters did not identify themselves with a precinct but with their neighborhood. This precinct focus was therefore challenging to organize. With the recently settled redistricting plan, my district now contained 52 precincts. Confusingly some precincts were split between two districts. For example, I shared one such precinct with Senator Vernon Malone. Many of these 52 precincts had been "organized" by the Democratic Party meaning they had identified precinct chairs and active voters, but the truth was that far fewer were actively engaged in the political process and there was no identifiable Democratic presence. My task would have been simpler had the Wake County Democratic Party's actions matched their rhetoric of the importance of precinct organization. But the reality was that the party had focused their resources more on fund raising.

With the limited resources I had available in my "war chest," I needed to target specific precincts within the district to turn out my base. There is a science to determining which voters within a district to target. Consultants are paid just to analyze these numbers. I selected the 28 precincts in which the Democratic candidates had performed most favorably. I started by looking at the party registration numbers. I next factored in the 2004 election results that had a heavier turnout due to the presidential and gubernatorial races. I then looked at the precincts that had supported Governor Mike Easley, a Democrat, even though they had also cast their vote for the Republican presidential candidate, George Bush, in the previous election. I also considered the 2002 "off-year" results. Finally, I examined the 2005 Raleigh City Council outcomes in these individual precincts. Furthermore, Democrat Charles Meeker's successful showing in the mayoral race, gave me further hope that I might make some inroads. My thinking was if I made a good showing in these precincts I would be successful. I always knew it would only take 1 more vote than my opponent to win. I had no expectation or goal of a landslide. My motto became "winning the election one precinct at a time."

With experience as a guide, I further prioritized these 28 precincts into 3 levels of people raising activities:

| Go To Precincts for November 2006 | | |
|---|---|---|
| 1st Priority | 2nd Priority | 3rd Priority |
| 07-04 | 01-29 | 08-01 |
| 08-06 | 01-30 | 08-02 |
| 01-43 | 01-39 | 08-09 |
| 01-51 | 01-44 | 13-02 |
| 07-09 | 01-45 | 01-17 |
| 07-12 | 19-07 | 01-18 |
| 07-13 | 07-02 | 01-36 |
| 13-05 | 07-03 | 01-37 |
| 01-15 | 07-05 | 13-06 |
|  | 07-07 |  |

Even though I recognized from the numbers that I was not likely to carry

47

the remaining 24 precincts, I continued to look for opportunities to include them nonetheless.

Getting the numbers to make these assessments proved to be beyond challenging. The Wake County Democratic headquarters responded to our request in March with a "disc" that we gave to a computer volunteer with the campaign. After multiple efforts at trying to decode this information and many follow-ups with headquarters, we were finally able to obtain manageable data. In the several weeks that passed trying to resolve this issue, we had to "reinvent the wheel" by gathering data from other sources.

## *Political Factors Favorable and Unfavorable*

Woven in with this targeted precinct approach were a variety of political factors with the potential to affect the race favorably and unfavorably. To my advantage, and one of the factors in my decision to run, was a changed political landscape. President Bush's popularity had suffered from lingering foreign wars and there was a perception of corruption in the Republican Party nationally. Notably were the Jack Abramoff and Mark Foley scandals. Jack Abramoff was a K Street lobbyist who was at the center of an extensive corruption investigation that led to his conviction and to 21 persons either pleading guilty or being found guilty, including White House officials J. Steven Griles and David Safavian, U.S. Representative Bob Ney and nine other lobbyists and Congressional aides. He had pled guilty in January to an Indian lobbying scandal with his dealings with SunCruz Casinos. He was sentenced to six years in federal prison for mail fraud, conspiracy to bribe public officials, and tax evasion. Mark Foley was a six-term Republican Congressman from Florida. He resigned in September amid reports that he had sent sexually explicit Internet messages to at least one underage male former page. The scandal had surfaced in the spring and was affirmed as being true when House Majority Leader John Boehner revealed to the Washington Post that he had learned of "inappropriate "contact" between Foley and a 16 year- old page.

Locally, there had been a particularly nasty Republican primary for a House seat that overlapped my district. The candidate who was more allied with religious conservatives had unseated the more moderate incumbent. I hoped to get the votes of those moderate Republicans who felt disenfranchised. As noted earlier, my opponent had not yet been

48

thoroughly tested. In the previous election, he had not faced a Democratic opponent nor had he had primary opposition this election. Dan's research had indicated that his only significant legislative vote to this point was against the budget and his primary focus had been to support legislation that defined marriage as a union between a man and a woman.

A potential challenge to my campaign was the unfolding scandal involving the Speaker of the North Carolina House, Democrat Jim Black. Allegations of corruption were swirling around him, of note, the solicitation of at least $25,000 in illegal campaign contributions from chiropractors between 2000 and 2005 to help shepherd legislation helpful to the profession through the General Assembly. It was being reported in the *News and Observer* that cash payments were made to Black in men's bathrooms, private clubs and elsewhere and that he deposited the money into his personal account and never reported the contributions to election officials. Another issue that had many Republicans and a good number of Unaffiliateds up in arms was the recent passage of contentious legislation allowing for a state lottery. These two factors had the potential to energize the Republican base. Indeed, this read of the political landscape was affirmed when close to Election Day my opponent's strategy to win involved airing commercials that ignored my presence and instead focused entirely on Black's transgressions.

# Section 2: Implementing the Strategy

Having embraced imbalance by favoring people and time over money, my campaign committee and I focused like a laser on our targeted precincts by growing our team with continued recruiting of volunteers, canvassing, initiating special projects, creating and participating in events, and communicating our message through multiple media outlets. Nonetheless, significant time and effort were also dedicated to the financial requirements of the campaign. Furthermore, a host of surrounding players impacted the ease with which we could implement our strategy.

The demands involved in undertaking the above tasks required multitasking to the nth degree. On any given day, I could be canvassing in the morning then organizing data received and preparing the walk lists for the next day, arranging invitations for a future event in the afternoon, responding to email and telephone inquiries from voters and volunteers, and preparing for an evening campaign meeting. For example, looking back at my calendar on June 21$^{st}$, one of the early days of summer, I canvassed one of my targeted precincts 01-15 with Andrea and Dan in the morning at which point I met one of my nuggets, Ellen Biedler, who invited me to an upcoming neighborhood event "Pig in the Park." In the afternoon, Dan and I dropped invitations for a "Pre Independence Day" meet and greet event in precinct 02-01. That evening, I held the first meeting for the chairs of one of my special projects, the Issue Advisory Committee (IAC). Implementing my strategy was never executed in a linear, sequential fashion but rather in a concurrent manner. Not only did these activities require a great deal of volunteer participation, but they also presented me with opportunities to spread my message and recruit and engage volunteers.

## Chapter Four – Volunteers

It goes without saying that by its very nature a grassroots campaign is fueled by volunteers. Clearly the earlier you start to grow your campaign team the better. In the 2000 election I had the advantage of starting 16 months out from Election Day. While initially I thought I was unique in having to start so early to build my network in my less than favorable district for Democrats, I have since come to appreciate how strategic it is to do so. First, the more time you have to connect with people, the more likely you are to engage them with your vision. Second, while many people assume the party will assist you in all things campaign related, the reality can be that with resources shared between multiple candidates and priority given to favorable districts, you may truly need to have your own group of supporters pledged to you as a candidate as much as to you as a representative of a party. With the last-minute nature of my 2006 campaign, I was fortunate to have a pre-existing structure to start from.

## *Recruiting Volunteers*

My overall approach to recruiting volunteers was one based on a ripple effect – you start with your close friends and family and expand from there.

### *Initial Recruiting Action*

As mentioned in Chapter Two, I sent an email announcement to many friends and acquaintances as a starting point for involving supporters, then proceeded to connect on a more personal level with my friends in various clubs and organizations: mystery book club, the Sassy Classics dance group, former members of the Wake County Citizens for Effective Government, the League of Women voters, members of the Wake County Democratic Men and Women, and my church family. Individually, I informed neighbors and the customers and staff at my soon to be unofficial headquarters at the Easy Street BP. One of the unexpected, but welcomed replies I received was from Claudia Kennedy, a Three Star General with whom I attended $9^{th}$ and $10^{th}$ grade of high school. In 1999, she was featured on the Feb $7^{th}$ cover of *Parade* magazine as one of "Five [Women] Who Could Be President." As quoted in the article, she "was the army's highest ranking woman ever, deputy chief of staff for intelligence, and responsible for intelligence of the entire Army." It had been 36 years since I had seen her in school but in reading the article our former high school and home town were mentioned and I knew it was her. I immediately sent her a letter congratulating her, reintroduced myself, and included photocopies of our yearbook pictures and sent it addressed to her at the Pentagon. A hand signed letter of response came back to me July $25^{th}$ of that year, including her email and post office address. We communicated some in the interim years and when the time came to announce my candidacy I opted to send word to her. Her supportive thoughts were appreciated. It never hurts to include all as you never know who might reply.

I followed my announcement with an invitation to anyone interested to join me for my first campaign meeting on March 16th. The turnout was gratifying. At this gathering, I presented my vision and secured the commitment of many to specific campaign roles. To build on the energy and interest of the meeting, I sent the following thank you email with action items to the starting contact list of 50 supporters:

*Subject: Gerry Bowles NC Senate Committee Update 3-19-06*

*Good Evening Campaign Volunteers,*

*A warm thank you to the close to twenty folks who were able to gather for our volunteer "kick-off" last Thursday. We were able to accomplish a great deal and are energized for the task at hand, winning a seat in the NC Senate. With your continued help this challenge will be met!*

*Special thanks to the following for volunteering ... Dan Williams, campaign manager; Diana Zandt and Sharon Norton, co-events coordinators and advance team; Andrea Bertole, volunteer coordinator and Bruce Northcutt, computer guru.*

*Many of you have volunteered to help with mailings, door-to-door canvassing, precinct organizing and yard sign distribution. Thanks.*

*We are still looking for volunteers to help with fund raising...a committee of three or four can be quite effective.*

*ACTION Item...*

*Our main focus now and in the future will be precinct organization. It is our hope to canvass the major precincts...25-30 of them. To that end we will need numbers to accomplish that goal.*

*Please email me the names of at least 5 folks that you know who live in our district. Include their address, phone number, and email address, [and] precinct number if you know it. Please get these names to me by April 1st.*

*I will contact these folks and then we will get them to bring in friends of their own. It is extremely important that you get me these names as soon as possible.*

*Our first "event" will be Primary Day, May 2nd. We want to have folks handing out literature in our key precincts. So if you know that you will be available to help in this manner, tell me that via email as well.*

*Once again, thanks for agreeing to be a part of the team...Gerry Bowles for NC Senate.*

*Gerry*

*PS. Good news...I have gotten the endorsement of the NC Association of Educators and the Triangle Labor Council.*

## 5 contacts for Gerry

Within 24 hours, my mailbox was filled with the names of potential volunteers. The number of responses to this announcement gratified me. The campaign then needed to contact these referrals personally to gauge their interest in becoming a part of the team. As the days passed, our list grew, as did the challenge of following up in as timely a manner as possible. Andrea, as Volunteer Coordinator, created the following script to use in making this initial contact and to share with other members of the team who volunteered to help.

*Script – Initial Calls*

*Hi - My name is _____ and I received your name from _____. We are both working with Gerry Bowles who is running for the North Carolina State Senate for District 15. I am just calling to let you know that Gerry is running and to ask if you might consider her candidacy.*

<u>Machine</u>: *If you are interested, I would enjoy speaking with you further about Gerry Bowles's campaign when you have a moment. My number is _____. If you are not interested, feel free to call and let me know and I will not trouble you further. Thank you.*

<u>Someone Answers:</u>
- *If <u>not interested</u>: Thank you for your time.*
- *If <u>interested</u>: We would love to be able to include you in our online newsletter (to keep you up to date with Gerry's activities.*
    - *Is there an <u>email address</u> we could use to include you in our updates (we will not be passing this info to anyone else)*
    - *As grassroots efforts we are looking for ways to minimize expenses and online communication helps with this.*

- *Confirm <u>precinct & address</u>*
- *As I have you on the line, may I ask if you would consider volunteering?*
    - *Might you be willing to have a Gerry Bowles for Senate lawn sign?*
    - *One of our first key events is coming up on Primary Day/polling day on May 2nd*
        - *Ask if available to volunteer on Primary Day (polling day) May 2nd*
        - *We are looking to have volunteers at the polls at 2 points in the day around 7-10am in the morning and 4:30-7pm in the evening*
        - *Can be flexible with the time to suit your schedule e.g. 4:30-6pm*
        - *We will be asking volunteers to hand out literature & collect the names of any folks at the polls who are also interested in volunteering*
        - *If you are interested, we are hoping to have 2 volunteers per polling station (1 to hand literature, 1 to collect names) - do you have someone else you could ask to join you?*

> o *Other volunteer activities: Canvassing opportunities, delivering and collecting signs, helping out at upcoming events, assist with administrative activities such as making calls and helping with mailings.*

This initial contact accomplished numerous goals. First and foremost, was to notify constituents of my candidacy and to ask for their consideration. Secondly, was to get their participation from as little as providing an email so we could more easily communicate with them in the future, to as much as volunteering to help us on Primary Day. From the outset, we focused on confirming the location of supporters so we could categorize volunteers with our precinct focused strategy in mind. Anticipating the reality of reaching answering machines rather than the people themselves, we provided a way they could contact the campaign later, if interested. Scripts for future calls included my website information as well.

### *Expanding the Ripple*

Beyond my immediate circle of friends and family and their friends and family, I set out to connect with registered Democrats in the district who may not have known me personally. The Wake County Democratic Party County Convention held in April provided the perfect opportunity for me to do so. As with our earlier supporters, we followed up with the contacts made through this convention. Andrea sent the following email on Friday, April 28th 1:22AM:

> *Hello- My name is Andrea Bertole and I received your name from Julia Lee's [Executive Director for the Wake County Democratic Party] list of registrants from the 2006 Wake County Democratic Party Convention. I am working as the Volunteer Coordinator for Gerry Bowles, who as you may recall from the Convention, is running in November as the Democrat for the North Carolina State Senate for District 15. As an active participant in one of the precincts that falls within Gerry's district, we would welcome your interest and participation in various activities over the next 6 months. I am going to include you in our updates on Gerry's campaign – I have provided a copy of our most recent update below.*
>
> *Given Primary Day is fast approaching, I imagine you are finding*

*things busy. If by chance you are available to hand out Gerry's literature to exiting voters on May 2$^{nd}$, we would be delighted for your assistance. We are hoping to inform voters that Gerry is the Democratic candidate for November. Also, if there are any precinct events coming up which Gerry could attend and introduce herself to your neighbors and answer their questions, please do let Gerry or myself know – she would welcome the opportunity.*

*If you would prefer to be removed from our email database, please feel free to email me or call to let me know and I will make sure to do so.*

<u>Gerry Bowles for NC Senate Campaign Update... 17-Apr-06</u>

*Greetings fellow Gerry Bowles supporters!*

*A warm welcome to those of you new to this update and continued thanks to existing team members – we appreciate your interest and involvement in winning Gerry a seat in the NC Senate.*

*Over the past couple of weeks Gerry has been active in introducing herself and the campaign to involved members of her district at the Wake County Democratic Party Convention, Citizen Advisory Council meetings, and a meeting of precinct 08-04. She looks forward to attending future gatherings to meet voters and describe further to those interested her plans for "effective. government. now." Is your neighborhood, faith community, or civic group having a get-together? Please invite Gerry to join you.*

*Work has continued on Gerry's web site (www.gerrybowles06.com), palm cards, campaign slogans and stationary. Timing is set for all to be in place by Primary Day.*

*The next couple of weeks contain some key activities. In addition to attending a meeting of the Senior Democrats, a banquet of the Raleigh Sports Club, a picnic of precinct 01-17, and the Jefferson-Jackson day activities, Gerry will be hosting an engagement party for her eldest son! Also, we will be sending out our first fundraising mailing. To this end, there will be a meeting for volunteers at Gerry's place (405 Amelia Avenue) on April 25th from 7-9pm to work on this mailing. Are you available to help? RSVP to andreabertole@hotmail.com or 793-0160.*

*The May $2^{nd}$ Primary Day is fast approaching and while we celebrate our first victory – Gerry has no opposition in running as the Democrat for District 15 – we are eager to build momentum and we need your help. Please let us know if you (and a friend if possible) can schedule time on May $2^{nd}$ to hand out Gerry's literature at polling stations and inform voters of her campaign (many thanks to those who have already indicated you can help).*

*With sincere gratitude we would like to acknowledge your interest in Gerry's campaign. Success depends on the participation of people like you. We greatly appreciate the contact information many have provided of friends or neighbors who live in the district. Our database now contains over 200 names! We have begun the effort to call each of these referrals and inform district members of Gerry's candidacy! Please do continue to send us the names, addresses, phone numbers, e-mail addresses, and precinct numbers of others you think will be open to Gerry's campaign.*

["Summary of Areas for Action" removed for space – an example of the list usually included at the end of the updates can be found in Chapter Eight's discussion of Campaign Updates]

*We look forward to working with you all over the next 6 months!!*

Many thanks,
Andrea Bertole

The response to the April $17^{th}$ Update was gratifying. One such example of the myriad responses came from the daughter of one of my volunteers during the campaign for the NC House.

*Hi Andrea,*

*Thanks for contacting me. I would be interested this summer in possibly volunteering; I worked as a paid intern for Rep. Brad Miller's campaign last summer and am very interested in politics. I am also looking for a part-time summer job. If you have any paid internship positions, I am very qualified and can get good references from both Mr. Miller and his previous campaign (manager) Martha Elder.*

*I know my Mom held a Gerry Bowles sign last time she ran (several years ago) at our polling place near Stonebridge (where I believe Gerry lived/lives?) And so she would probably be interested in doing something again. Her email address is [name and email address removed for privacy]*

*I will not be home from college until the beginning of July 7, but feel free to contact me with volunteer opportunities then.*

*Sincerely,*
*[Name removed for privacy]*

I received many requests from folks wishing to serve as interns for the campaign. This one from the first of June came from someone recently credentialed by the more conservative side of the spectrum.

*Dear Ms. Bowles,*

*I was wondering if you were in need of someone to assist you in your upcoming election campaign. I have a wealth of experience working in the political arena in my homeland of Scotland and have recently completed the John William Pope Civitas Certification in Campaign Management. In matters of strategy and campaign management I have an extremely sharp mind and I fully believe I would be an asset to any campaign.*

*Thank you for your time.*
*[Name and contact information removed for privacy]*

To push to the outer limits of the ripples of potential supporters, I actively employed numerous methods. I started planning events with my team including a dance performance and fundraiser with my fellow Sassy

Classics in May. The May 2$^{nd}$ Primary Day offered a chance to meet active voters. As mentioned in Chapter Two, I regularly distributed volunteer cards to people I met during the day as a tool to further expand the pool of volunteers. And, most importantly for my campaign, I started door-to-door canvassing immediately following the Primary. The decision to start post-Primary was made to avoid confusion among the electorate as to when they should cast their vote for me as I had no Primary opposition. The results of all these activities were both satisfying and energizing. Our database continued to grow.

## *Retaining Our Volunteers*

It's not enough to just attract volunteers, you need to build a relationship with them as best possible to maintain their energy and interest and keep them connected. As has been noted before, we always followed up an initial contact with further communication and invitations to participate in the campaign.

### *Keeping Supporters Enthused*

A key approach we used to engage the volunteers we had collected through the recruitment process was to follow up in both a general and targeted fashion. Our database was helpful in the latter respect. We kept track of the specific interests of supporters and tried our best to contact them when those needs arose. For example, we had many people offer to help distribute yard signs over the course of the summer and then contacted them when our signs were ready at the end of August. Unfortunately, there were times we could not make use of a volunteer's stated skills. In one instance we had a generous offer to do a taping for a commercial. The volunteer said he could donate his expertise, time and equipment to this end but we sadly did not have the funds to air it if produced. Our goal was to ensure that all volunteer offers were acknowledged and as many as possible were utilized.

When thinking about your team of supporters and how to keep them on board, there was much to be said for the basic rules of hospitality you would apply in your home – welcoming all, being open and inclusive, expressing gratitude, respecting time and making guests feel comfortable.

### *Updates*

One of the tools that was effective in helping supporters feel connected and energized was our Campaign Update which we sent by email roughly every 2 weeks. We didn't want to flood inboxes with multiple notices of activity. Rather, we wanted to provide a regular way for our supporters to plan their calendars and feel informed. Andrea assembled a list of events and volunteer activities that supporters could partake in and follow along to know what the campaign was doing. Knowing both that the general content of these communications was similar from one update to the next and knowing these folks were being bombarded with all type of political information, we hoped to distinguish our updates from the rest by making them entertaining and as fun to read as possible. Even so, we were aware that not everyone would wish to receive these updates and respected their right to opt out of being on our mailing list. Whereas there was a consistent structure to the updates (general thanks to supporters, recognition of specific volunteers, list of upcoming events, volunteer opportunities, a pitch for funds, contact information and a quick summary of new and ongoing areas for action), the theme would vary from one to the next. For example, the following July update was created around the notion of music and summer:

*Gerry Bowles for NC Senate Campaign Update... 23-July-06*

**Roll out those lazy, hazy, crazy days of summer**
*You may have wondered, you may have speculated, you may have begged the question: "Where is Gerry's July Campaign Update and will it finally incorporate some musical references?" Well, at long last, here it is – what's been happening, what's going to happen, and what soundtrack could be playing when it does...*

**Summer in the City**
*Not to worry if this hot town has got the back of your neck dirty and gritty – we want to see you anyway! So, please join us at our Campaign Update meeting on Thursday, July 27$^{th}$ from 6:30 to 8:00pm at Gerry's home (405 Amelia Ave, Raleigh, 27615). As always, all are welcome!*

**Memories Are Made of This (Sweet, sweet memories you gave-a me...)**
*If you have been feeling soured by the democratic process, Pam and Ken Green would like to invite you to get involved and hear*

how Gerry plans to earn your vote and sweeten political lemons to make lemonade! Come participate in this:

Meet & Greet for Gerry Bowles
Hosted by Pam & Ken Green
1913 Hamrick Drive, Raleigh 27615
Thursday, August 3$^{rd}$ from 6:00-7:30pm
Please RSVP by August 1$^{st}$ to gerry@gerrybowles06.com; 919-847-9901

### Summer Nights
Gerry is looking forward to spending the summer night of August 7$^{th}$ speaking to members of the North Raleigh Lions Club. If you have community events (morning, noon, or night) which you would like Gerry to attend to meet and speak with friends and neighbors, please contact Gerry, Dan or Andrea to arrange the details.

### Twist and Shout
The countdown is on to Gerry's August Campaign Kick-off! Set the date aside to support Gerry's plans to "shake up" the influence of special interest groups, to "work issues on out" and to "get folks goin'" and get citizens involved in their process of representation. Please take part in:

Gerry Bowles' Campaign Kick-off
With Special Guest Congressman David Price
Hosted & With Jazz Performance
by Lola and Dave Youngman
(www.daveandlolayoungman.com)
4908 Boulder Creek Lane, Raleigh, 27613
Tuesday, August 8$^{th}$ from 6:30-8:00pm
Suggested Guest Contribution: $25
RSVP to Andrea Bertole (see contact info below)

Sponsorship Levels:
Platinum $1,000 * Gold $500 * Silver $250 * Bronze $100

### Heard it through the Grapevine
As you know there is great value in receiving a recommendation from someone you know, be it regarding a good restaurant, a

*"must-see" movie*, and certainly a candidate you feel can make a difference. Word of mouth is tremendously helpful in connecting with members of Gerry's district. In the last Update, we put out the call for ideas to you, our great group of supporters, on how to connect with people in your neighborhood and we are delighted to pass along a wonderful suggestion from Herbert Reichlin. In walking his adorable dog each day (not just Herb's assessment, I have met Robby and fully concur he is Disney cute), Herb mentioned he ends up meeting and chatting with many of his neighbors who are unable to resist the charms of Robby. Herb observed that there exists an opportunity to pass out Gerry's business cards as conversation eventually turns from Robby to Herb and the activities he is involved in. Happily, we have recently provided Herb with said cards and offer the same to any others of you who may be out with your dogs. But the concept is flexible and if you are out looking for your cat, or taking your kids to the park, or simply out getting some air, and would like some cards to pass along to your neighbors, we would be happy to provide you with the materials. If you have other suggestions on good ways to connect with members of your community, please pass them along!

**Hot Fun in the Summertime**
Canvassing has been one of the key approaches we have depended on to meet people, introduce them to Gerry, and engage them in the process of choosing their representative. We are truly energized by the response at the doors we have received and invite you to take part this August in our "Four on Friday" canvassing plan. In each of the 4 upcoming Fridays in August, we will spend 4 hours devoted to canvassing precincts in Gerry's district. Please join us on August $4^{th}$, $11^{th}$, $18^{th}$, and/or $25^{th}$ at the BP located at Six Forks and Newton Rd for a 10:00 to 12:00pm and/or a 2:00-4:00pm canvass of nearby neighborhoods. Please let Andrea know if you plan to take part (see contact information below). No need to feel blue if Fridays don't work for you – we have other canvassing times available and would welcome your company! Simply contact Andrea for further details.

**RESPECT**
*It often can be the case that we get so busy with our day-to-day lives and involved in our future goals that we forget to take a moment to reflect on our past and how far we have come in our personal lives and in our lives as a community. In reflecting on her run for the Senate, Gerry wanted to take a moment to acknowledge the important role played by Betty Ann Knudsen in paving the way for the involvement of women in political office in Wake County. It is with great pleasure we announce that Betty Ann will be acting as Gerry's Honorary Chair for the campaign. Stay tuned for details on an upcoming event to celebrate the link between Betty Ann's contributions and the options that exist now for many of us in the political realm as a result.*

**Thank You For The Music**
*With the heightened impact one vote is expected to make this November given the low turnout anticipated for this "blue-moon election," with no race for president, governor or U.S. Senate at the top of the ballot, we are so thankful to you all for your interest in Gerry's campaign. Our strategy of winning the election "one precinct at a time" through a grassroots effort depends on your continued support, energy, ideas, and involvement. Offers to volunteer a couple of hours of your time and pledge "2-for-Gerry", time you take to organize or participate in meet & greets, energy you direct to working as part of Gerry's Issue Advisory Committees all represent "music" to our ears. Our sincere thanks! To that end, may we also offer additional thanks to:*

*\* Susan & John Dellinger and Mayor Charles Meeker for supporting Gerry with a wonderful reception on July 18$^{th}$ – the energy from those attending was inspiring!*
*\* Volunteers from the Phone Canvass/Update Meeting July 12$^{th}$ – your help in connecting with active Democrats was invaluable.*

**If I Had $1,000,000**
*Community involvement has been and continues strongly as the primary focus of Gerry's campaign. Our time and energy is directed in large part to earning voter support. Nonetheless, funds do assist in this process by facilitating mailings, yard sign*

*production, web site maintenance, event promotion, and other mobilization undertakings. If you find your budget can absorb a contribution, your donations are of tremendous help, and each dollar is gratefully received and thoughtfully applied to campaign expenses. Checks can be made payable to "Gerry Bowles NC Senate" and sent to 405 Amelia Ave, Raleigh, NC 27615.*

*So long, farewell, auf Wiedersehen, adieu...*

*Andrea*

["Summary of Areas for Action" removed for space – an example of the list usually included at the end of the updates can be found in Chapter Eight's discussion of Campaign Updates]

## Transparency and Inclusiveness - Campaign Meetings

With my passion for bringing people into the political process and in modeling how I hoped to govern if elected, I tried to run my campaign in a transparent and inclusive manner. I never wanted anyone to be left out or feel they were not part of the "inner circle." To this end, I always welcomed returning and new supporters to my campaign meetings, during which I would be open about the ongoing challenges faced as well as the successes. I figured if I was facing challenges in my interactions with potential voters, my supporters may be as well, so I would share with humor my incidents to humanize the experience. In a similar vein, the email updates sent every couple of weeks were comprehensive despite being sent to an ever-growing number of interested voters. With concern about what news might reach my opponent, a well-meaning supporter cautioned me about sharing too much in the updates regarding campaign activities, However, my priority was openness over fear of what my opponent might learn. In addition, I aimed to always be egalitarian in my requests of volunteers – anything I was asking someone else to do, I was first in line to start myself. It was helpful that Andrea, in her role as Volunteer Coordinator, had her finger on the pulse of the campaign's activities and provided another point of accessibility to supporters. In instances where a volunteer had a concern, she offered another ear for those who might have felt uncomfortable contacting me directly. Finally, perhaps less common among candidates, I hosted numerous meetings and events at my home.

*Campaign Update Meetings*

When you set up your team you arrange for regular meetings. I had meetings at my home. It was a place I was comfortable and felt could convey a welcoming atmosphere and was fairly central within my district. I held my meetings early evening (after work hours) and provided food and beverage. I would set an agenda and try to keep the meeting to an hour. In this campaign we had a core group of regular folks who volunteered in various capacities, but I also wanted to keep things open and inclusive and would welcome any interested folks to join in the meetings. The advantage of this approach was to realize my intent to involve all. The time challenge came in having to bring new attendees up to speed, as I did not have the same folks attending each meeting. But I purposely wanted to allow for flexibility in how people could participate. I also wanted it to be enjoyable for people involved in the campaign. I didn't think that having fun and being serious were at odds. I could be serious as a heart attack about the issues but I also had seen in my life that some who were very strident about a cause and their beliefs could often appear self-righteous and fail to enlist people in their cause.

*Showing Appreciation*

Always mindful that there are numerous demands on people's time and that there are many choices in how they spend that time, I never wanted it to seem that I took my volunteers for granted. In addition to the regular thanks offered in the campaign updates, following any volunteer activity, Andrea would send an email to the participants acknowledging the help provided. Furthermore, I sent hand written notes of thanks to those who hosted a meet and greet or provided baked goods for an event. Another way I tried to show my appreciation of volunteers was to welcome their attendance at any of my events without a monetary contribution. For most occasions requiring volunteers, I made sure there were refreshments with the idea of making people feel like guests not just workers. Beyond serving as a form of thanks, refreshments provided an opportunity to strengthen the fellowship among those present.

In addition, on September 30th, after several months of volunteer help and leading up to election day on November 7th, Andrea and I organized a thank you event for all who had offered their help to celebrate the super successes the campaign had achieved and to renew energy for the final phase of the campaign. Our hope had been that after some ice cream and camaraderie, we along with available volunteers could either canvass the immediate neighborhood or distribute yard signs. While we would not rethink the sentiment behind planning this "Cheer for Volunteers," it was a bust. Apart from the two of us, we had only 2 volunteers show up. In hindsight, perhaps it was too much to ask people to give up more of their time to be thanked. Turnout may also have been affected by the timing (the event was scheduled for a Saturday afternoon) and a last minute change in location. On reflection, we hoped there was some value in people knowing we attempted to actively thank our folks.

## *Respecting Time*

Recalling my emphasis on time and people in the campaign formula of *time-people-money*, we were ever mindful of doing all we could to make sure every moment counted for volunteers. If we were asking someone to choose to help us instead of spending time with friends or family, then we did not want that time to be wasted. Organization was key to any volunteer activity. We had agendas to keep meetings on track, we had materials at the ready including scripts for things like phone canvassing or fund raising, addresses, envelopes, and stamps for mailings, etc. We always had more activities available on hand than we anticipated getting accomplished to ensure there would be something to do if we finished early or had more volunteers show up than expected. In recognizing that some of the volunteers were just able to drop in for a short while and that others might not be able to come at the "start", we tried to be flexible in our structuring of the time. An example of the preparation that would go into planning a volunteer event follows:

> *Subject: My attempt to map out Tuesday logistics*
> *From: Andrea Bertole*
> *To: Gerry Bowles*
> *Date: Monday, April 24, 2006 7:42 AM*
>
> *Hi Gerry,*
>
> *I just am trying to get organized in my mind for Tuesday to be sure (as we chatted about) that we are ready to use any volunteer who arrives. From our conversation Sunday here is my sense of the logistics...does this sound right?*

*Hope you are getting some rest today!*

*Andrea*

*Volunteer Night – 25$^{th}$ April 2006 – Mailing re Fundraising*

*RSVPs:*
*[List of 9 volunteers who planned to attend]*

*General Materials Needed: 1) Sign in sheet/Volunteer sheet (I will bring these); 2) Name tags/stickers (do you have any?) 3) Refreshments (I will bring some Toll House Brownies – shall I bring napkins, cups or anything of that nature?)*

*Materials Needed for Mailing:*
    *Pens (black or blue)*
    *Lists of addresses for tables*
    *Tables*
    *Stamps*
    *Letters*
    *Envelopes to Mail*
    *Donation Envelopes*
    *Volunteer Cards*
    *Palm cards to be added later*

*Volunteer Activities:*
*1. Mailing: Instruct not to seal envelopes as will need to add Palm Cards on weekend*
*a. Address envelopes by hand:*
    *-First, target list of addresses of people who gave money in the past*
    *-Second, Church members*
    *-Third, Other*
*-To avoid duplication, divide past donor list by letters (e.g. a-f for one table, g-l for another, m-r, s-z etc.) (shall we make photocopies of these lists so each table has its portion?)*
*-When a table moves onto a new list (e.g. Church members), they target the same letters of last names and check first that they have not already addressed an envelope to that person while working*

on the first grouping.
-Gerry to monitor to help avoid duplication

b. *Affix Stamps on Addressed Envelopes*

c. *Donation Envelopes:*
*Affix stamps*
*Affix/Stamp with Gerry's address*

d. *Cut Volunteer Cards to correct size for mailing (Gerry – should we have some samples ready to go so someone can just replicate the size desired)*

e. *Fold/Assemble materials – letter, stamped & addressed donation envelope, volunteer cards, palm cards (to be added on the weekend) (Shall we prep a sample of how this package should look?)*

2. *"Why vote Gerry" cards – these need to be cut in half (I have printed these now so they are ready to go)*

3. *Affix www.GerryBowles06.com labels to back of business cards (I have about 100 labels printed with this info ready to go)*

4. *Call contacts e.g. Julia Lee's list of delegates (I have printed the list of those not yet contacted & a suggested script) & Gail's long list for 08-04 (I have printed the list of those not yet contacted & a suggested script). We could also contact those on Bill Robinson's Long List for 02-05 (over 200 people) but I will just bring the excel file on disk rather than printing it out and we can assess it if we have enough volunteers & phones to tackle it.*

5. *Find precincts for contacts where this info is missing in our database – using modified database listing ask volunteers to find an address on the map and note the precinct. (I will print out a copy of this list with just the contact info on it – e.g. excluding my "comment" section [used to remind us of where the contact was made and any concerns expressed by contact]*

> 6. Assemble Canvassing Walking Lists *(Gerry, I am unclear if there is anything further to be done with this prior to receiving more info from Perry – not sure what would be required here)*

In addition to any initial call for volunteer help, we would send a reminder on the day of the meeting and provide driving directions (pre-GPS) to the volunteer location. We recognized that people might get busy and forget. Appreciating that time was required to get to and from a volunteer event, we were flexible in offering volunteers the opportunity to help from their homes. We tried to fit our volunteers' circumstances rather than making them fit ours. For example, for our phone canvassing evenings which were held at my son's place of business near downtown Raleigh, a hike for folks living in North Raleigh, we provided scripts and lists to volunteers willing to participate off site.

## *Training*

My own experience volunteering with the John Edwards campaign for President in Iowa in January 2004 was instructive in terms of what makes volunteers want to be part of and continue with a campaign. I had volunteered online and talked by phone to the fellow in charge of recruiting volunteers for the Iowa campaign. I had indicated I could afford the transportation from Raleigh to my assigned city of Des Moines, but not my board. He assured me that would be perfect and that I could stay with volunteers who had offered to host. Relying on that assurance, I got my ticket as my Christmas gift and set off. As promised there was an Edwards' staffer waiting with transportation at the airport to meet and collect John Edwards' volunteers. We were immediately taken to the Des Moines headquarters, luggage in hand, located in an industrial area of the city. They asked how I wanted to help and I expressed a preference for door-to-door campaigning rather than phone canvassing (I figured I could have done that from Raleigh). That afternoon, however, the job at hand was making phone calls.

We started this task at the headquarters but were divided into groups and transported off site once the business day had ended and other locations became available to use. There was a network of attorneys supportive of Edwards and my group was sent to one of their offices to make more calls. We were directed to the basement and at one point I was the only one there.

I couldn't help but feel uncomfortable that I didn't know how I would get my luggage from headquarters or even where I would be sleeping that night. I wanted to know what the plan was. Eventually we, along with other groups of volunteers, returned to headquarters and assembled for our first joint meeting. It was late in the evening, close to 10:00 when a "senior" campaign official came to thank us all and to then inform us excitedly that for the duration of our stay we would be sleeping on the floor at the YMCA – I thought at first he was joking, but he was not. Had I known, I would have brought my sleeping bag and a towel. I felt sick. My luggage would not even have fit in the locker of the YMCA. My discomfort was noticed and it turned out I was able to stay at a volunteer's family home. I didn't want to stand out from the other volunteers and seem a Prima Donna amongst this group of largely younger volunteers, but I was so grateful for this exception being made. We were not able to leave headquarters for this volunteer's home until he had "met his numbers." It was close to midnight when we reached his home and I was introduced to his mother. She was a delight. She was close to my age and we hit it off immediately which dramatically helped raise my comfort level.

Of course the logistics of managing volunteers for a campaign on a national level differ from those of a more local campaign, but some observations made an impression. One of my takeaways to keeping volunteers engaged was to ensure that they felt comfortable with the tasks being asked of them; what exactly was required, were there guidelines, who could be called upon to answer questions that might arise, and what was the plan of action? Many of my early volunteers did not have experience in the political arena but had experience volunteering in other areas and had transferable skill sets. I tried to impress upon them that politics was not so unique and their abilities were well suited to the needs of a campaign. I think Andrea's reaction to taking on the Volunteer Coordinator role at the beginning of my campaign was typical of many volunteers:

>  *Subject: Volunteer Coordinator Role & Action Items*
> *From: andrea Bertole*
> *To: gerry bowles*
> *Date: Tuesday, March 21, 2006 2:28 PM*
>
> *Hi Gerry,*

*I really enjoyed being part of your "kick off" last week and meeting your wonderful group of friends, family, and campaign supporters.*

*I am looking forward to the role of Volunteer Coordinator. To that end, I thought I should improve my sense of what this role entails. My recollection from talking with Dan and Adrian (I hope I have recalled his name correctly) is that this role involves putting together packages, training volunteers (for which there is an existing structure that may be built upon) and I presume arranging volunteers to assist with certain events and coordinating their canvassing undertakings. Is this sense of the role what you have in mind and are there other responsibilities I should anticipate?*

*Being new to the process, I thought I should also get some insight regarding the how and when to dive in – for example, do you want me to help organize the responses you get from your request for precinct contacts and Primary Day volunteers? When I have questions such as these or ideas should I be consulting you or Dan or both of you? I did wonder whether your literature and web site would have information for potential volunteers – for example, I noticed an old campaign link on the web for a candidate who listed and described their 3 different volunteer "strike forces:" lawn signs, events, and literature drops along with a contact number and e-mail address.*

*In terms of the action items, I will be happy to hand out literature on May 2$^{nd}$ [Primary Day]. Regarding precinct contacts, having just been in the US for 3 years and in our new town home since the end of January, I do not have much of a network yet. I may have a couple of people from my former apartment complex I could check with – do you know if the area around the Brier Creek shopping complex is in your district (e.g. Hwy 70 & Hwy 540 area)? I know you mentioned you are working on some talking points, but in introducing your names to others, are there some key points you would like conveyed? Also, if you think it might encourage others, I could mention at our next book club meeting* *that I am the volunteer coordinator with your campaign and we are looking for others in the district who may be interested in assisting/canvassing?*

*I am very excited to begin helping in your election to the NC Senate!*

*Andrea*

To instill comfort among our volunteers, Andrea and I tried to support them in a variety of ways. Specific to the campaign roles, I copied relevant chapters out of my go-to book, *How to Win a Local Election*, which detailed each of these roles and provided a structure to serve as a starting point. More generally, Andrea and I created kits and scripts for activities like canvassing door-to-door or by phone that outlined step by step what to do and tried to anticipate possible stumbling blocks. We never wanted any volunteer to worry about failing at a task. Given we were always a part of the volunteer activities ourselves, we were available for mentoring as part of the training process. Perhaps most importantly, we looked to set an environment of camaraderie to create a team feeling amongst our volunteers. For example, if we were gathered for a phone canvassing evening, we would have a social component to the night so folks had the chance to interact with the others present. When someone spoke to a potential voter and received a hostile response, we were there to lend a sympathetic ear and bring a touch of humor to the moment. Likewise, when the calls were met with enthusiasm and promises of support, we would celebrate together.

### *Seeking Input from Volunteers*
Given the importance of volunteers to our grassroots approach, it was incumbent on us to encourage them to share their ideas for the campaign. Our hope was to empower them to contribute in ways we may not have thought of. For example, with our early volunteer undertaking on Primary Day, Andrea sent out an email to all who participated seeking feedback as we used this event as a dry run for Election Day. Not receiving any negative response, we interpreted that things went smoothly. We continued this model of seeking volunteer opinions through the Campaign Updates. Andrea usually asked for recommendations from supporters for ways to build contacts and fund raise and we would act upon and recognize

these suggestions whenever possible. An excerpt from the July 23rd Update (included above in its entirety under "Updates") illustrates this process:

> *As you know there is great value in receiving a recommendation from someone you know, be it regarding a good restaurant, a "must-see" movie, and certainly a candidate you feel can make a difference. Word of mouth is tremendously helpful in connecting with members of Gerry's district. In the last Update, we put out the call for ideas to you, our great group of supporters, on how to connect with people in your neighborhood and we are delighted to pass along a wonderful suggestion from Herbert Reichlin. In walking his adorable dog each day (not just Herb's assessment, I have met Robby and fully concur he is Disney cute), Herb mentioned he ends up meeting and chatting with many of his neighbors who are unable to resist the charms of Robby. Herb observed that there exists an opportunity to pass out Gerry's business cards as conversation eventually turns from Robby to Herb and the activities he is involved in. Happily, we have recently provided Herb with said cards and offer the same to any others of you who may be out with your dogs. But the concept is flexible and if you are out looking for your cat, or taking your kids to the park, or simply out getting some air, and would like some cards to pass along to your neighbors, we would be happy to provide you with the materials. If you have other suggestions on good ways to connect with members of your community, please pass them along!*

Another of our volunteers, Nell Whitlock, initiated a literature drop of "reasons to vote for Gerry" which she created and delivered to the 54 mailboxes in her neighborhood close to Election Day. In addition, she was helpful in forwarding information to assist the campaign, such as news about my opponent. Likewise, in early October, Harry Hurd, an Unaffiliated supporter and his wife, Marcia, took it upon themselves to make their own door hanger entitled "Why an UNAFILIATED will vote democratic" and planned to deliver them to other Unaffiliated voters in their precinct.

> *In the past I have voted for democrats and republicans, depending*

*on the candidates and the issues of the moment. I take myself to be a serious citizen, believing that our country has been the land of opportunity, fairness, caring, innovation, political and religious freedom. I hope it continues to be these things, but the following things worry me considerably.*

***The record:*** *The way we were sold the need for attacking Iraq, the continued misjudgment and mismanagement of the war itself; the deaths of almost 3000 US soldiers; the serious disabling wounds of 20,000 US soldiers; the deaths of 50,000 Iraq citizens; the loss of respect for the US throughout the world, the Abramoff scandal; the inability of the federal government to act aggressively to help those put in peril by Katrina (good job, Brownie); Tom Delay; closed door meetings re energy policies; weakened environmental policies; a drug program that is much too expensive because of special treatment given to drug companies; a congress that gives the executive branch free reign; spending a surplus into record debt; the tactic of hyping issues that divide us, rather than finding ways to unite us;*

***How did we get here? One big picture view.*** *The republicans, at least the neo-cons, so dislike government that they are willing to put mediocre people or ideologues in high government positions, while the most competent republicans are off running big companies. The democrats are more likely to put competent people in charge because they see that the functions we decide to organize centrally should be led by highly competent people.*

***A solution. Ensure checks and balances are working.*** *The republicans' control of both house and the executive together with 9/11 have made for a big erosion of the checks and balances. If we get a democratic congress or senate, more reasonable solutions and legislation will result....*

In knowing we too were targeting this demographic, they sought to coordinate with our efforts and to further help my candidacy in whatever manner possible. Later, in response to our November 1$^{st}$ Update, they offered financial support, help at the polls, and reported that they had finished distributing the campaign fliers, which we had provided. While a more top down campaign structure may have discouraged participation that was not dictated by the campaign itself, we welcomed these proactive and independent ways of contributing.

## Challenges Encountered with Volunteers

In all honesty, there are some volunteers you may wish you hadn't attracted. It's best in circumstances such as these to keep a sense of humor and to recognize the diversity of the world you have opened yourself up to. We were to find that some people came to the campaign with their own soon to be revealed agendas. One potential volunteer's email in response to a call for volunteers we had posted on the Wake County Democratic Party's website proved to be less promising than we hoped.

> *I saw your name on the Wake County Dem party site and would like [to]get involved more to help win in the next election. Let me know about the meeting Wednesday July 12.*

However, his interest took an unexpected turn within a few email exchanges aimed at trying to involve him in the campaign. His response to Andrea demonstrated that he had something more "base" on his mind than stuffing envelopes.

> *From [email address removed for privacy]*
> *Date: Sat, 22 Jul 2006*
>
> *I am looking to meet you but look at videos, mags, pic, of nude men that are well hung wile[sic] we are together and having fun. Let me know when you can do this especially this weekend it is a fantasy of mine so if you are interested let me know and we can meet thanks a lot*

Andrea's response was spot on:

> *Hey Gerry,*
> *I think it is safe to say that I will not be adding [name removed for privacy] to our database of contacts...guess I was naïve with the first email he sent saying he wanted to help with the campaign.*

Another challenge posed with some volunteers was that they required more of my time and emotion than they contributed. One example involved a volunteer who responded with great excitement about helping and hoped to do so in many ways, but in the end never committed to a single opportunity. In the meantime, much of my time was spent in trying to set up something for her to help with. A separate case involved a volunteer who got involved in the political system to address systemic problems she had encountered in the past. However, these issues were so personally consuming for her that while she did contribute in a few important ways, she was unable to see through all her promised commitments.

Unrealistic expectations can present another challenge with recruiting volunteers. As previously mentioned, we received internship inquiries from several students, one located as far away as Scotland. Our budget clearly didn't allow for paid staff let alone student interns. Other student inquiries while welcome came too late in the campaign to be of use. While speaking locally to the students at Peace and Meredith College in October, just weeks before the election. I had a few offers to assist at campaign headquarters. We did not have a physical "office" downtown, and at that time in the campaign our needs were targeted and didn't suit their schedules. There was also confusion as to what a small business could contribute to a campaign. There were folks who wanted to offer their business services to the campaign as a personal contribution. For example, one supporter wished to provide food from his restaurant at an event. As election law forbids corporate contributions in any manner, regrettably, I had to explain that I could not accept this type of help.

# Chapter Five - Canvassing

## *2000 Experience*

Canvassing was the strength of my campaign. A large part of my political education began in 2000 when I ran for a legislative seat in the NC House. There was no Democratic precinct organization in most of my district at that time. With just a Wake County map, over which I would lay out the precinct boundaries, I selected subdivisions to canvass with the hope of identifying one or two people who might help me connect with others in their neighborhood. To begin, I started in the areas closest to my home so that I could say I lived just down the street and hopefully connect on a personal level as a neighbor rather than simply as a Democrat. With the high growth in the area, the map I had did not list many of the newer subdivisions I ultimately found in my district. I didn't follow the conventional wisdom of visiting only registered Democrats; instead, I went to each door as I was in an area in which I needed to appeal to Republican and Unaffiliated voters. Also, I found many households had a mix of Democrats, Republicans, and Unaffiliated voters. In addition, many folks had moved to the district from other states and while they identified themselves as Republican, their concerns were more geared to the economy and less to social issues.

For the most part, I canvassed by myself, though I did have the welcome help of volunteers on a couple of occasions. I chose to hit the doors on Saturdays. From the people I met I collected contact information and sent a personal letter containing a contribution request and volunteer sign up card. As a method to grow my base it was labor intensive. If no one was home, I wrote a note on the literature I left at the door, with the hope that the homeowner would read it and tell his or her friends. My goal was to cover 100 houses each Saturday. On average, I found only 10-15% of the homes occupied. I also found much of my district in North Raleigh was not so conducive to door-to-door campaigning. Many of the homes in the district were situated on acre lots that necessitated my walking as much as a ¼ acre just to get to the door. In addition, some of the precincts in the district were located in Durham County. Even though these homes were close together and easier to canvass, I didn't feel a connection with the voters as their issues and concerns were different and their focus was directed to Durham's politics.

## *Improved Scenario for 2006*

In 2006, I had a much better sense for the political lay of the land in my Senate district given my previous experience as a candidate and as a volunteer for Mayor Charles Meeker. Redistricting made my district much easier to canvass. Geographically, Durham was no longer a part of my area. The new make-up of my Senate district contained a higher percentage of registered Democrat and Unaffiliated voters. Consequently, this time I had a Democratic base to rally and in some cases an organized precinct structure to tap into. Recalling my strategic motto of winning the election one precinct at a time, and within the three-level framework of prioritization of the 28 targeted precincts, I identified which areas to focus on first for canvassing. I started by looking at those precincts within the district that coincided with my past campaign and those areas in which I had lived, worked, and worshiped. My district included precincts in the City of Raleigh, Wake County and the town of Wake Forest. I began my first canvass in the most geographically central precinct that had the best voting performance by the Democrats. It had the additional benefit of containing neighborhoods with sidewalks and houses close together. I eliminated some precincts for *canvassing* because the population was sparse and the voting patterns were strongly Republican.

In contrast to my previous door-to-door experience, I had a regular canvassing partner, Andrea Bertole, who helped anchor this activity that was the heart of the campaign. Traditionally, campaigns begin canvassing after Labor Day fearful that their efforts over the summer will be forgotten. Recalling the people-time-money balance, and having more volunteers and time than money, we bucked convention and began our canvassing in early May rather than waiting until September. We ended up growing a lot of support from May to August. It may be that it was hard to forget someone walking to the door in one of the hottest summers on record. Whereas, I had sent personal letters in 2000 to reconnect with people I met at the doors, in 2006 Andrea followed up with an introductory email and regular campaign email updates.

## *Schedule of Canvassing*

Andrea and I chose to knock on doors weekday mornings rather than take the Saturday approach I had employed in 2000. At that time, many assumed only weekends worked for canvassing, however, I found few people at home. When I did catch folks, they were often en route to soccer games, the Home Depot, college football games, and general errand running. I felt like I was imposing on their busy Saturday schedule. Even though I was leaving behind literature, I had fewer face-to-face opportunities.

On most weekdays, we would try to start after 10am in the morning. Needing to prepare for our evening campaign activities, we usually wrapped up by 1:00 p.m. This approach gave us time to review the canvassing information afterward so data could be added to our database and emails could be sent. We were pleasantly surprised with our weekday approach. There were any number of people at home – retirees, stay at home moms, folks on vacation, those working from home, shift-workers, and pet owners who popped in to care for their animals. It seemed that three times as many people answered the door during the week as compared to my 2000 experience. In addition, we had a great deal of success in recruiting people to help with the campaign, examples of which ran the gamut from finding folks interested in receiving updates, willing to display my yard sign, open to making phone calls, and/or happy to host meet and greets. Clearly, this approach may not work for all candidates due to their work schedules and other commitments. I had decided that the campaign was my job. Fortunately, Andrea was able to make this her job too.

As we had such success going door-to-door during the week, we didn't set-up regular weekend canvassing. That said, we always encouraged volunteers to let us know of canvassing times that worked with their schedules. Our reality was that weekends were not a popular choice. We only canvassed on the weekend twice. Both of those occasions were organized by either the Democratic Party or another candidate.

## *Walk Lists*

When planning each precinct's canvass, our approach was to use a walk list, which we created from data received from the Wake County Board of Elections' list of registered voters. Information was organized by precinct and contained each voter's name, address, race, gender, party affiliation, and date of birth. Andrea would alphabetically organize this data by streets for the precincts targeted. The night before canvassing, depending on how many volunteers were joining Andrea and myself and how much time we planned to canvass, I would assess which part of the precinct we would focus on and organize the walk sheets for the streets I anticipated we could cover. We had precinct maps to help plan the canvass, but often they did not reveal the full picture of life on the ground. For example, in one area an entire apartment complex was vacated in anticipation of a future shopping mall. Fortunately, having familiarized myself with the area through my previous canvassing in 2000, I was better prepared in terms of where to go and how to get there.

## *Targeting All Doors*

Most campaigns target certain doors aligned with the demographics they feel are most important to their particular election. I had incorporated demographics into my assessment by way of my targeted precinct focus. But, within that framework, I chose to go to every door. Just as in the 2000 campaign, strategically I needed to reach voters of all party affiliations and I recognized that if elected I would be serving the full mix. To cherry pick whom I would offer my message to seemed contrary to the kind of representative I aspired to be. As previously noted, we witnessed the growing and changing nature of the district. Often the information provided on the walk list no longer reflected the current occupants of the home. Also, new roads, subdivisions, and neighborhoods continued to pop up. If we skipped certain homes, we may have missed capturing receptive voters. As observed earlier, a further discovery was the large number of households that contained members of various party affiliations. When walking a street, it did not seem to take any longer to visit each door than it did to leap frog homes. This approach avoided the awkwardness of bypassing people in the yards of homes not targeted. There were exceptions to my every door approach when common sense dictated differently. If a home had a yard filled with Republican yard signs or a W'04 sticker on the bumper of the car (indicating support for George "Walker" Bush for president in 2004), I usually assumed support for my candidacy would probably be low.

## *Team Approach*

Ideally, I would have liked to have 3-4 volunteers to knock on doors each canvassing occasion. By mid-summer, Andrea and I were often joined by a third person, Katherine Morgan, which worked incredibly well. While it might have been beneficial to have a larger group regularly available to increase the coverage, there would have been a trade-off. While I could have covered more territory, I would have needed to spend more time in organizing and orchestrating the canvass. I found I had more flexibility with a small group in that I, too, could canvass and reach more doors instead of spending all my time dropping and collecting volunteers. Regardless of the number involved in a canvass, I always wanted to ensure my volunteers felt comfortable. I liked to partner with volunteers as opposed to sending them off on their own so that we might develop camaraderie and hopefully create a desire in them to return for more. In addition, this approach meant I was available to respond to questions canvassers got at the doors and to provide them with guidance and reassurance.

In contrast to past elections where I often canvassed alone, having the company of volunteers allowed me a chance to share my stories about interactions with voters at the door. When someone had been rude (which was infrequent, but did occur) or was eccentric (coming to the door with only a towel around his waist) I had others nearby to revel in the experience. Furthermore, people sometimes were more candid with volunteers than they were with me, which gave me a better sense of how the campaign was being received. That said, nothing could diminish the value of having the candidate herself at the doors. I heard from volunteers how helpful it was for them to be able to say to voters, especially those with questions, that I was in the area, just on another street, if they wanted to speak to me personally. I felt a sense of security knowing that I was not alone, even if we were in different parts of the neighborhood. I perceived that having additional volunteers offered my campaign further credibility in that others, not just me, were out speaking on my behalf.

## *Canvassing Approach*

The prospect of canvassing can be daunting to some people. Depending on the ease a volunteer had with going to the doors, I selected streets that kept the group close to one another and to me rather than leaving people in more remote areas. To offer further support, Andrea and I developed a canvassing package that included:

- campaign literature
- a map of the precinct being canvassed

- a map of the district
- a suggested script with a brief "how to" on canvassing (see Canvassing Volunteer Guide sample below)
- information about where to vote and about other candidates running in the precinct (see Things to Review with Canvassing Volunteers sample below)
- cell phone contact information to reach us if needed
- a list of upcoming events
- a Gerry Bowles campaign sticker
- a name badge
- voter registration forms

We provided our *Canvassing Volunteer Guide* to our volunteers to help ensure that those new to canvassing had some direction and that veterans knew what our campaign hoped for in their canvassing activities.

**Canvassing Volunteer Guide**

**Importance of your efforts:**
- With Gerry's campaign strategy of winning this election "*one precinct at a time*," meeting people door-to-door is a key way to mobilize members of her district.
- This year will be a "*blue moon election*" with no race for president, governor or U.S. Senate at the top of the ballot – turnout is expected to be low which means one vote will count for more.
- In canvassing today, you are playing a vital role in introducing Gerry's candidacy to voters and demonstrating your support for her – our heartfelt thanks!!

**What's involved?**
- You will receive a map of the precinct in which we are walking & a "walk list" (a list of households for you to visit).
- Please go to all households on your list (democratic, republican, and unaffiliated).
- If a home is for sale, do not worry about leaving materials at this time – we will try to revisit it closer to the election date.

**A guide on what to do & say**
- Knock on door and/or ring the doorbell.

- If <u>someone answers</u>,
    - Offer your hand and/or hold out the palm card
    - Offer your greeting – feel free to personalize it – a suggested approach is:

        - *"Hello, I am canvassing today with Gerry Bowles who is running as the Democrat for the NC State Senate in your district – may I leave you some information about Gerry for your review and ask you to consider voting for Gerry in November?"*

        - If the person at the door seems interested, ask if we could have his/her e-mail address to send campaign updates and inquire about placing a "Gerry Bowles" sign in the yard.

- If there is <u>no answer</u> – leave the palm card tucked in door.
- Be safe – do not go to any home you are uncomfortable with.

**Recording information on the Walk List**
- Please date & note your name at the top of your walk list.
- Please put a check mark (√) to indicate you went to a home and left literature.
- Please place an "X" by any home you did not leave literature at.
- Please place an "*" beside the name of anyone you speak in person with.
- Please note the street number of any homes you see which are not on your list and include them in your canvass.
- Please write any other observations about a particular household, for example:
    - E-mail address
    - Bumper stickers supporting democrats
    - Issues raised
    - Yes to a yard sign
    - Particularly receptive response at the door
    - Other yard signs

In addition to this guide, we prepared and used a *Things to Review with Canvassing Volunteers* facts sheet of sorts for the precinct we were targeting to help provide our volunteers with context and anticipate questions they might have.

## Things to Review with Canvassing Volunteers

- **Review bullet points in "Canvassing Volunteer Guide"**

- **Relevant Statistics:**
  - In District 15 there are 126,776 voters: 45,589 Democrats, 51,777 Republicans & 29,410 Unaffiliateds

  - We expect approximately 50,000 total voters in the district this coming election which means that to ensure victory we need 26,000 votes - spread across all of the precincts in our district, this is certainly achievable.
    - If we can get 60% of registered Democrats in the district to vote, we would win. If 40% of Democrats turnout then we need 50% of the Unaffiliated turnout to reach the margin of victory.

  - 01-51 Total registered voters = 1,211 → 509 D + 456 R + 246 U

- **Possible Questions you will be asked at the door:**
  - Am I in Gerry's district?
    - Use the District Maps to show that the person is in Gerry's district (recognize that is can be confusing as House, Congress, and Senate districts are different from one another, though they do overlap).

  - Who is Gerry running against – Republican Incumbent Neal Hunt
    - Some say not to give your opponent's name but we are finding people are confused about Senate vs. House Representatives and so we find it is better to offer Neal's name so folks know Gerry is not running against the person they want to support in the House race.

- If someone at the door seems engaged, then this question can be used to lead into Gerry's position on Representation e.g. "You ask a good question and we have heard that one a lot which is partly why Gerry is running – she will stay connected with her voters once in office and you will know her name."
  - What is Gerry's view on the environment, abortion, etc?
    - "Gerry recognizes there are many issues of importance to the people in her district – she is focusing primarily on Education, Transportation, and Representation but if you wish to contact her about a particular concern of yours, please visit her web site at www.GerryBowles.com or email her (gerry@gerrybowles06.com) or call her (847-9901)."
- Other candidates:
  - The Democratic Incumbent House Candidate for 01-51 is <u>Grier Martin</u> who is being challenged by Republican J(oseph) H Ross.
  - The Democratic Congress Incumbent for 01-51 is <u>Brad Miller</u> who is being challenged by Republican Vernon Robinson.
- Where to vote?
  - 01-51 The Achievement School at 400 Cedarview Ct, Raleigh, NC 27609
- Canvassing Kit Contents:
  - Walk Lists
  - "Why Vote Gerry" Talking Points
  - Voting Information
  - Precinct Map
  - Volunteer Sign Up sheets and/or cards
  - Pen
  - District Map
  - "Gerry Bowles" Sticker for right side of volunteer's shirt
  - Palm Cards
  - Name Tag Stickers
  - "No Toll" Stickers for those who will put them on their cars

I told volunteers that they did not need to be an expert on all things "Gerry Bowles" and that they could refer any questions they received back to me to follow-up with after the canvassing event. The campaign literature contained my website and e-mail address. I also tried to set a reasonable time limit given the physical and emotional nature of the endeavor. I would often arrange to canvass from 10am-1pm or 2pm, with the actual time at the doors usually being 2-3 hours. At the start of each canvass, when I had new volunteers, I would take time to make them feel welcome, go over the plan for that day, answer their questions, and share experiences to help develop camaraderie. At the end of the canvass, I would collect the walk sheets, highlight the streets we had completed on the precinct map, assess which areas still needed coverage, select the streets to be tackled next, and restock the kits for the following canvass. I would also give Andrea the completed walk sheets upon which volunteers would have written their findings at the door so she could include in our database the contact information for those who had offered their e-mail address, requested a yard sign, or indicated some other form of support.

## *Database*

Our database was both an important tool for organizing our campaign and a tangible way to measure growth and success. As we have noted previously, this Excel spreadsheet was employed to keep track of our supporters, their location and precinct, phone number and email information, how we met them and any preferences they outlined for volunteer activities. It was a useful way to organize potential volunteers in a precinct focused campaign and to identify which precincts needed more coverage. One initial challenge was identifying the precinct numbers for our various supporters. Many knew their voting location but not necessarily their precinct. Fortunately, at that time we could use Wake County's webpage to enter a supporter's name and address and determine his or her precinct number. This website was a great tool particularly given our precinct-based strategy. As we watched our list expand after canvassing outings and events, we felt encouraged that the campaign was making headway. From our database, we could tell that our email list of *engaged* supporters numbered 1,101 by the end of the campaign.

## *Including Event Information*

One technique we found effective as the campaign progressed was to include invitations to upcoming events along with the literature we distributed to the folks in the neighborhood being canvassed. For example, when Susan and John Dellinger graciously hosted a meet and greet featuring me and Mayor Meeker, I scheduled our canvassing of the surrounding targeted precincts to precede the event. Andrea created an invitation on her computer, I printed copies out at home on decorative paper, and then we attached them to my campaign literature to leave at the doors. This simple, no-frills practice offered a non-threatening way to approach people. In inviting them to an event, the campaign was providing a chance for folks to meet and take their measure of me. Also, the invitation served as a great icebreaker. After all, who is offended at being invited to a party, particularly given that most of my events had no admission fee? Our invitation personalized the campaign in that a neighbor was supportive enough of me to open his or her home for an event. It further gave folks a local contact for the campaign whom they could approach if they wanted more information.

## *Positive Response and Nuggets*

From precinct to precinct the response at the doors was overwhelmingly positive. On more than one occasion, I was told by residents that they had lived in their community a long time and had never had a candidate come to their door before and were appreciative of my doing so. People of all affiliations seemed open to my campaign. In this election, my being a Democrat was not a deal breaker. Many were willing to offer an email address to receive my campaign updates. Others volunteered to display a yard sign. The following email passed along from Andrea shows that our efforts in May were not in vain and made a lasting impression:

> *Hi Gerry - thought you might like to see you made an impact - I have it in our notes that we canvassed his neighborhood May 22/23.*
>
> *Andrea*
>
> *----- Original Message -----*
> *From: [name removed for privacy]*
> *To: Andrea Bertole*
> *Sent: Sunday, August 06, 2006 8:37 PM*
> *Subject: RE: Don't forget - Tuesday, August 8th Campaign Kick-*

*off for Gerry Bowles*

*Hello, and thanks for the reminder!*

*Unfortunately, I will be at a Chiropractic workshop that evening. Sounds like a rollicking good time is to be had!*

*Please let Gerry know she can count on me in the next election. I very much enjoyed chatting with her when she came through the neighborhood.*

*She may remember one of my biggest concerns is that Community College staff (all teachers, professional and administrative staff) that are paid with State funds should come under the State Employment act, and State pay scale. They don't now. They are considered non-State employees paid with State funds, and their salaries are arbitrarily set by the President and/or the local board(s) of trustees for each college. I'm retired now, so it won't help me, but future employees will benefit.*

*[name removed for privacy]*

Of great delight were the occasions when I discovered what I referred to as "the nuggets," those who I had not previously known, but who showed a desire for greater involvement in my campaign. One of the first nuggets I met at the door was Ellen Beidler. After introducing myself and having a brief conversation, she pulled out her checkbook and wrote a contribution on the spot, apologizing that it could not be larger. I was blown away, particularly as I had not even asked. Then, in discussing the boundaries of my district, she came to realize I not only represented her central Raleigh location but also her mother's Wake Forest neighborhood. She explained how incredibly active a Democrat her mother was and how important it was for us to meet. This conversation led to her mother hosting a wonderful meet and greet for me. In addition, Ellen invited me to attend a community "Pig in the Park" gathering later that week so I could meet her neighbors. I had noticed the fliers for this event while canvassing, but would have felt less comfortable just showing up without this personal invitation.

Another nugget was a middle aged Republican woman who had lived in her community for over 30 years and had come to be protective of many of her elderly neighbors. She was out in her yard when I visited the house next to hers and received no response. In noticing me, she declared that no one was at home. She further stated that she had advised her neighbors not to come to their doors as many had been preyed upon in the past by sales people. We got to talking and I shared my literature. She was excited that I was female and she liked my issues. She took my materials, said she would vouch for me to her neighbors, and suggested ways to contact others who lived nearby.

I met a third nugget, Mr. Hunter Tapscott who was eager to talk about issues when I went to his door. During our conversation, I learned that he was a Westinghouse retiree and that we had a mutual friend who had also retired from the company. He shared that the retirees met monthly and, as program chair, he asked if I would be interested in speaking at their next gathering.

While a day with these markers of success was particularly satisfying, a day where many people answered their door could also be energizing. Simple conversations could offer an emotional boost. For example, Andrea reported that a lady she met while canvassing on June 7th told her that her friend had just received my information and the two of them were chatting about me and noted that my issues crossed party lines, especially my stand against double taxing with tolls on the I-540. On another occasion in late August, a man wanted a yard sign immediately delivered and volunteered to work the polls on Election Day. On the 24th of August, Andrea met someone she thought might be a possible nugget. This woman worked from home, helped in the Kerry 2004 presidential campaign, was active in Connecticut and Maryland and wanted to get more involved in Raleigh. In addition, she had voted in the May primary and asked for information about becoming a precinct chair to be sent her way. Unfortunately, this was a nugget that never materialized, but in fairness she had a new one-year-old baby, and regardless provided a great feeling of energy. Another encounter at the doors that proved invigorating on October 21st, came about when I spoke to a gentleman who was open to voting for me and recalled meeting me when I spoke at an event for the Lion's Club held in early August. How encouraging to learn I was making a good impression on different fronts.

Though infrequent, ugly encounters did occur but often ultimately proved to be more entertaining than disturbing. On one occasion, I knocked on a door, waited but got no response so moved on to the next house. I was a few doors down the way when a man from the first home came out across the street waving my literature in his hand and demanding to know if I had left it at his door. With my picture prominently on my materials, I could see no way to deny it. He ranted that he would never vote for a candidate who came to his door, called him, sent him material in the mail, or put an ad on T.V. I could only hope that my opponent would contact the man in one of these ways. I also wondered how this man could learn of his electoral options. In mid-August, someone tried to "sic" a dog on Dan! A further canvassing outcome involved my receiving an email from a voter frustrated that it wasn't clear from my literature and website if I was a Democrat or a Republican. The tone of the communication was negative, but the lemonade from this email was that the voter had read my material and visited my website rather than just throwing out the material left at his door. I did subsequently clarify my party affiliation on my website in response to his concern and surprised him with a personal call to thank him for noting the omission. In late October, after introducing myself while going door-to-door, a not so friendly (it turned out) Republican commented, "I know - I've seen the signs all over the place." Hooray for the power of signage!

The more positive the reception, the more our enthusiasm to canvass grew and the more I felt affirmed in continuing with this strategy. Canvassing became a source of energy and the driving force of the campaign, so much so, that I felt conflicted in undertaking obligations that took me away from the doors. An added benefit of this primary focus on canvassing was that we effectively did our own polling. By summer's end, with 47 days of door-to-door activity under our belt and approximately 13 precincts covered, I had a strong sense of the district's receptiveness to my candidacy and what issues were important to them. This insight informed decisions I made as to the efficient use of the campaign's limited resources. For example, as my assessment of which issues mattered to people in the district was affirmed, I chose not to spend $8,000 on a poll to identify issues important to my district as had been described by Perry Woods as a step the Senate Caucus would expect before offering monetary support.

## *Canvassing Etiquette*

Being sensitive to the discomfort that political discussion might evoke, I encouraged an informative and conversational approach by my canvassing volunteers and discouraged any confrontational interactions. Much advice exists on how to approach voters at the doors. The wisdom of specifically asking each person you meet for his or her vote was a tactic I never mastered. While it may in part have reflected my own fear of being rejected, it largely seemed presumptuous to me, and an exercise in poor manners, to put someone on the spot about his or her vote. I preferred asking folks to consider my candidacy while offering materials that outlined my issues. Success came when there was an engaged voter at the door, not so much whether that person specified that he or she was voting for me.

## *Common Questions*

One of the questions I was most often asked was "why are you running." I am still trying to figure that one out! What I felt they really wanted to know was what made you get out of your house and expose yourself to public scrutiny and the negative environment that we have come to expect in the political arena today. Given that all of us have concerns, what did I care about so much that had led me to this choice? For me, the motivating issues of engaging people in the political process and improving education policy required a legislative response. The conversations which developed from such discussions revealed a deep-seated cynicism about politics. Follow-up questions from these voters often challenged my ability to affect change in a system they viewed as corrupt. If I got elected, how would I keep from being steamrolled by the "big boys?" My response was simply to paraphrase "the only way for evil to flourish is for good men [or women] to do nothing."

A second common question was about party identification. During the 2000 House campaign, there was a hostile attitude that characterized many of the Republicans at the door. After introducing myself, I would inevitably be asked by these voters "are you a Democrat" (insert accusatory tone) or are you a "Republican"? (insert mild friendly tone). I decided that humor was the best defense to such negativity so I would reply, "I am a Democrat, but I sleep with a Republican" (my husband Harry being a registered Republican at that time). The humor had an impact. Many would chuckle and confess to being part of a "mixed marriage" as well. Their preconceived notion of all Democrats being "wild eyed liberals" was tempered. Our interaction then proceeded on a more personal and less political level. Indeed, such humor resulted in a "mixed marriage" couple attending my Wake Forest fundraiser as shown in this email I received:

> *Gerry,*
> *It was nice to meet you last week when you knocked on my door on [removed street for privacy]. I told my husband you "also sleep with a Republican" and so I'm pretty sure he'll accompany me to the Massenburg's on Sunday! Of course the Republicans have been mailing him about Neal Hunt, but I told him I'd already agreed to put a yard sign up for you, so .... now it's up to you on Sunday to convince him personally with your message!*
>
> *Looking forward to seeing you Sunday.*
>
> *Blessings,*
> *[name removed for privacy]*

In 2000, the Bill Clinton-Monica Lewinsky scandal was still big news and I was told by more than one potential voter, "I will never vote for a Democrat again after what Bill Clinton did in the Oval Office." To these men I would politely respond, "Well sir, I did not sleep with Bill Clinton." By contrast, in 2006, President Clinton's transgressions were less troubling in light of six years of having "W" in the White House. The question was still asked, but the hostility was absent. In fact, many Republican candidates, including my opponent, did not broadcast their party affiliation in their literature, on their website, or on their yard signs (I wondered if they were queried on this absence).

As mentioned previously, I was often asked if I was related to Erskine Bowles. I loved this suggestion from one of my dear supporters when he was asked the same question about me:

> *I have given out two Gerry cards. The woman who got the first asked if she [Gerry] was related to Erskine Bowles. I said, "No" but immediately thought what a great mnemonic that was. From*

*now on, when giving the card, I will say she is not related to Erskine Bowles. That "not related to" part will tend to stick in memory and be called up when trying to remember, "Who was [it] that I wanted to remember to vote for [?]"*

## Political Educator

A good bit of my time at the doors was spent clarifying the responsibilities of a State Senator and in identifying the district I hoped to represent. I found myself frequently distinguishing my candidacy from that of Elizabeth "Liddy" Dole, one of North Carolina's US Senators, which spoke to the confusion surrounding different elected offices. Another example I encountered involved US and North Carolina House races. David Price and Brad Miller were both congressmen running for re-election in districts that overlapped mine. Likewise, Grier Martin and Ty Harrell shared parts of my district for their House races. At the doors, it was not uncommon for me to be asked if I was running against Representative Grier Martin. My hope was that by taking the time to educate voters more fully about legislative positions, I would engage them further in the political process.

## Combined Canvassing Efforts

Throughout the campaign, opportunities arose to participate in joint canvassing events. In one instance, the Wake County Democratic Party (WCDP) set up a countywide canvassing day in October where volunteers could meet in different locations and help the candidates on the ballots in that area. Of my 52 precincts the only one covered by this venture was not favorable to door-to-door canvassing, or to our targeted list (it was in a highly Republican area). I had chosen to just do literature drops in this precinct. It would have been helpful if the party had consulted candidates as to which areas might be best served by this volunteer effort. Nonetheless, I was grateful that the party had initiated a volunteer effort, and planned to arrive early at the specified location. I had taken my own materials to combine with those supplied by the WCDP. Unfortunately, it fell to me to organize the canvass at this site. The party organizer didn't even have a map of the area. Apart from Andrea and myself, no one else showed up. We proceeded to make the best of the situation by gathering the materials provided (door hangers produced by the WCDP) and included them in our canvassing materials, hoping to help other candidates while doing our broader canvassing.

A second instance of a less than stellar joint canvassing experience occurred in early October after being invited to join a canvass for another candidate whose precincts overlapped mine. This candidate was joined himself by Congressman David Price. Andrea had coordinated with their campaign manager the night before, assembling packages for canvassing, using some of our scarce materials to do so. On the day of the canvass, it was unclear whether Andrea and I were helping or intruding on the event. We were not able to choose our area and the one assigned to us that day was not strategic as we had already canvassed many of the shared precincts and had chosen to avoid the apartments and condominiums found on our walk list (these households have a higher turnover of voters and there is an awkwardness to accessing each door). Many of the volunteers were college students coming in support of the other candidate. We felt more like taggers on than guests. We were purposefully not included with the Congressman and the candidate and were sent off with just one other volunteer. It felt like we were not wanted and yet the candidate had asked us to take part. I had accepted the invitation to show support to another campaign and to be considered a team player, but I ended up feeling drained, embarrassed and frustrated emotionally. Rather than being a collaborative effort, it felt like we were just volunteers. In addition, Andrea ended up having to spend a great deal of time retrieving much of our unused materials from the campaign packages that hadn't been distributed.

In retrospect, the lesson in these two experiences was that I needed to assume less and assert more. In both instances, I imagined I was part of a team with the standing of a candidate and yet ended up feeling like more of a workhorse, whose interests were not considered.

By contrast we had a successful, collaborative canvass with the Chair of the North Carolina Democratic Party, Jerry Meeks. Following a conversation we had after his special appearance at *Quail Ridge Books and Music* early in August, Jerry asked me to contact him to schedule a date he might join our door-to-door canvass. In organizing this event, we knew what to expect, could advertise to the broader Democratic base and set the agenda for the morning. We arranged this canvass to be part of our Four on Friday August canvassing efforts and sent out the following update to our contact list:

> **2 G/Jerry's for the price of one:**
> Jerry Meek, Chair of the North Carolina Democratic Party, will be joining Gerry and volunteers in the morning of our "Four on Friday" canvass this week on August 25th from 10 a.m. -12p.m. If you have not yet had a chance to take part in one of these invigorating opportunities to connect with neighbors, we invite you to do so with Gerry and Jerry on Friday! We will be meeting at the BP located at Six Forks and Newton Rd. Please let Andrea Bertole know if you can take part (919-793-0160 or andreabertole@hotmail.com).

We had a great turnout of volunteers and the energy and enthusiasm provided a good boost as we headed into the fall.

## *Literature Drops*

During the first week of November we switched our strategy from canvassing to literature drops, as there was not the same need to get email addresses and signs. We had volunteers initiate drops. In addition to help offered by Nell Whitlock and the Hurds noted in our Volunteer section, the Mainwarings distributed our literature in conjunction with that of Grier Martin and Brad Miller). Being in palm card deficit, we were retrieving unused materials from volunteers that they may have had from helping on previous occasions. To supplement our supplies, we used the Wake County Democratic Party's door hanger, a mock ballot that listed all the Democratic candidates running for election in November. We highlighted my name and attached our self-printed "Why Vote Gerry" handout (a sample can be found under "Political Campaign Products" in Chapter Eight). Our goal was to exhaust our supply of campaign literature and have nothing remaining come Election Day. This pared down approach still had an impact as evidence by the following emails received after one such literature drop:

> Mrs. Bowles,
> You have my vote!!! And I would love to support your campaign by putting your sign(s) in my yard! I live at the corner of [omitted for privacy], right at the corner where a lot of voters will turn to vote at Hudson Memorial. My address is [omitted for privacy] I know you are extremely busy in these last days before the election, so feel free to have someone from your campaign staff put your

*signs in my yard!*

*Also, my mother was a first grade teacher for over 30 years in Her[t]ford, NC where I was raised and my parents still live!*

*Good Luck next Tuesday!!!!!!!*

*Sincerely,*

*[Name, cell, and home number omitted for privacy]*

And

*Ms. Bowles*

*My wife mentioned that you stopped by the other day to discuss the upcoming election. I wish that I would have had the opportunity to speak with you. What I am curious to know is this: What is your opinion on charter schools? I normally vote Democratic, however I am the board chair of a charter school in Raleigh, which cause me to rub elbows with many Republicans. I would really like to see charter schools "de-poloticized" (sic) because it does not benefit the children of Wake county to have partisan fighting over school models.*

*Anyway, I guess I have shown my hand a bit, but would be interested in hearing your views. If you would prefer not to respond via email, you could call me [phone number removed for privacy]*

*Thanks,*

*[name removed for privacy]*

*P.S. I will be out of town on election day so I have to vote absentee this weekend.*

## Phone Canvassing

> *Canvassing by Phone October 3rd & 4th from home at your convenience*
> Travel the telephone wires and unearth new campaign supporters. Spring into action and join the phone canvass expeditions on Tuesday, October 3rd & Wednesday, October 4th from 6:30 – 8:30pm at Hardin & Bowles located at 1514 Glenwood Avenue, Suite 201 in the 2-story yellow building on Glenwood between the Wade Avenue underpass and the Rialto Theatre at Five Points. No cause for disappointment if these dates conflict with your schedule. Excursions can also begin at home with scripts and phone lists supplied happily by the campaign.
> - from Sep 29, 2006 Campaign Update

As the above excerpt from one of our Campaign Updates illustrates, a variation on our door-to-door recruitment efforts was to contact potential voters by phone. While many campaigns refer to this activity as phone banking, we chose to describe it as phone canvassing. We felt this terminology better reflected our approach that was less about banks of volunteers calling in an isolated, sterile setting, and more about camaraderie and team building. We had several sessions planned and felt it afforded volunteers who might otherwise not be able to canvass by foot an opportunity to help grow the campaign. One such example can be found with our first phone canvass in July in which a few senior citizens showed up with walkers, hearing aids, and missing glasses (hard to read the phone lists) but with plenty of enthusiasm and good humor. We recognized that it is not everyone's cup of tea to make calls for a campaign, so we really tried to share the victories and defeats with one another. For example, on one occasion, our campaign manager, Dan, was having an unusual run of bad luck. Much to his chagrin, people kept hanging up on him. To sooth his sensibilities, my husband, Harry, offered to treat him to a beer at the end of the evening as a reward for his perseverance which turned this adverse experience into something fun, with all of us checking in to see how many more hang ups he would receive.

Most of these events were offered with the kind help of my son, Hal Bowles, who let us use his business location at Hardin Bowles and multiple phone lines to make calls. By situating phone canvassing at this more downtown location, in the evenings, we hoped to attract volunteers whose work schedule prevented daytime canvassing and who could drop by on their way home from work. As with all our volunteer activities refreshments and time for social interaction were part of the agenda. This approach generated additional benefits. For example, it allowed two of our key volunteers, Herb Reichlin and Betty Ann Knudsen, to get to know one another, leading to Herb's suggestion of featuring Betty Ann more prominently in the campaign, naming her as honorary chair and eventually celebrating her contributions to local politics with our Strong Women's Tea event (described later). The goals of each phone canvass varied from seeking sponsorships for fund raisers to the more traditional get out the vote effort.

We were quick also to recognize that not all could attend at a certain location or at a particular time but might like to help. For those volunteers, we happily provided call lists and scripts to be used at home. In late October, close to the election, we had more requests for scripts to use at home than we had volunteers show up at a designated location. In response, we shifted our final phone canvass in early November from Hardin Bowles to being at homes. An example of the positive response we had from our volunteers calling from home is as follows:

> *From: [names removed for privacy]*
> *To: abertole@nc.rr.com*
> *Sent: Wednesday, October 25, 2006 8:02 PM*
> *Subject: calls made*
>
> *Andrea,*
>
> *From the list you sent, we called the ones on the first page.*
>
> *Sorry, we didn't call more, but every little bit helps.*
>
> *"unscientific" results:*
>
> *you've got my vote!, several*
> *not interested, several*
> *left message, several*
> *and several folks were interested in visiting the web site. That's a*

*tell-tale sign of how people expect to get information or do research these days!*

As with most volunteer activities, to be sure to make the best use of everyone's time and ensure their comfort, preparation was key, particularly as some volunteers were only able to stay for a brief amount of time, and others were not able to come at the start. When volunteers arrived, we had a sign in sheet (used later to help send thanks), a script, a list of names to be called, a phone log to record responses, and a calendar of upcoming campaign events. As part of our welcome, I would offer brief remarks regarding my approach to phone etiquette. For instance, while in the past I might have avoided calling during the dinner hour, I was less concerned in 2006 as dinnertime was not so defined. By contrast, I did not want to make calls too late at night and risk interrupting bedtime routines so we tried to wrap up all our calls by 9pm. We asked volunteers working from home to be mindful of these guidelines and use their best judgment.

A sample of our phone canvassing script from our first canvass in July and an example of the information sought in a phone log are provided below:

## Activist Phone Canvass Script – July 12th

*Please personalize your greeting to those on your call list as you feel appropriate – a suggested script for your call includes the following:*

Good evening – May I please speak with _____ ? My name is _____ and I am working with Gerry Bowles who is running as the Democrat for the North Carolina State Senate for District 15. We would like to involve you, as an active Democrat, in Gerry's campaign and earn your vote for November $7^{th}$. As you may have heard, this year is a "blue-moon election" with no race for president, governor or U.S. Senate at the top of the ballot. As such, turnout is expected to be low and the impact of one vote is heightened.

<u>Machine</u>: We invite you to visit Gerry's web site at GerryBowles06.com and contact Gerry to become involved through this web site, or at 847-9901 or gerrybowles@yahoo.com. Thank you.

Someone Answers:
- If <u>not interested</u>: Thank you for your time.
- If <u>interested</u>:
1. We would love to be able to include you in our online newsletter to keep you up-to-date with Gerry's activities.
    - May I have your <u>email address</u> to include you in our updates (we will not be passing this info to anyone else)
    - As a grassroots campaign we are looking for ways to minimize expenses and online communication helps with this.

2. May I confirm your <u>mailing address</u>?

3. Would you be willing to display a <u>yard sign</u> for Gerry Bowles later this summer?

4. Could I include you as a member of our growing network of <u>volunteers</u> for Gerry's campaign - Would you pledge "2-for-Gerry" by offering 2 hours of your time to our volunteer activities ranging from canvassing, to helping out at upcoming events, phoning other voters, and helping with mailings.

5. While Gerry's primary campaign focus is community mobilization, the <u>need for funds</u> is inescapable. We are preparing a mailing for Gerry's Campaign Kick-off with special guest David Price on August $8^{th}$ - We are seeking sponsors for this event at levels ranging from $100 to $1,000 OR if your budget can better absorb a smaller form of support, your contribution at perhaps $10 would help us reach our $1,500 fundraising goal for the mailing. Checks can be made payable to "Gerry Bowles NC Senate."

6. Please join us for a reception with Mayor Meeker on July $18^{th}$ or for Gerry's Campaign Kick-off with Congressman Price on August $8^{th}$ *(see Event Listing for details)*

Thank you so much for your time this evening and hopefully your vote for Gerry November $7^{th}$. On a final note, I encourage you to visit Gerry's web site at GerryBowles06.com.

## Gerry Bowles - Democrat for District 15's North Carolina State Senate - November 2006

*Phone Canvass Log*

LM=Left Message   NR=No Response   B=busy signal   SL=Send Literature   O=Other (specify)

|   | Name | Phone # | E-mail | Precinct | Lawn Sign | Volunteer | Comment |
|---|------|---------|--------|----------|-----------|-----------|---------|
| 1 |      |         |        |          |           |           |         |
| 2 |      |         |        |          |           |           |         |
| 3 |      |         |        |          |           |           |         |
| 4 |      |         |        |          |           |           |         |

# Chapter Six – Events

Events offered another important approach to winning the election one precinct at a time. These included meet and greets, my Campaign Kickoff, community events I participated in, political forums I attended, and Democratic Party gatherings.

## *Meet & Greets*

If canvassing was the meat of my campaign, then meet and greets served as the potatoes. These events were social gatherings generated by the campaign or set up by supporters that enabled me to meet the public in a more intimate fashion.

### *Goals*

My approach to meet and greets was the idea they be multifaceted. There was certainly a monetary goal for each event. However, even for the high-ticket occasions, I insisted that someone with limited means be afforded an opportunity to attend. The campaign also planned many events in which contributions were welcomed but there was no "admission" charged. As I alluded to in Chapter Two when describing my goals for my campaign kickoff, my distinctly grassroots campaign recognized the value in "people raising" as well as fund raising. Whether growing a business or a campaign, relationships are key and networking was always a goal. Other goals included creating opportunities to promote my name recognition (visibility) and to grow the campaign (recruit more volunteers). A final goal of my campaign was to maintain the morale of my campaign committee by providing venues in which they could participate.

### *Invitation*

I used a variety of means to invite people to these events. The information was always posted on my website and highlighted in my electronic newsletter. The campaign requested that these events be included on the Wake County Democratic Party's website calendar of events and campaign updates. As a matter of course the campaign also notified the local print media, the *News and Observer* and the *Independent*. In the instances where the meet and greet was held in a private home, the host would be encouraged to invite his or her friends and family. My primary approach, as mentioned in the canvassing section, was to include invitations with my campaign materials that I would hand deliver or leave at the doors. They would usually include a suggested contribution amount and request an RSVP so I could ensure having enough food and beverage.

## *Set-up*

In terms of the flow at any given event, there always was a loose structure involved. For my comfort, sense of support to the hosts, and grassroots focus, I liked to arrive early to help greet and set-up. With any of the meet and greets, regardless of whether there were ten people or ten times that amount, I followed a basic checklist for event preparations:
- setting up my banner outside the home
- placing balloons at key intersections to guide attendees to the event
- ensuring yard signs were available for distribution [once we had them],
- setting up a welcome table for guests where they could:
  - sign in, on a sign in sheet
  - get a name tag
  - offer a monetary contribution if desired
  - sign up to volunteer
  - pick up campaign literature

## *Program*

By arriving early, I could introduce attendees I already knew to others and help create a conversational setting. An added benefit to being at the event ahead of time was that anyone new showing up would feel more comfortable with others already in attendance, as opposed to being the first at the event. After allowing some time for folks to arrive and mingle, I would assess when the time was right to say a few words, generally midway through the event. The host would introduce me, I would acknowledge the elected officials and any other candidates and allow them to briefly introduce themselves. While I had a short "stump" speech based on my key issues, I would tailor my remarks to the concerns of those at the event I had heard earlier while mingling. This approach was not universal to all candidates. While attending a peer candidate's meet and greet in September, I arrived early to find no evidence of an upcoming event. Where we would have had balloons out to mark the way, there was nothing to show I was at the right location. The candidate arrived late and the attendance was sparse. To my thinking it lacked the comfort and welcome I strived to create at my functions.

### Markers of Success
Given my multiple goals for any meet and greet, the markers of success were various. The funds raised or the number of attendees did not solely determine success of an event. Equally important were:
- engaging new people in the campaign (first time attendees and those who took the time to RSVP regrets instead of simply ignoring the invitation)
- expanding the demographic of supporters (for example, registered Republican women, high school students, folks from precincts outside the event)
- creating a contagious enthusiastic spirit among attendees (willingness to take yard signs, give e-mail information, and share news of the campaign with their friends and family)

### Fringe Benefit
In addition to the benefits that came from the successes above, the meet and greets led to an unexpected benefit of heightening the campaign's profile and credibility among the North Carolina Senate Caucus, North Carolina Democratic Party, the media, political followers, and other candidates. The number and success of these events created a buzz and an appreciation of how active our campaign was, which in turn generated energy and momentum amongst the broader voting community.

### Experiences with Meet & Greets
Over the course of my campaign, I took part in more than a dozen meet and greets, each providing their own learning opportunities, energy, and success.

### Dessert and Dancing - May 24, 2006
In sharing the news of my candidacy to my circle of friends, I announced I was running for office to the Sassy Classics, a senior Rockette-style dance troupe that I danced with. Sharon, my events coordinator, and Carole Guld, a fellow dancer and passionate Democrat, proposed that the "Sassies" perform at a fundraiser by way of support. Carole suggested using the Raleigh Jewish Community Center as a venue, knowing it was located within my district. The reality was that this site was not in a favorable precinct, in fact in terms of my targeted list, it was in the bottom

tier. However, we hoped given Carole's prominent connection to the larger Jewish community, that we would generate interest beyond the precinct's geographic boundary. We had invitations printed and arranged our first volunteer meeting in late April to address envelopes. Carole had a directory in which she highlighted the names of her friends within the Jewish Community. In addition, we sent invitations to registered voters within the vicinity of the Community Center.

The RSVP response was underwhelming given the large number of invitations sent. We were aware that people do not always reply and felt compelled to have sufficient refreshments for a potentially large turnout. We had arranged for volunteers to provide the desserts, but through miscommunication we were unsure enough would be provided which led to a last minute S.O.S to additional volunteers to supply more. In fact, the underwhelming number of RSVP's would have been preferable to the actual turnout we experienced! There were more "entertainers" than audience members. However, there was a silver lining to our less than stellar first "fundraiser." We ended up having enough refreshments to take us through the remainder of the campaign and we connected with Lola Youngman, an engaged member of the 08-04 precinct. Lola became an active volunteer and ended up hosting, with her husband, my campaign kickoff in early August. Moving forward from this event, we realized that we couldn't afford a conventional approach to fund raisers. For the majority, we adopted the aforementioned strategy to meet and greets and passed up the added expense of mailing.

## *High School Reunion Event - June 17-19, 2006*

In thinking of possible event locations that would tap into broader circles of support, I thought of planning something in my hometown around my high school's 50th birthday celebration (a reunion of all the classes) which was being held in Williamsburg, Virginia, in mid-June. I thought to hold a casual hot dog event at my family's home. It is amazing how going back to your home can put you back into your childhood roles and instead of feeling like Gerry Bowles, NC Senate Candidate, I felt more like "Gerry from the hood." My Daddy was 85 years old at that time and not of my political persuasion. On a good day, he was not a social animal and in addition his health had been a bit compromised. I mailed invitations for the event to my classmates, but kept waiting for the right moment to run this idea by my Daddy. Only a handful of RSVPs came in and those that did come wished me well but regretted not being able to attend. Given that my reaction was one of relief to each "regret" and having said nothing to my Daddy, I realized it didn't make sense to carry on with this event. At the opening night of the Reunion, I made sure to let as many people know as possible that there would be no cookout the next day. That said, I felt a great deal of stress when the event time came around hoping that no one would show up (no one did).

For all that angst, there were positive moments that resulted from attending this reunion. The first was connecting with a friend, Tommy Norment, who had graduated a year ahead of me and was the current Virginia General Assembly Republican Senator representing the Williamsburg area. Tommy was wearing two hats that night – he was there as an attendee and as the keynote speaker for the event. In having an opportunity to catch up, I shared that I was running as a Democrat for State Senate in North Carolina. After offering condolences, he wished me well even though he was on the other side of the aisle. Surprisingly, and so kindly, he sent me the following email on June 29th:

> *I enjoyed seeing you at the JBHS $50^{th}$ event. I was excited to see your enthusiasm in running for the NC Senate, even if it is against a fellow Republican! I know you are an experienced campaigner, but here are some approaches that have worked for me:*
> *1. Money: while you have to do a lot of direct "asks" get a finance committee of folks who have not necessarily been involved in politics, but know how to ask for money without being discouraged at the first "No" response.*
> *2. Money: spend it wisely. Consultants can sometimes consume a disproportionate share and direct mail is still a "weapon of choice".*
> *3. Message: you have to give voters a reason to "change". Trying to "out good guy" the other guy seldom if ever works.*
> *4. Message: negative works, but it can be done in a politically acceptable way without coming across as being "nasty".*
> *5. Message: keep the message simple, limited and stay on message always.*

6. *Consultants: honest ones have value in providing objectivity and expertise. It is kind of like being a lawyer and avoiding having yourself as a client.*

7. *As a challenger: you can make up in manpower by friends and people who believe in you to overcome money.*

> *A. Groups going door-to-door with you. Frequently, I only personally hit every other or third house and let a volunteer kno[ck] on the other doors asking for their vote and leaving a flyer..*
> *B. Phone banks manned by volunteers from banks, realtor offices or other places with multiple phone lines that can save money.*
> *C. Small, neighborhood meet and greets in people's homes.*
> *D. Lit drops that save postage.*

8. *The "BIG ASK": Always ask for their vote. Never, ever forget to ask for their vote as you look them in the eye and shake their hands. It creates a "moral" bond.*

*Good luck and all this is worth exactly what you paid for it.*

An additional positive boost was an outgrowth of my communication with Tommy. He had shared news of my candidacy with a former classmate and friend, Frank Smith, who was not in attendance. He sent me the following email message on June 18th:

*Dear Gerry,*

*Tommy Norment sent me a note which included your political aspirations. Are you crazy? I guess that happens to lawyers.*

*I went on from W&M to the Army and then to the University of Kentucky for graduate school in (sit down for this) Library Science. Felsie Riddle [our high school librarian] would be still spinning in her grave if she knew that. Worked most of my career in Va. Beach Public Library where I retired in '01. Married a librarian, Laurel Mancini, (also retired) and we live in a little house with our three cats in Va. Beach and try to keep beneath the radar.*

*Hope you regain your senses before you get elected!!*

Sincerely,

*Frank Smith*
*Class of '64*
*JBHS*

Finally, though unexpectedly, my fund raising aspirations for this trip were achieved. Despite having canceled the hot dog cook out/fund raiser, financial support was realized within a week of returning to Raleigh. A letter arrived with a check for $1,000 from a dear childhood friend, Arthur, who I had encountered at the reunion and enjoyed reminiscing with.

### *Pre-Independence Day Ice Cream Social - June 27, 2006*

I hosted one of the first meet and greet events, a "Pre-Independence Day" ice cream social, at my home in late June. I hadn't chosen to target my precinct as part of my 25 most favorable. However, having lived in the area for 27 years I felt the need to introduce my candidacy to my neighbors in a more personal manner. I adjusted the canvassing schedule to allow enough time to cover my area while continuing with the targeted precincts. Within a short time, from June 15th to June 26th, I along with volunteers, left invitations to this celebration attached to my campaign literature at homes throughout my neighborhood. For the most part, we canvassed by car as most of the homes sit on acre lots. In addition to opening my home to neighbors, I also welcomed others to attend by announcing this event through the media outlets previously detailed. Happily, this celebration was one of the few events mentioned on one of the *News and Observer's* blog sites. By contrast to the Dessert and Dancing event, the response to this social hit most of our markers of success.

### *Rodham Meet and Greet - July 9, 2006*

The pace quickened after the 4th of July as more folks were beginning to focus on the campaigns and the upcoming election. On July $9^{th}$, Andrea and I attended a meeting of the 08-04 precinct in which Rodger Koopman, candidate for the Wake County Commissioners, and I were guests of honor. A large turnout enabled me to enlist additional folks to help with the campaign. This event at the home of Joyce and John Rodham was an example of the value in having organized, energized, and active precincts. My treasurer, Gail Christensen, was the catalyst of this group. As precinct chair, she kept her neighbors informed and involved through her communications, spirit, and activism. Geographically located in one of the most hostile (for a Democrat) precincts in my district, this group gave my campaign an entrée into this area and provided nurturing and continuing volunteer support.

### *Meet the Mayor - Dellinger Meet and Greet - July 18, 2006*

From the beginning, I was on the look-out for supporters in my district who would feel comfortable hosting a meet and greet for me in their home. Not only did such events help complement my canvassing plans, but they also presented a strong endorsement of my campaign to others who lived in the district. Whenever possible, I mentioned hosting as a volunteer activity and encouraged committee members to suggest people who might be willing to host. Our fourth meet and greet came about through one such suggestion. While preparing for the ice cream social, I confirmed with Susan and John Dellinger their willingness to open their home to me in mid-July. Their home is in the North Hills area and was centrally located among three of my first-tier targeted precincts. As they were located within the Raleigh city limits it occurred to me that if Mayor Meeker's schedule permitted his attendance, his presence alongside me would offer folks another reason to attend. Fortunately, the timing worked and the Dellingers were comfortable with this development. The morning after the ice cream social, I joined volunteers in distributing invitations along with my campaign materials on the street where the Dellingers lived, then spread out from there to the surrounding precincts.

As with the ice cream social, this event was not intended as a fundraiser. The invitation did not require a donation but did mention a reasonable suggested contribution of $25. It invited the recipient to "Join Mayor Charles Meeker and Susan and John Dellinger for a reception supporting Gerry Bowles, Democratic Candidate, NC State Senate, District 15 on Tuesday July 18th from 5:30-7:00 p.m. and to please RSVP by July 14th to gerry@gerrybowles06 919-847-9901." Whether a person could attend or not, my hope was that the invitation would accomplish conveying who I was, what office I was running for and how that person could reach me to learn more. While the literature might have been dismissed, I hoped the invitation was a more personal inducement to find out about me. Invitations were also sent to the Dellinger's friends, church community and business associates and the event was posted in various venues as had been done with the ice cream social.

Prior to the event, we had not received many responses and my hosts were concerned. I was always so grateful to have someone willing to host a meet and greet and was sympathetic to how responsible the host felt about turnout. One of the anecdotes I often shared with them concerned one of John Edwards' first meet and greets in his 1998 primary campaign for the North Carolina U.S. Senate seat. I received a postcard invitation to an open house that was being held in a location convenient to my work commute. It was pouring rain when I arrived at the start of the event. Much to my surprise, I was one of the first guests to arrive and one of the few in attendance. However, the low attendance did not keep John Edwards from winning this primary and becoming one of North Carolina's US Senators. It taught me the valuable lesson that I would witness in my campaign: the success of an event is not solely determined by the number of attendees, or the amount of money raised. Even so, we were delighted that the number of responses to the Dellinger meet and greet increased after the RSVP request date and within 48 hours of the event. We were to find this pattern of late response was not limited to this event.

What varied from event to event was what and how much to serve to eat and drink. With a tight budget, I did not have the luxury of catering events so I counted on the hosts and volunteers to supply the refreshments, relying on RSVPs to guide quantity planning. Of course, the hosts are partners and have their own concerns about the condition of their home and coordination of the event with their personal friends and family. The day before the Dellinger event, Susan sent me an email that shows how much work can be involved:

> *Gerry, I hope you enjoyed the play last night.*
> 
> *My next phone calls will be to Sharon and Diana* [the campaign's event coordinators]. *John and I worked all weekend to finish yard projects, clean and cook. Thank you for the motivation to get things in better shape!*

*Steven Beck* [their precinct chair] *is out of town and his wife Kristin is coming – and bringing crab dip! Bill Page has a 5:30 meeting downtown but hopes to be here by 6:15. And, he's bringing a neighbor (whose name I can't remember).*

*About 6 to 10 folks from St. Marks Episcopal will be there. Eve and Tom Vatagliona, Betty Jo and Jim Jacobs, John and Mary Mainwaring, Gene Brown, Deborah and Clay Clark.*

*John and Mary and Betty Jo and Jim might be able to host meet and greets in their precincts later.*

*My mother and her neighbor, Barbara Gutknecht, will attend. I told them I'd make the donation for them since they're seniors on fixed incomes and they're out of the district, but I knew they'd enjoy the event.*

*My neighbors, Mary and Joseph Covington, are back in town and may be there.*

*Adrian* [their son] *confirmed that Lindy Brown* [candidate for Wake County Commissioner] *is coming. My daughter-in-law, Kayla, will be coming for sure. Adrian may miss class and attend.*

*I'm so glad the Perry's are attending. I'm sure I've seen them in the neighborhood, but look forward to putting the faces with the names.*

*John and I are planning from anywhere from 20 to 50 people.* [There were over 60 who signed in] *I do believe we'll have more voters than candidates. Not bad for July!*

*I'm going to ask Sharon and Diana about a card table and a person out front to take the donations and to see if one of them could bring red, white, and blue balloons for the mailbox. John and I have a note to put the flag out.*

*Feel free to call me at work ... if you need right of way in the next couple of days.*

*-Susan*

We seemed to have had the "perfect storm" for this event. We had wonderful, involved hosts who engaged their community and whose warmth provided a welcoming environment. Furthermore, we had a great location, an outstanding guest, and enough lead-time for our canvassing work to make headway. The turnout was huge and not only included our known supporters but also people new to the campaign. The event provided a boost of energy and generated a buzz in the political community and an excitement that spread to new supporters. It was a public affirmation of what we had been sensing while canvassing and helped give the campaign further credibility.

On July 26th, Susan emailed us this whimsical headline, touting the success of our fundraiser in contrast to that of Liddy Dole's on the same evening!

**Meeker/Bowles beat Liddy Dole in fundraising :-)**

*Thought you two would enjoy this tidbit. I look forward to seeing you Thursday night. -- Susan*

*From The New York Times: WASHINGTON, July 22 " The tables were loaded with untouched platters of food as Senator Elizabeth Dole rose this week to introduce her party's Senate candidate from Nebraska. Sixty people were supposed to be at the fund-raiser, but Mrs. Dole, the host and leader of the Republican effort to hold the Senate this fall, found just 18 people scattered across an expanse of empty carpet.*

### Making Lemonade – August 3, 2006

The great success of the Dellinger event encouraged other people to feel comfortable in opening their homes to me. One of my more recent volunteers, Pam Green, who had joined the campaign committee, indicated her and her husband, Ken's, willingness to host a Lemonade Social on August 3rd from 6:00 to 7:30 in the evening. Their house was situated in one of the targeted 28 precincts. I directed our canvassing to include a radius around their home, advertising this lemonade party. With the temperatures hovering over 90°F, I encouraged them to keep the gathering informal by offering just lemonade and cookies. However, the hostess told me her husband would insist on providing more. Communication was a little less clear for this event. While I had understood the hosts would be taking care of all the food and drink, her desire to offer more caused some of the basics to be overlooked. As it turned out, I ended up supplying the *lemonade*. The evening was well received and gave me a chance to meet new voters from my district. The turnout to this event (about 15 attendees), while not as large as the Dellinger event, was encouraging for the more neighborhood feel and for the short time available to plan it. In addition, in posting this event in the usual sites, people heretofore less involved in the campaign sent replies to say they could not attend which indicated they were engaged enough to be aware of the event and take time to respond. It felt like I had connected in a more intimate manner with these folks even though they could not attend.

### *Oakforest Event - August 20, 2006*

While the next larger meet and greet took place August 20th in Wake Forest, the planning began two months earlier after meeting Ellen Beidler while canvassing in her North Hills community. As I described in my section on canvassing, Ellen's enthusiasm and support for my candidacy included involving her mother in my campaign. She insisted that I call her mom after learning that my district included Wake Forest where her mother lived. By Ellen's admission her mom was a political enthusiast and a life-long Democrat. As soon as I returned home from canvassing on June 21$^{st}$ I called her mom, Barbara Massenburg, to introduce myself. Our conversation involved a lot of "who do you know?" and a bit about current events as a means to discover common ground and shared beliefs. As is often the case when we find someone who shares our passion, in this case politics, the conversation came freely and without hesitation. In no time at all, I felt a kinship with her. She indicated that she would be delighted to host a meet and greet for me at her home in Wake Forest and gave me the names of six couples to call and introduce myself to whom she thought might want to contribute to the event.

I must admit that calling these folks was indeed a stretch. I was to call someone who I had not met at the behest of someone that I had just met "on the phone" and ask them to support me in my political campaign. My awkwardness was dispelled by the response of the first contact. After introducing myself as their Democratic candidate for the North Carolina Senate seat to represent Wake Forest in the legislature, I explained that I was calling them at the request of Barbara Massenburg, and would like to have their support with a meet and greet. The gist of the conversation can be summed up in this contact's response, "If Barbara Massenburg says you're ok, that's good enough for me." It was as if I had been given the Duncan Hines seal of approval!

In chatting with Barbara, I mentioned that I had heard Frank Drake, the newly elected Wake Forest Town Counselor, speak as a panelist during a political workshop hosted by the Wake County Democratic Party. He had been outspent by three other candidates in a four-way race. He had run a grassroots campaign, going door-to-door every evening after work and on Saturdays during the fall. I had been so impressed by him and was encouraged because I knew that even though some of the precincts we shared were not at first glance favorable to a Democrat, he had been elected. Barbara responded that she had hosted an event for Frank and that I should phone his wife, Kathy, to bring her on board my campaign. Kathy's response to my request for support was similar to that of the other folks that Barbara had listed. Barbara was indeed the recognized doyen of Wake Forest Democratic circles.

In addition to agreeing that she and Frank would co-host the event to be held at the Massenburg home on the 20th of August, Kathy shared the names of supporters of Franks' campaign that I might invite to the event and names on call lists that I might use for the general election. With just under 60 days to go, we started planning for this "meet and greet." Once more we combined our canvassing with invitation distribution. This gave me an opportunity to make inroads into part of my district that may not have been normally open to me.

Barbara and her husband, Speed, lived in an historic home, "Oakforest." Early on, Andrea and I had the opportunity to visit and prepare for the event. Part of the delight of the home was the "ghostly presence" of an earlier inhabitant. "She" did not make her presence known the afternoon of the party, but our knowledge of her existence added a different "dimension" to the event. In our true meet and greet fashion there was no charge, but contributions were welcomed. Our invitation was to "Get involved and hear how Gerry plans to earn your vote!"

This event on Sunday evening from 5:00 to 7:00 pm was a success. The setting was warm and comfortable, and the refreshments (contributed by Barbara's friends and a few of my campaign committee members) were delicious and abundant. We had planned to be outside for most of the afternoon, but heat and a later thunderstorm sent us inside where I took the opportunity to offer a few remarks. One of my fellow candidates in offering "constructive" criticism told me that I had talked too long. I was not oblivious to the fact that my remarks were lengthy, but had observed the body language and knew many folks in the crowd had not met me previously. Fully aware that folks were not captive in the area where I was speaking, and were free to move to another room if they tired of listening, I made a conscious decision to give them a full personal introduction and an overview of the political scene.

The turnout at this event was positive. There were people I didn't know, always a positive sign, some regulars, other candidates for office, and most rewarding, people that I had met while canvassing the Wake Forest neighborhoods. One such attendee was Ginny Fleming. As mentioned earlier, I had met Ginny while canvassing and we instantly formed a bond in that we both had husbands who were registered Republicans. When she and her husband arrived at the meet and greet I was especially gratified because he was most excited to meet someone like his wife "who slept with a Republican."

As previously mentioned, the "bottom line" definition of success for most political events is "how much money did you raise?" The monetary contributions were significant at this event. Equally important to me were the folks who I might not have had an opportunity to meet who were now a part of the campaign. I had even enlisted the support of a Republican. In addition, one of the attendees invited me to be his guest at the upcoming monthly meeting of his book club. My yard signs (which had just arrived) were available for distribution at the end of the event and were soon a part of the Wake Forest landscape, thereby advertising my name and showing a commitment by the homeowner to my election. The campaign continued to gather momentum. So on that June day when I knocked on Ellen's door in the North Hills community, a seed was sown and in August yielded a bumper crop in the community of Wake Forest!

## *Strong Women Tea – September 10, 2006*

I was always pondering unique and personal ways to raise awareness of and funds for my campaign. I continually brainstormed with my committee to think of ideas. We looked for opportunities to meet people in informal settings. The hope was to reach folks that might not ordinarily attend a political event. The belief was that it can be more comfortable for the "non-political" individual to meet a candidate for public office in the home of their neighbor than in a less intimate public location. One result of this approach was our "Strong Women's Tea".

The idea of a strong women's tea had its genesis in the early summer. Having met Andrea through a book club, it was not unusual for us to discuss books that we had heard about or were reading. The focus of one such discussion was Elizabeth Edwards', wife of John Edwards, new book, Saving Graces. Our discussion led to planning an event that celebrated strong women in politics. I thought initially of asking Elizabeth to be our featured "guest of honor".

I had a couple of connections to Elizabeth. I had traveled to Iowa in January 2004 to campaign door-to-door in her husband John's presidential campaign. The following June I had spoken with her at the wedding of John's goddaughter to the son of one of my close friends. More recently, Elizabeth and I had exchanged greetings and best wishes when we ran into one another at the doctor's office. I was there for an annual checkup and she was undergoing treatment for cancer.

I called the goddaughter's mother to find out how Elizabeth was feeling. Even though we knew that Elizabeth was extremely busy and was planning a book tour after Labor Day, we were of the mind, "nothing ventured, nothing gained." She gave us the telephone number of Elizabeth's scheduler and the following odyssey began.

> *To: ayoung@young.us*
> *Thursday, June 29, 2006*
> *Strong Women for Gerry*

Hi Andrew,

As per our phone conversation on June 28$^{th}$ I would very much like to have Elizabeth as my guest of honor at a fundraiser for my candidacy for NC Senate in District 15. That is the district where John and Elizabeth have resided in Raleigh.

I met Elizabeth at one of the first meet and greet events for John in the Country Club Hills neighborhood when he was making a bid for the US Senate in the primary campaign.

I was taken by her warmth and intelligence! Subsequently, my friend and co-worker at the legislature, Cornelia McMillan, shared more wonderful stories about Elizabeth and her strength of character.

When John made a bid for the presidency, I volunteered to campaign in Iowa. The trip was a Christmas present from my husband!

I campaigned door-to-door in Iowa and South Carolina and was present when victory was declared in South Carolina. Since the campaign, I have followed Elizabeth's fight against breast cancer and had occasion to see her in the doctor's office on one of her check-ups.

I am thankful that she is winning this greatest battle.

I am not alone in wishing and praying for Elizabeth's complete recovery. I have many friends who share her struggle against breast cancer.

They would love to have the opportunity to meet her and share their stories. Thus, it is my hope that Elizabeth might be a guest at an event which would focus on "Strong Women for Gerry."
I understand that time is a precious commodity and that Elizabeth has more on her plate than most, but I would very much appreciate her willingness to try to squeeze in an hour or two to "headline" our event.

> *Thank you for your time. My best to Elizabeth and the entire family.*
>
> *Gerry Bowles.*

Andrew's response was encouraging in that it was not dismissive:

> *Enjoyed talking with you! I have forwarded this to our scheduler and she will see what she can do.*
>
> *If you need to reach her before then, her name is Lori Krause and her number is 202-955-4553.*
>
> *Best, Andrew*

The return names on the email from Cheri and Andrew Young didn't resonate at the time but would in hindsight. Just two years later, Andrew claimed paternity of a child that was in reality, the result of a union between John Edwards, the then Democratic candidate for U.S. President and Rielle Hunter, his campaign videographer. He became fodder for the tabloids and part of one of the more intriguing attempted cover-ups in American electoral history.

In subsequent conversations with Ms. Krause I discovered that I was competing with Oprah and Larry King! Even though her schedule did not fit mine, the idea of honoring strong women did bear fruit.

As is often the case, my quest ended in my own backyard. While discussing the "Strong Women" concept at a combined phone canvassing/campaign committee meeting, Herb Reichlin, the transportation chair (IOC), looked over to our honorary campaign chair, Betty Ann Knudsen, and suggested that she be our guest of honor. We all agreed enthusiastically. What an inspired idea! She was known as a political activist and feminist. She was the first woman to chair the Wake County Board of Commissioners and to run for a North Carolina Council of State office. Furthermore, she had mentored many women who subsequently held political office.

My note to Betty Ann reflected our thinking:

> Dear Betty Ann,
>
> Thank you so much for joining my phone canvassing event on July 13$^{th}$. I am truly grateful for your support with my run for the Senate. I am really moved to think of you as an Honorary Chair for the campaign. I have such appreciation for your role in paving the way for my involvement in politics today. I would very much like to take the opportunity to honor the link between your remarkable contributions and the options that exist now for many of us in the political realm as a result. Upon reflection, rather than announcing you as Honorary Chair of my campaign this Tuesday at the event hosted by the Dellingers with Mayor Meeker, I would like to take a bit more time to plan a more significant event where you are the focus. I hope this suits. I am excited at the prospect to reflect on and celebrate the transitions from past to present times to which you were such an important contributor.
>
> Warmest regards,
> Gerry

Betty Ann graciously accepted and the planning began in earnest! Vivian Bowman Edwards a local filmmaker, visual artist, and video producer helped us immensely in this endeavor. Vivian was a part-time instructor at Duke University's Center for Documentary Studies and it was through that association that she met Betty Ann and began working on a documentary film about her, "Show Up. Speak Out: The Public Life of Betty Ann Knudsen."

We decided to have this event as our post Labor Day kickoff. Cognizant of Saturday afternoon ACC football games, we chose the date of September 10th, a Sunday, and the time, early afternoon, that fit nicely with having tea. For the location, we chose an intimate venue at the home of Becky Burmester, a neighbor, mystery book club member and supporter.

Next we broadened our scope to include women in the political arena whom had been influenced by Betty Ann: Secretary of State, Elaine

Marshall; Wake County Chief District Court Judge, Joy Hamilton; former Raleigh City Councilwoman, Jessie Taliaferro; and Lindy Brown, candidate and future winner of a seat on the Wake County Board of Commissioners. Each of our assembled "guests" was asked to give testimony to Betty Ann, sharing what she had meant to them in their own respective challenges to win elective office.

Our August 30th update detailed the specifics of the event:

**Strong Women's Tea September 10th**

*History: Afternoon Tea with Strong Women (and Strong Men who Support Strong Women)*
*If you haven't set the date aside yet, now is the time to do so. You are invited to join a line-up of strong women influenced by Betty Ann Knudsen who are currently active in politics, including Secretary of State, Elaine Marshall, and Wake County Chief District Court Judge, Joy Hamilton, in reflecting on the past remarkable contributions of Betty Ann and to honor the options that exist now for many of us in the political realm as a result. Take part in embracing Betty Ann's spirit of determination for change and join Gerry in her enthusiastic acceptance of the torch passed from this wonderful living legend.*

"To honor where I've come from, to celebrate how I got here, and to claim where I'm going."
– Oprah Winfrey speaking on her "Legends" Celebration

**Strong Women Afternoon Tea**
to celebrate the contributions of

## Betty Ann Knudsen,
*(Honorary Chair, Gerry Bowles' Campaign)*

in paving the way for the involvement of women in political office in Wake County and to mark the "passing of the torch" to

## Gerry Bowles,
Democratic Candidate NC State Senate, District 15

*Home of Becky and Joe Burmester*
*625 Downpatrick Lane, Raleigh*
*Sunday, September 10th from 3:00 to 5:00 p.m.*
*Please RSVP by September 7th to gerry@gerrybowles06.com or 919-847-9901*
*Sponsors: $100 Guests: $25*

The event was a success by every measure - social, economic and spiritual. Even though the focus was on Betty Ann, I was honored by being inducted into her Royal Order of Butterflies.

When Betty Ann won the first of two terms as a Wake County Commissioner in 1976, she started the Royal Order of Butterflies. It was inspired by a line in a poem she had read: "You can fly, but that cocoon has got to go." She thought it was a good motto for women running for public office and that year began inducting female politicians and nonprofit leaders into the Royal Order. There were no meetings, no dues and no bylaws. Betty Ann presented each new member with a small butterfly pin. She estimated that there were hundreds of members.

Betty Ann read the poem to all of us as she passed the torch of leadership to me:

*Lord,*

*The words were
on a poster - -
and I can't get
them out of my
mind:
YOU CAN FLY...
BUT THAT
COCOON
HAS GOT TO
GO.*

*And I don't think
it was talking about
butterflies.*

*But the risk - - oh the risk of leaving the
swaddling warmth of a cocoon. MY cocoon.
MY status quo. MY ... deadening security.
To leave the known,
no matter how
confining it may be
 - - a totally new life-style - -
oh, the risk!*

*Lord, my cocoon
chafes,
sometimes. But I
KNOW
its restriction. And it's scary
to consider the awful
implications of flight.
I'm leery of heights,
(Even your heights.) But Lord,
I could SEE so much wider,
clearer from
heights. And
there's an
exhilaration
about flight
that I have
always
longed
for.*

*I WANT TO FLY...
If I could just have the cocoon to come back to. Butterflies can't.
I can't.*

*Probably butterflies don't even want to - -
once they have tasted flight.*

*It's the risk that makes me
hesitate. The knowing I can't
come back to the warm,*

*understanding status quo.*

*Lord...about butterflies...the cocoon has
only two choices - - risk or die.*

*What about me?
If I refuse to risk,
Do I, too, die inside, still wrapped in the
swaddling web?*

*Lord?*

*Written by Imjean Sorley and Jo Carr*

Not only was this a great honor for me but also the poem resonated with all the attendees. The large turnout exceeded our expectations. There were people from Betty Ann's past: friends from the League of Women Voters, where she had "cut her teeth," and neighbors who had worked in her early political campaigns for the Wake County Board of Commissioners. In 1976, some had joined her in the fight for passage of the Equal Rights Amendment in North Carolina. Others had volunteered in her historic race to be the first woman in North Carolina to run for election to a statewide post. In 1984, she mounted a strong primary challenge to the "oldest rat in the barn," Secretary of State, Thad Eure, the longest serving Democrat in North Carolina at the time.

Particularly gratifying to me was the presence of high school students whose moms I had met at the BP and invited to the event. It felt more like a spiritual gathering than a traditional fundraiser though in fact it was one of my most successful ventures in that respect. In addition to giving financial support, many left with yard signs and a renewed or newly declared commitment to the campaign. Having all these women share their stories was informative, instructive and inspiring.

Andrea's words from the September 29th Update "Final Sprint" section captured our sentiment regarding the event.

*A particular word of appreciation to:
\* Becky and Joe Burmester for providing a most welcoming venue*

*for the Strong Women Afternoon Tea Honoring Betty Ann Knudsen; Betty Ann Knudsen for her inspirational past and current roles involving women in public office; the line up of strong women who spoke passionately of the influence of Betty Ann; and the guests who shared in this motivational afternoon illustrating the impact one person can have with persistence and courage.*

## *Goodberry's - October 1, 2006*

On Sunday, October 1st we had an event at Goodberry's, an open air ice cream store within my district and close to my home. I had spoken with the manager and received permission to meet folks who stopped by for an ice cream cone. He was delighted for us to do so but, unfortunately, what seemed on its face to be a good way to engage the public turned out to be awkward. For our program that afternoon, we decided to assemble yard signs as a conversation starter and entrée with customers. However, few of them were interested in the campaign and seemed most uncomfortable when being engaged. It seemed as if they were wondering if what I was doing was permitted. Their expectation had been to get an ice cream cone and not to go to a political event. In short order I "read the room" and we left the area. I recognized there was a risk with this kind of outreach effort, but knew also that it would be hard to run a grassroots campaign if I was not willing to take it.

## *Fall into the Voting Habit Meet & Greet (Katherine Morgan) - October 10, 2006*

On October 10th Andrea and I canvassed 01-37 (a precinct in our $3^{rd}$ tier), then attended a meet and greet in the evening at the home of one of our friends and active volunteers, Katherine Morgan, located in a first-tier precinct, 01-43. It was a small, intimate gathering of her friends. I was reminded of college dorm bull sessions. Our conversations covered a wide range of issues. One of her friends was interested in history and it was enjoyable to chat with someone who shared a similar background. Once more we had more than enough food to enjoy. Even though the turnout was small the event provided further insight to the notion that our campaign was gathering more supporters as evidenced by this response Katherine received from her canvassing for the event.

*Hey, ya'll*

*When I got home I had a message from [name removed for privacy] who wants a yard sign at [contact information removed for privacy]. She was real sweet and would love to meet you, Gerry. I'm going to send her my invitation to the meet and greet but she thinks she may be busy that night. She has a broken foot, so if you want to give her a call, Gerry, I'm sure she would love it.*

### Coachman's Trail Meet and Greet – October 11, 2006

The following evening I shared the billing at an event with Wake County Commissioner candidate, Rodger Koopman. This meet and greet in Coachman's Trail was planned by three activist moms, Alison Donnelly, Jennifer Tisdale, and Patti Pilarinos. Andrea and I met Jennifer at the Jefferson-Jackson Breakfast in April and she had indicated an interest in the campaign and had communicated with us throughout the summer. After school started, I bumped into her again when she served as one of the panelists at a rally in support of the Wake County School Bond. I was interested in gathering others of like mind to be a part of my campaign, and asked if she might introduce me to her friends as we all shared a common vision of improving the Wake County Schools. She asked if I could do a joint event with Rodger and I said, "absolutely." With a good turnout of enthusiastic attendees, this event resulted in engaging many supporters who took our signs, shared their contact information and volunteered to help on Election Day.

## *Campaign Kickoff – August 8, 2006*

Of the many meet and greets I was fortunate enough to plan and/or attend, the flagship one of the campaign was my Campaign Kickoff event with Congressman David Price, hosted by Lola and David Youngman. As described in Chapter Two's, *Getting Started,* though contacting Congressman Price's office in early April, my later than usual campaign launch in August was dictated by his busy schedule. Understanding the fund raising and name recognition goals of a kickoff, I turned this later "start" to my advantage. As a quick review of the events above and below show, I was far from idle in the months leading up to the kickoff in terms of raising funds and building connections with voters. I used the kickoff to follow-up with new supporters by including them in the invitations and reminding them of my candidacy. I was able to extensively promote my kickoff and broaden its scope through canvassing and the many other activities I was a part of.

With Congressman Price committed to the kickoff, I was hopeful to find a safe, easy-to-get-to venue, having the warmth of a home rather than a business, and located centrally within my district. Lola Youngman answered the call and her home fit the bill. Even though her home was situated closer to the outskirts of District 15, it had the benefit of being part of both my and Congressman Price's districts. Lola was an active member of the engaged and supportive precinct 08-04 and her willingness to host this event was made even better by her offer to lend her musical talents and those of her husband to the night with a vocal and instrumental jazz and blues performance! Her precinct generously provided the refreshments for the evening.

As fund raising was to be the goal of this particular event, I planned a more formal invitation process, though I supplemented this more casually, and sought sponsorships from invitees. While seeking larger contributions to this event at tiered levels, I still wanted it to feel inclusive and not beyond the means of supporters. While I recognized the financial support of Platinum, Gold, Silver and Bronze levels of sponsorship on a display board at the kickoff and with inserts included with the invitations, I offered a suggested guest admission of just $25 as noted in the informal electronic invitation sent to our supporters in our July $23^{rd}$ campaign update:

*Gerry Bowles' Campaign Kick-off*
*With Special Guest Congressman David Price*
*Hosted & With Jazz Performance*
*by Lola and Dave Youngman*
*(www.daveandlolayoungman.com)*
*4908 Boulder Creek Lane, Raleigh, 27613*
*Tuesday, August $8^{th}$ from 6:30-8:00pm*
*Suggested Guest Contribution: $25*
*RSVP to Andrea Bertole (see contact info below)*

*Sponsorship Levels:*
*Platinum $1,000 * Gold $500 * Silver $250 * Bronze $100*

*A special word of acknowledgement to precinct 08-04's involvement in hosting this event.*

Lacking a volunteer in charge of fund raising, I sought the support of my campaign committee to make calls to possible sponsors and guests. Andrea prepared the following script to offer a guideline for calls and efforts began at the start of June with an anticipated completion date of mid-June:

**Call guideline for fundraising telephone volunteers for Gerry Bowles' Campaign Kick-off with special guest Congressman, David Price Place: Hosted by Lola and Dave Youngman 4908 Boulder Creek Lane, Raleigh, 27613 Time: 6:30-8:00pm**

*Please personalize your greeting to those on your call list as you feel appropriate – a suggested script for your call includes the following:*

*Hello – This is _____ calling on behalf of Gerry Bowles who as you may know is running as the Democrat for the North Carolina State Senate for District 15. I am calling to let you know that Congressman, David Price, will be Gerry's guest at her campaign kick-off on August $8^{th}$. Gerry asked me to call and invite you to be a sponsor of this event at one of our 4 levels of contribution:*

*Platinum - with a $1,000 contribution*
*Gold - with a $500 contribution*
*Silver – with a $250 contribution*
*Bronze – with a $100 contribution*

*In addition to recognizing sponsors at the event itself, we will be including a note of appreciation with the invitations we will be sending out. May we include you as one of our sponsors?*

> *Yes:*
> *Thank you so much – Please make your check payable to "Gerry Bowles NC Senate." When would be a convenient time for us to pick up your contribution?*

> *Prefer to mail contribution:*
> *Please send check payable to "Gerry Bowles NC Senate" to 405 Amelia Ave, Raleigh, NC 27615*

> *No:*
> *Thank you for your time and we hope the event itself will fit into your schedule later this summer.*

> *Machine: Hello – This is _____ calling on behalf of Gerry Bowles who as you may know is running as the Democrat for the North Carolina State Senate for District 15. I am calling to let you know Congressman David Price will be Gerry's guest at her campaign kick-off on August 8$^{th}$. Gerry asked me to call and invite you to be a sponsor of this event at one of our 4 levels of contribution. Please call me back at _____ to let me know of your interest and for further details. Thank you.*

Reflecting the more formal nature of this event, I arranged to print and mail paper invitations to targeted primary voters in precincts shared by Congressman Price and me and to active Democrats in some of my other precincts who I thought might take note of David Price's involvement. Having a friend who worked at *Barefoot Press*, I chose it to print the invitations. A fellow candidate recommended using *Triangle Mailing Services* to send them which saved some time in sorting the invitations by zip code and was not noticeably more expensive in postage. Amid canvassing and other event logistics, I had to pay closer attention to the timing involved in getting these invitations mailed in sufficient time before the event. Not only did this require coordinating with the vendors involved, but Andrea and I needed to allow sufficient time to insert a list of future sponsors of the event so that their support would be recognized. In addition to requiring a larger time commitment than many of our less formal events, the invitations took a sizeable portion of our early funds to cover their expense. I was grateful that I could add to my guest list by emailing my database of campaign contacts and posting the event on the Wake County Democratic party website and requesting inclusion in their news blast of events.

The night itself was everything I hoped for. The weather was cooperative enough to have our usual welcome table outside and the event was well attended. The evening had a festive feel bolstered in no small part by the music delivered wonderfully by my hosts. As he did in the coffee shop back when I first met him during my 2000 campaign, Congressman Price modeled a warmth in his engagement with all the guests that created a comfortable atmosphere. While there was no set program, he and I took time part way through to share our message and allowed time for other candidates in attendance to do the same. Importantly, I had a chance to formally introduce myself and describe my goals to an enthused crowd. Following soon after the success of the Dellinger event with Mayor Meeker, the kickoff added increased credibility and generated further buzz about my campaign. In terms of fund raising, this event generated more contributions than any other. As a sidebar regarding coordinating with Congressman Price's campaign, after this event, they requested a list of the attendees so that they might contact them. Congressman Price acknowledged in his remarks that night that he appreciated our campaign's hard work in building support for Democrats in an otherwise unfriendly voting environment.

## *Community Events*

As a candidate, one is invited to participate in any number of organizations' "Meet the Candidates" forums, but I also looked for ways to engage folks in non-structured settings that would not be threatening or intrusive to them. There were many venues to choose from. To discover them, I scoured The *News and Observer,* The *Independent*, listened to local radio (WPTF, WRAL), and monitored the Wake County Democratic Party's website. I tried to think outside of the box and not attend just "political events." Given these events tended not to have a political focus, compared with a meet and greet arranged specifically for me or a political forum, I always had to balance the wish to introduce myself to and engage potential voters with the desire to respect the intention behind the event itself.

It was a fine line that I tried to walk. Even though I am completely comfortable with political discussion, most of my friends and fellow citizens are less so. I have observed my neighbors' reluctance to engage in political discourse. On many occasions, this discomfort was verbalized to the detriment of my ability to pass out literature in public places. I find it ironic that in our zest for political correctness, the fear that "someone" might be offended, we often muzzle attempts by candidates to get their message out.

## Wake Forest Festival– May 6, 2006

One of the first community events I attended as a candidate was the Wake Forest Festival. Wake Forest is a small town in Wake County just north of Raleigh and a number of electoral precincts in the town were a part of my district. So that I might introduce myself to some of the town's citizens, Andrea and I walked the Main Street, met some of the festival's volunteers and were able to get a number of email contacts. We spent the better part of the afternoon strolling down the main street "visiting" with folks that along with us were milling about and enjoying the different displays. We met the fire and police chiefs, bought raffle tickets to support worthy causes, admired the young children with painted faces and just generally relished this slice of small town living. At each booth we visited, I introduced myself as the Democratic candidate for the NC State Senate to represent their area in the legislature. I then offered them my literature. Of note, when filling our stomachs at *Shorty's* famous hot dogs, we had the good fortune to meet Lois and Charles Shirley who were excited about my candidacy and would come to support my campaign.

## Pig in the Park – June 24, 2006

Andrea and I attended this early evening *Pig in the Park* neighborhood celebration in the targeted 01-15 precinct. This event was not a political gathering and we were not "neighbors" in the strict definition of the word; but we had been invited by a resident, Ellen Beidler. I hoped that attending would add an extra memory note to the people living there and bolster the canvassing work we had done earlier.

Once again, I found myself walking a fine line as a candidate attending a function that was non-political in nature. This type of semi "gate crashing" required gumption and both Andrea and I had butterflies in our stomachs when we drove up to the park. Our initial discomfort soon abated as we caught the eye of Ellen who introduced us to some of the neighbors and they, in the tradition of true southern hospitality, made us feel quite welcome so that we could relax.

I was fortunate to have had Andrea by my side. Having been a "lone ranger" at many events, I can report that it was less stressful on me, the candidate, to have a partner with whom to share the stage. Not only was it helpful that there were two of us to engage in conversation and to spread the campaign message, but also it made me seem more approachable to have a guest. I recruited some great new volunteers at this event and left with many email addresses.

### Wake Forest – July 4, 2006

There were two specific instances as a candidate when I had to bite my tongue and not cause a stir, as it would have been counterproductive for my candidacy. While the second occurred in August with the League of Women Voters, the first took place at the 4th of July celebration in the town of Wake Forest. Andrea and I arrived early in the afternoon prior to the evening's fireworks. There was a small admission charge to the fireworks display that we paid. At that moment, I felt that Thomas Jefferson, author of our most famous historical document, the Declaration of Independence, was smiling down upon us!

As we entered the stadium to witness the upcoming fireworks, we distributed literature to folks who were seated and awaiting the upcoming show. Out of the corner of my eye, I noticed a woman who looked distressed to see me handing out literature. As I followed her with my eyes, I saw her approach one of the gate attendants and felt certain that she was complaining about my activities. Sure enough, within moments the attendant, with whom I had spoken earlier, sheepishly approached me. I relieved him of having to ask me to stop handing out literature by telling him that I had seen what had transpired and would stop "soliciting."

The patriotic fervor that I had felt was deflated – my bubble was burst. Imagine bringing politics into a 4th of July celebration! What would our founding fathers have said? It was reminiscent of the line spoken by Claude Rains in the movie, Casablanca, 'I'm shocked, shocked that there's gambling in Casablanca. To paraphrase, 'I'm shocked, shocked that there's politics at a 4th of July celebration!

*Lion's Club August 7, 2006*

Since the day in March when I announced to my monthly mystery book club that I was running for office, and attracted Andrea to my team, the two of us would update the group on our campaign experiences before our book club discussion began. A fellow member, Donald Rosenbaum, who also served as the program chair for the North Raleigh Lion's Club, approached me. He asked if I might be their guest at the upcoming August meeting. I happily obliged and spent a delightful evening, met a lot of new friends, and hopefully earned a few votes.

*Quail Ridge Books Event – August 13, 2006*

In scanning the daily paper, I noticed that Jerry Meeks, the Chair of the North Carolina Democratic Party, was to be the upcoming speaker at Quail Ridge Books and Music. He was going to lead a discussion about the book *"Don't Think of An Elephant."* Even though the store location was not in my district, I figured that there might be lots of like-minded folks to introduce myself to. I arrived early and collected some new supporters. One emailed me later in the week in response to an outreach from Andrea and passed on some interesting news:

> *Thank you,*
> *Living in Lee County, there is not much I can do on a daily basis to assist you. However Chris Lizak noted on Tues, that Gerry is polling 50-50. For other efforts I am involved in, I would like to get this type of info.*
> *Txs*
> *eugene.b*

Hooray! Good news indeed! In addition to generating this email, the event gave me an opportunity to talk with Jerry during which he offered to join me in canvassing. Soon after we were knocking on doors together on our "2 G/Jerry's for the price of one" canvass.

*League of Women Voters Annual Celebration – August 28, 2006*

On the heels of the Wake Forest July 4th celebration, the second event that caused me a great sense of consternation occurred at the League of Women's Voters' annual gathering. Each year, this group honors the passage of the 24th Amendment to the US Constitution which conferred upon women the right to vote. I have had the honor to attend this celebration on many occasions both as a candidate and as a proud citizen. Generally, at this non-partisan and well attended event, the female candidates for public office are especially honored, recognized and given a moment to introduce themselves. While there are usually a few men in attendance, especially candidates, they are not acknowledged officially. Candidates are also provided space in the foyer to display campaign literature.

By August 28th my campaign was definitely picking up steam. We had literature and yard signs available for distribution. The challenge on this occasion was getting the literature into attendees' hands. Our assigned space was in a small foyer that led into the large reception area. The crowds were so great that our materials were bypassed because of congestion.

Recognizing that if I was going to distribute any literature I would need to do so personally. I started introducing myself to the guests and offering them invitations to the upcoming *Strong Women's Tea* event. I was astounded when one of the ladies "in charge" made a beeline over to me complaining and pointing out that materials were to be left in the foyer. Once again there was a flashback to Casablanca - Shock, Shock, campaigning at a celebration to honor a woman's right to vote. I know that Cady Stanton and Susan B Anthony looked down from above with tears in their eyes. Irony of ironies, one of my fellow candidates, a male running for the state house, continued to hand out his literature in a more discreet fashion without objection. He would soon be called Representative.

## *Westinghouse Event – September 5, 2006*

A further opportunity to meet voters materialized as the result of my door-to-door canvassing. As mentioned in the canvassing section, Hunter Tapscott became one of the "nuggets' that I collected on the trail. He served as the program chair for a group of *Westinghouse* retirees and asked if I might be the speaker for one of their fall meetings. Our conversation in early summer resulted in my being the guest speaker at the group's September monthly meeting. Having a liberal arts background, I was at a loss at how to speak to the issues that a group of engineers might be most interested in and was helped significantly by my husband Harry, a nuclear trained engineer. Having worked with *Carolina Power and Light* (currently *Duke Energy*) in his early years he had called on the folks at Westinghouse and thus was familiar with the connections between Thomas Edison, Westinghouse and the nuclear industry. In addressing the group, I could sense their surprise at my knowledge of AC/DC and was certain that I had "garnered" the support of many of these gentlemen (older white businessmen) who might otherwise not have been a part of my natural constituency. My remarks were so well received that we later posted them on our web site so that our supporters could follow my campaign more closely, which in turn generated many favorable responses.

## *Sweet Tomatoes – September 12, 2006*

Leading into autumn, I was a guest at the monthly meeting of a men's history book club sponsored by the Wake County Public Library. They met at Sweet Tomatoes, a restaurant on Capital Boulevard. I was invited by a member who I had met at Barbara and Speed Massenberg's home in Wake Forest.

The setting was quite intimate. There were just six of us. In an example of living in a small world, I discovered one of the members also belonged to the mystery book club that Andrea and I attended. As we sat over lunch, they talked about the book and I listened to their discussion and commented when asked a question (as opposed to going with prepared remarks like at the Lion's Club event). The members covered the spectrum of political allegiance but none were highly partisan. Most were retired and all were very gracious and polite. The discussion questions were generic and I could draw parallels to my candidacy. My views could be discerned from the conversation rather than having to respond to specific political questions. Two of the members volunteered to display my yard signs and work the polls on Election Day. It was a wonderful use of my time.

## *Church Events –September 23 & September 24, 2006*

On the 23rd of September, I was a guest of Reverend Paul Anderson, pastor of Bethlehem Baptist Church located within the district. This Saturday afternoon event was their homecoming and Reverend Anderson invited me to attend so that I could introduce myself to members of his congregation. I was not entirely comfortable with "politicking" at a church event. As it turned out Reverend Anderson was delayed with an emergency, so his wife Tina escorted me around. She was a great hostess and introduced me to many people. I was able to distribute a number of yard signs and collect a few supporters. As such, the notion of "imposing" at a church event was tempered by being an escorted guest.

The following day, Sunday the 24th, I was again a guest of one of the churches in the area. All candidates had been invited to the First Baptist Church downtown to introduce ourselves to the congregation. As I was a member of a group I did not experience the discomfort I had felt the day before. In fact, my opponent was also in attendance. After the service, members of the congregation were free to come and visit with us. I enjoyed the conversation.

### *Wakefield 5k Run – October 14, 2006*

Mid October provided me another unusual event to experience. Sharon, one of the campaign's event coordinators, Andrea, and I participated in the Wake Booster 5k walk/run in Wakefield. This event was held to raise public awareness of and to remember young people who had lost their lives because of drunk driving. A group of parents led by the PTA President, Mr. Yahyapour had spear headed a campaign against driving while under the influence after the Wakefield community had lost four of its teens to this tragedy. I had met Mr. Yahyapour while waiting in line at *Justins*, one of our favorite lunch spots in the district. Andrea and I were rewarding ourselves after a morning canvass. I introduced myself and offered him my palm card. He asked questions about some of my key issues and admitted that he was a registered Republican but asked me to call him about a contribution as he cared about the same issues I did.

A few days after our meeting he left a phone message about the upcoming Wakefield event and asked me to attend and to help him contact some of our local officials so that they might also attend and be honored. His request affirmed what I had suspected that there were folks, even those who have been successful in their business endeavors, who were not comfortable in communicating with their elected officials. I was happy to share Mayor Meeker's contact information and agreed to be at this event.

On the day of the race we met a nice young highway patrol woman who was so excited to meet me that she asked if we might have our picture taken together. She shared that her office mate had his picture taken with a Republican politician displayed in their office. She wanted one of her own political leaning. The next week I sent her a copy of the photo!

### *Difficulties in Getting Your Message Out Via Community Events*

In my first campaign for state office I realized just how difficult it can be to communicate your message. The summer before the November election I visited the now defunct *Borders*, my neighborhood bookstore. Operating on the assumption that folks who visited a bookstore might have more of an interest in what was going on in their community and be inclined to be more informed, I introduced myself to the store's manager and proposed participating in a political forum to be hosted by the bookstore. I explained about the district and the office I was campaigning for and suggested that the forum could be a part of other scheduled activities. I expressed a willingness to organize the event. The manager was quite excited with the proposition but noted that he would need to include my opponent. I agreed wholeheartedly and replied that having us both would make for a more enlightening experience for the public. I volunteered to have Nell, my media guru, contact my opponent, Representative Russell Capps, to set this up. Capps' response to her was "this is a little early to be campaigning." I was both aggravated and dismayed with his reluctance to meet the public in this manner. My reaction was to move forward with the event alone. In following up with the manager the next week I found his tone to be quite different. He shared that *Borders* couldn't host this forum. His boss at the corporate office had decided that it was not a good idea to be involved in this type of "political" event. I personally believe that my opponent may have had something to do with that decision. Instead of embracing the opportunity to debate, Capps nixed the idea. Why else would corporate have even been called? Why the distancing from local and/or political issues at a bookstore – a place of ideas? With this experience as a guide, I tried to avail myself to any group who might have organized an event embracing it as a chance to connect with voters.

## Political Forums

Adding to the opportunities to meet voters through meet and greets and community events, there also existed a variety of gatherings specifically organized for candidates.

## Triangle Apartment Association -September 19, 2006

In mid-September, I was the guest of the Triangle Apartment Association's "Meet the Candidates" reception, a cocktail event that did not require any public speaking. The association, a local affiliate of the National Apartment Association, was an 800+ member trade association of owners, builders, investors, developers, managers and allied service representatives. It was also the natural constituency of my opponent, his home base of support. It was here that I met my opponent's wife, Duden, for the first time. Someone had pointed her out and I just turned and extended my hand and said "how do you do, I am Gerry Bowles." She seemed rattled and discomforted by my hand, as though she was thinking, "should I shake her hand?" She said, "I'm Neal Hunt's wife" (not I am "Duden") and I said "yes, I know."

The welcome I received from my son Matt and his coworkers who were also a part of this "alliance" overcame my disquiet in this situation considerably. Matt was part of the political action group of his company and so I was accepted and embraced as "Matt's Mom," which was a familiar role for me. They took me under their wings, carrying yard signs and literature from my car and introducing me to some of their friends who whispered in hushed tones that they were voting for me. So, what could have been a very difficult evening turned out to be quite nice. I made a lot of contacts and recruited new volunteers for the campaign. Many agreed to display my yard sign and to work the polls. The reception, held at the North Hills Mall, in the heart of my district, provided an added benefit of my being able to display my yard signs in a heavily trafficked area during the course of the event.

## 6$^{th}$ Women's Political Candidate Forum at Peace College- October 2, 2006

The forums I attended at Peace College as a candidate were more intimate than any of the other forums, and as a woman's college, they were more personal. The college was founded in 1857 and had been long associated with politics and leadership in North Carolina and the southeast. It counts among its graduates the first female judge in the southeast and the first female State Senator from North Carolina. At the time, it was the only college in North Carolina with an undergraduate major in leadership studies. It had been an all girls' school until the last few years and thus the participants at the forum were all female candidates for public office.

Andrea brought Betty Ann, the campaign's honorary chair, and there was something spiritual about her presence as an octogenarian amongst all these young women. We were provided a spot to set up our materials and time to engage the students informally prior to the forum. The more formal part of the evening involved the candidates sharing our experiences as female leaders with these young women, many who hoped to become future leaders of North Carolina. We were asked questions about the challenges we had faced in our political careers and how we had made a difference in our community.

After our remarks, the floor was opened to questions from the audience. By far, this was my favorite part of the evening. Not only was it interesting to know what was on the mind of this Generation Y, but also it was revealing to know more about the other female candidates who shared the journey I had taken. I felt more of a sense of sisterhood that evening than at any time on the trail. The camaraderie provided a timely boost. Even though we recruited a number of volunteers, their subsequent participation in our events proved to be a logistical problem. Peace College, located in downtown Raleigh, was not in my district and accessibility and transportation to my more suburban activities were an issue for the students.

### *Meredith College Meet the Candidates - October 17, 2006*

On October 17th, I had interaction with two separate groups of folks. During the first part of the evening I traveled to Meredith College in response to their invitation to participate in a Meet the Candidates event. This non-partisan event allowed candidates to meet Meredith students during their dinner hour and to display our campaign materials, Even though the college was not in my district, Andrea and I attended as I wanted to be supportive of their efforts. We were the first to interact with the dining students. It was a bit awkward as I wasn't sure that they knew who we were and what was going on! At the time, none of the other candidates had introduced themselves in this manner. Shortly thereafter other candidates followed suit and joined some of the diners. At one table I introduced myself and one of the "guests" was the *News and Observer* reporter who had interviewed me by phone. She did not acknowledge me in any way or ask me any questions which struck me as odd. What kind of reporter was she? Another curious event that evening was the appearance of Vernon Robinson followed by an entourage of TV cameras. Robinson, a candidate trying to unseat Congressman Brad Miller, was a harbinger of Tea Party mentality and was prone to making outrageous comments about the congressman.

### *McKimmon Forum: Wake County Town Hall Meeting on Senior Issues- October 17, 2006*

During the second part of the evening, I traveled to the McKimmon Center for a forum hosted by the NC Assisted Living Association. The format of this town hall was intended to give lawmakers and candidates an opportunity to hear from professionals involved in elder care. Following the presentation, we were able to share our views and to react to the ideas presented in the initial discussion. The moderator then asked each of us questions about the covered topics. I recall two of my fellow Democratic candidates, Lindy Brown and Don Mial, responding well and with humor. My opponent, seated on the other side of the stage, answered his question in such a confident, incumbent manner that by contrast, I felt my response insufficient. He was smooth, perhaps a bit smug. On the positive side, I was able to play to my strength and to interact with many members of the audience and to distribute a number of my yard signs.

An appreciated thank you note arrived the following day from one of the town hall organizers which spoke to the many competing options for candidate gatherings:

> *Greetings!*
>
> *On behalf of the volunteers and organizers of "Caring for Our Elders: A Town Hall Meeting", thank you for participating in the thoughtful discussion we had last night. I hope that you agree that we had a good discussion and that there are ideas that you can use in the upcoming session of the North Carolina General Assembly.*

*When I watched the television news last night, I was surprised to see how many other important meetings were going on simultaneous to our Town Hall Meeting – one in Apex about the recent event there and two events about the upcoming school bond vote. Looking back, it was great to see that you stood by your commitment to participate in our event. You could have easily called to cancel because of the other events. The result would have been a panel of empty seats, which would have been a disaster. So I hope that you know how truly grateful we are for your participation and for your interest in and commitment to the seniors in our community.*

*Sincerely,*
*Evelyn Hawthorne*
*Government and Public Relations*

## *Triangle Community Coalition-October 19, 2006*

A couple of days later, I attended a Political Pig Pickin' hosted by the Triangle Community Coalition. The most recognized and politically powerful group in this coalition was the Home Builders Association of Raleigh-Wake County. These were the folks who had endorsed my opponent, one of their own. All the candidates were given the opportunity to make a three-minute "stump" speech while standing on the provided bale of hay. The setting was wide open, yet intimate. My opponent delivered his remarks right beside me. A straw poll was part of the night's activities and the results were posted after I left. To no one's surprise I came in second. I never received the final tally.

## *Professional Engineers of NC- October 24, 2006*

I was a guest of the Central Chapter of the Professional Engineers of NC at a "Meet the Candidates Night." The organization represented thousands of members and described themselves as having a "vital interest in our community and the political process." I was able to talk informally with some of the members during a complimentary 6:30 dinner and then along with other candidates speak in a more formal setting. We were able to present a short (two to five minute) statement concerning our qualifications and platform. Cullen Browder from WRAL-TV moderated the event. As this group was composed of members from across the state, I spent a great bit of time explaining the parameters of my district. The experience was positive in that many of the folks I spoke with knew my husband Harry from his days working at *Carolina Power & Light*, now known as *Duke Energy*, and had fond memories of that time.

## *Democratic Party*

I tried to take advantage of as many events sponsored by the Democratic Party as I could, seeing them as a way to broaden my reach, connect with active voters, raise funds, and be a team player. While many of these events offered a great chance to achieve these goals, I had to weigh some against the emotional costs that may not have been evident from the outside looking in.

I was comfortable when I had control of my campaign and my message, but any time that was threatened, I was less than happy. The party apparatus tried to manage all the campaigns for the Senate through the NC Senate Caucus. This Caucus was comprised of the Senate leadership and a few representatives from the Senate. They determined who received monetary support and how much. This determination was not based on anything "personal" but on polling data that revealed who might have the best chance of electoral success and therefore might be in a better position to help the party. From the get go I knew that "the numbers" were seen as god. I felt and still do that a singular focus on these numbers missed the point of furthering the party's and the public's interest. The more distance there was between our campaign and this "Inner Sanctum" the better I felt. So, when it came to attending events sponsored by the state and the county parties, I weighed how much my attendance might benefit my campaign's success in my district against how much discomfort I might feel in participating.

The exception to my uneasiness within the party apparatus was when I interacted with the local organizations, the groups known as "the Democratic Men, Democratic Women and the Wake County Senior Democrats." The folks in all these organizations embraced me emotionally and financially. It was always a delight to attend their meetings both as a candidate and as a friend.

## *Jefferson-Jackson Day - April 29, 2006*

Jefferson Jackson Day is an annual event celebrated by the NC Democratic Party to honor the Democratic Party roots. The Democratic Women of Wake County hosted a breakfast in the morning and the NC Democratic Party hosted a dinner that same evening. Each event featured a nationally prominent political speaker. As a member of the council of the women's organization, I had chaired one of the event committees in the past and had attended many. As a candidate, I was eager to be able to use the occasion as a "coming out party" among familiar faces. Andrea and I attended the breakfast together and were able to recruit some early volunteers to the campaign, one of whom would later host a meet and greet.

## *Primary Day – May 2, 2006*

One circumstance that I did not have to worry about was having to win the primary election to be chosen as the Democratic candidate for this office. The benefit of having to face primary opposition is having your name become familiar to the active electorate. The downside is the need to devote resources to that initial campaign.

In 2000, though I had no competition from another Democrat for the House position, I took the novel approach of using the primary election as a campaign event. My strategy behind using Primary Day was to increase my visibility to voters who were most likely to vote on Election Day. I assessed it was a safe bet that those voting in the Primary could be counted on for November.

When it came to getting help, I found people were more willing to volunteer to work the polls for the primary than for the general election. I think they were more comfortable just asking the voters as they were exiting the polls for their consideration of my candidacy rather than asking them for their vote on Election Day. My volunteers and I did not try to single out Democrats as I was aware that I needed to reach both Unaffiliated and Republican voters. As a follow up to this primary "event," using data supplied by the Board of Elections, I sent a letter of introduction and of thanks for voting to the Unaffiliated voters in my district who had cast a vote on Primary Day.

As I had started the 2000 campaign 19 months before the November election, I had knocked on scores of doors before the primary. To increase my name recognition, I decided to hand out refrigerator magnets that had my name, the office I was seeking and the dates of the primary and the general election on them. The end result was puzzlement and disappointment among many of my hoped for constituents who expected to find my name on the primary ballot but didn't see it. Despite this confusion, the good news was that my message had reached folks.

In 2006, again having no primary opposition, I decided to use Primary Day once more to spread my message. I chose not to hand out magnets ahead of time because we started our campaigning later in the election cycle. I would revisit that decision in the future as it was surprising how many people still had them on their fridges long after the 2000 race was over. With just 2 months of campaigning under my belt, Andrea and I sent out a call for volunteers to help at polling places within our 28 targeted precincts. While we would have liked to have covered each of the 28, we considered who was available to help and balanced our desire for targeted coverage with the personal touch of having a volunteer situated at their own polling place greeting neighbors. The number of volunteers available and their location flexibility determined our coverage.

I floated amongst different polling stations, where I tried to greet voters and thank our volunteers. Andrea and I had prepared a bag of greeting tools for volunteers that included my palm card and a guide for volunteering which in part instructed our volunteers to greet voters only as they *exited* the polls so voters wouldn't enter thinking I would be on the primary ballot (see sample below). The guide also offered a possible greeting of *"Gerry Bowles thanks you for voting and hopes you will consider her in November."* This event served as good practice for November in terms of volunteer logistics and it helped give the campaign some early energy.

## Primary Day – May 2nd

In the apt words of Elvis "Thank you …Thank you very much." Your help in handing out Gerry Bowles' literature this primary day is truly appreciated!!

Just a couple of things to note:

- Gerry is unopposed as the Democrat running for District 15's NC State Senate seat so she is *not* on the primary ballot – we just want to introduce her name to active voters May 2$^{nd}$.
- To avoid confusing folks going into vote for primary candidates, we suggest approaching them on their way out of the polls.
- Please personalize your greeting to voters as you feel appropriate – our suggestion is "Gerry Bowles thanks you for voting and hopes you consider her in November" or something to that effect.
- Gerry's website is now up and active! Please invite folks to visit it.
- There should be signs indicating where campaigning/distributing literature is allowed and where it is not.
- I too will be at the polls, but if you encounter any difficulties or have any questions, I will have my cell phone with me – please feel free to call (741-8690).

Leftovers:

- If you have leftover materials and/or signatures on the supporter/volunteer sheets, please drop them off to Gerry's at 405 Amelia Ave, Raleigh (just off the 540 and Six Forks Road) at some point in the week following May 2$^{nd}$. Feel free to leave these materials on Gerry's covered front porch if she is not at home. If it will be difficult for you to drop these materials off, please just let me know and we can arrange another way to pick them up from you.

Comments please:
- I would love to hear if you have any advice for future polling day volunteering efforts.
- Did you have some interesting comments from voters? Please share them with us.
- Any other observations from your time at the polls? Please let us know.
- I would welcome your input – please offer comments with your returned materials, by phone, or by e-mail.

With great appreciation,
Andrea
(andreabertole@hotmail.com; 919-793-0160)


### *Eleanor Roosevelt Luncheon - May 20, 2006*

The Eleanor Roosevelt Luncheon is an annual affair held for a select group of members of the Democratic Women of Wake County who pay extra each year for their membership and receive this designation. As a member, I attended and found myself amongst friends. Happily, I left this event with a few monetary contributions to the campaign.

## *07-11 Precinct's Ice Cream Social - June 25, 2006*

A neighborhood gathering organized by the Democratic activists in the 07-11 precinct offered an interesting contrast to the community *Pig in the Park* event I discussed earlier and went to the evening before this event, on June 24th. Instead of beginning the event with a case of nerves at the prospect of "crashing" the gathering, I attended the ice cream social as an honored guest. As a candidate whose name would appear on the November ballot, I was afforded an opportunity to give a speech and meet some of the constituents I was hoping to serve.

Even though the weather did not cooperate, with unrelenting rain requiring us all to huddle under a shelter at Lynn Road School, our spirits were high. I was also gratified that this precinct had taken the initiative to arrange this event that allowed me to spread my message and to meet folks that were impassioned about the political process. As my campaign celebrated and encouraged generating energy and excitement, I was delighted to find kindred spirits who shared my interests. Even though most everyone at the ice cream social may have been disposed to vote for me regardless of my attendance, my participation recharged my batteries and I was energized to go forth into areas that were not as welcoming. Furthermore, we were able to add to our list of volunteers new folks willing to canvass, make phone calls and display yard signs.

Grier Martin, candidate for the NC House, was also a guest at this event as we shared this precinct. His district included a lot of precincts that favored Democrats, but none, I would guess, more enthusiastically. Grier and I were to share the spotlight at a number of events and the experiences were always positive and comfortable.

There is often an individual leader that is the organizing force behind an energized active precinct such as this one. This person spearheads the efforts that help provide not only boots on the ground but the emotional support that is needed to sustain campaigns. In this precinct, Terry Grunwald stood as a model of precinct leadership, and her warmth and activism as well as the evident admiration her precinct members had for her continually impressed me.

## 08-04 Precinct Events – Various

Another beacon of support throughout the campaign came continually from precinct 08-04. My treasurer, Gail Christensen, had been its chair in previous years and her leadership along with the activism and commitment of the membership led to a strong base of support in an otherwise generally unreceptive voting territory within my district. Like 07-11, this precinct was of such value and represented the best of what precinct organization could look like. Given Gail's involvement in both my campaign and her precinct's activities, I had the good fortune of receiving a more personal link to this group and as such have included their events in my "Meet and Greet" section.

## Ty Harrell's Neighborhood BBQ – July 15, 2006

Later that week I attended a neighborhood cookout in support of Ty Harrell, a candidate for the NC House. As was the case with Grier Martin, Ty and I shared a number of precincts in North Raleigh. This event was held in one of those precincts. As often as possible, I invited and encouraged other Democrats on the ballot to join me at my scheduled meet and greets. Most offered a reciprocal invitation. I felt that the presence of other candidates enriched these events for those in attendance as well as for me. Ty was of the same mind and there were many candidates in attendance.

An example of the tangible benefit to my campaign was the discovery of a "nugget" at this cookout. Arriving before Ty, Andrea and I had an opportunity to introduce ourselves and my campaign to the gathered guests. One of those attending, Katherine Morgan, had volunteered to help with Ty's campaign, but we were able to make a personal connection with her that led to friendship and many hours of door-to-door canvassing, and an October meet and greet held at her home (as described earlier).

## Wake County Democratic Party (WCDP) Candidates Event - July 20, 2006

On the following Thursday evening, I attended an event sponsored by the WCDP at Artspace, an area set aside for artists to share their creations. Even though the downtown location was not likely to be a venue that would attract a lot of the folks in my district, I wanted to be a team player and support this Democratic event by attending. A number of factors contributed to the night not being a success for me or my campaign. First off, the temperature (mid-July in Raleigh) was in the 90's, and the air conditioner in my van had just quit. I was soaked upon arrival and quickly made my way to the ladies' room to try to repair my hair and makeup. I never really recovered from feeling "a mess." The venue was not an easy one in which to mingle as it was comprised of a number of cubicles. Therefore, I was never able to meet folks with any amount of ease or comfort as it was unclear whether someone was there to see or show art or whether someone was open to meeting a candidate. All in all, this event was a bust for me and I left feeling that even if my teammates were there, they were not in evidence.

### *Wake Democrats Countywide Rally - August 18, 2006*

In mid-August, the Wake County Democratic Party sponsored a countywide campaign rally. This evening event held from 5:00-8:30 at the State Fairgrounds featured all candidates running for office. It provided the opportunity for rank and file members of the party to meet and talk with candidates in an informal setting. In addition, for a small fee, one could have a delicious BBQ dinner. I arrived early so that I could claim a strategic location for my campaign materials - near the food! This rally was one of the more enjoyable events in which I participated. I always felt energized by the folks who were closest to the ground. These were the real grass roots activists.

### *Candidates' Breakfast - August 23, 2006*

A few days later, I chose *not* to attend a candidates' breakfast sponsored by the Wake County Democrats at the Goodwin House, our party's headquarters. The 8:00 am event was a little early for me particularly given its location a good distance from my home. I appreciated the party providing us with an opportunity for fellowship, but felt a better use of my time that Wednesday morning was to be spent canvassing closer to home in my district.

### *Young Democrats Banquet – August 24, 2006*

On the evening of the 24th after canvassing in the 01-44 precinct I attended a banquet in honor of P.R. Latta. This event, sponsored by the NC Young Democrats is another annual affair that recognizes the lifetime accomplishments of individual Democrats. I wanted to attend because P.R. was the epitome of grassroots activism. P.R. was an original. There is a story that goes that some avid Democrats would vote for "a yellow dog" if that was the Democrat on the ballot. P.R. was the poster child of a Yellow Dog Democrat. There have been many times when I have been disgusted with fellow Democrats and have felt the urge to change my registration to Unaffiliated and have not done so because of folks like P.R. A World War II veteran, he cut his teeth as a union organizer after the war. His support for all Democratic candidates in the area is legendary. I made his acquaintance when I ran for the NC House. He tutored me in all things political as we sat in his basement workshop while he was cutting stakes for yard signs. He was a dear friend and the model of integrity and passion for all things political. Even though the evening was all about him and his contributions to the party, P.R. spent a good portion of his time handing out invitations to my upcoming "Strong Women's Tea." Need I say more about the supportive nature of P.R.?

### *07-11 Neighborhood Open House- August 29, 2006*
Tuesday evening Kate Dieter-Maradei and Nick Maradei opened their home to all Democratic candidates with precinct 07-11 in their districts. Orchestrated in part by this active precinct, this well attended open house enabled me, once again, to add a lot of contacts and to grow our campaign. Furthermore, it reminded me of the value of having strong precinct organization for educating voters of their electoral choices. There were many down ticket lower profile candidates in attendance whom I had not often encountered at other functions that were offered a platform at this open house.

### *Wake County Democrats Bar Association - August 31, 2006*
The next party event occurred on Thursday evening. I attended an affair downtown at the Raleigh City Museum hosted by the Bar Association. My presence at this event was mainly to wave the flag as a Democratic candidate. Most of the lawyers at this event were predisposed to vote for a Democrat, however I hoped to be able to get a few monetary contributions for the campaign. Sadly, I did not. The attendees at this event

consisted of attorneys from the entire county as opposed to the relatively small district that I was seeking to represent.

### *Meet and Greet for Rodger Koopman – September 6, 2006*

In early September, I attended an event at the home of Stan Norwalk. Stan was an activist in the newly formed group, Wake Up Wake County which aimed to "be a voice for people who believe we need to plan well for growth, development and healthy, vibrant communities" in the high growth Wake County. He was hosting a meet and greet for Rodger Koopman, candidate for the Wake County Commissioners. Even though the event was in Cary, definitely a distance from my home and not within my district, I attended in part as there was no conflict with my schedule and also to support Stan's event. The turnout was small, but it was time well spent personally and for the campaign, as I was able to reconnect with a friend who lived in that area and who made a generous contribution to my campaign.

### *Wake County Democrats Annual Labor Day Picnic – September 9, 2006*

I chose *not* to participate in the annual picnic as it was located well outside my district and I believed that those who would be attending were folks that I already knew or would be in my camp already. I decided on this occasion that a better use of the campaign's time that day was to be involved in sign distribution. We assembled and distributed signs from 10:00 to noon at the B.P. In addition, we prepared for our big event the next day, the *Strong Women's Tea* honoring Betty Ann Knudsen.

### *Democratic Women of Wake County (DWWC) Monthly Meeting – September 28, 2006*

On the 28th of September, I was one of the featured speakers at the monthly luncheon of the DWWC. All the Democratic candidates for the state legislature were guests and were offered five minutes of time to speak. As is always the case, I felt like I was with family and was completely relaxed. The following, indicative of my "stump" speech, is a copy of my remarks.

> *Government is a relationship between "We the People" and their representatives. The Founding Fathers in their infinite wisdom established an election system that would best serve the interest*

*of the people by holding their representatives accountable for their actions every two years.*

*This contract sealed in our Constitution has served us well for over 200 years. I am saddened and our body politic suffers when the people's interest is superseded by our representatives taking care of special interests.*

*My campaign has been about putting people's interest first. We have knocked on over 4500 doors in our district. I have listened to the concerns of folks who have never been approached by anyone before. We have conducted polling the old fashioned way - one door at a time.*

*I worship, as did the majority of our founding fathers, the God of Abraham. Their faith informed and enriched their lives. Perhaps because of this or because they had left European theocracies, they were careful to make sure that the government they were establishing was free of religious litmus tests.*

*While my opponent spent time making sure that students in our schools cite the Pledge of Allegiance, the citizens have concerns about their students having a seat to sit in and quality educators that are paid better than a living wage. With only 9 out of 12 students who begin our high schools as freshmen graduating, I believe we have more important issues to tackle.*

*My opponent sponsored an amendment to our NC Constitution that would protect "traditional" marriage. Once again, the folks I have spoken with are more concerned about affordable housing and health care, educating their children and providing the infrastructure that ensures the quality of life that we have come to cherish.*

*In short, I believe that there is a disconnect between our current senator and the people that he represents. That is why I am running to be the next senator in our area.*

*I ask that you share my message with your friends and neighbors.*

*Tell them that I offer political courage, personal integrity and public service.*

*With your help I can be the next Senator from District 15.*

### Dogs with David – October 8, 2006

Demonstrating again camaraderie among candidates, I was invited to a casual event for Congressman David Price in early October. As I was attending an out of town wedding, Andrea and her husband, Chris, represented our campaign at this "Dogs with David" cookout. The event, held in the driveway of one of David Price's supporters, was small but intimate. Andrea shared that everyone was nice, but in comparison to the canvassing experience, it felt a bit uncomfortable. There was a different pace to socializing with new acquaintances at a small event as compared to greeting potential voters at the doors. At this juncture in the campaign we had definitely hit a rhythm in our door-to-door experience that felt both easy and rewarding.

### Meet and Greet for Grier Martin – October 9, 2006

On October 9th, Katherine Morgan and I canvassed in the morning and in the evening I attended a meet and greet for Grier Martin at the home of Susan and John Dellinger. As described under "Meet and Greets," the Dellinger's had been so kind to open their home earlier in the summer for my event with the Mayor. I was happy to return to an environment that was open, warm and friendly. Even though Grier was the "headliner," I didn't feel awkward or uncomfortable. This event also gave me the added benefit of returning to a targeted precinct to meet or reconnect with voters.

### North Carolina State Fair – Mid October, 2006

The NC State Fair is an annual event held for a 10-day period in October in Raleigh. The NC Democratic Party always has a booth to be used as a form of outreach to the larger state community. Volunteers working this event answer questions about the party, its policies and the candidates. Democratic candidates were invited to display their literature and I provided some of my, by that time, scarce materials for this purpose. A member of my campaign volunteered to cover a weekday morning shift from 9am-noon and reported that she had to search for my campaign literature. The materials were either poorly positioned or not displayed at all. She eventually found some of my fliers on the floor! Given I was running low on my campaign materials and had any number of folks in the district interested in learning about the campaign, I was distressed to hear of this treatment of resources. I was left regretting my choice to contribute materials to this party run event rather than directing them to other activities sponsored specifically by my campaign.

## *Conclusion*

Generally, my multi-pronged approach worked well in using events to bolster my canvassing efforts to implement my campaign strategy. In detailing the variety of events I participated in during the campaign, I wanted to give a sense of the pace of events, and the need to balance competing demands on my time particularly when integrating these with other "implementation" activities. With my grassroots focus and more local district (as compared to statewide office), meet and greets stood out as my preferred way to engage voters personally and directly. These events paired well with my canvassing activities. Community events, political forums and Democratic Party functions all gave welcome opportunities to broaden my reach, enthuse my base, build camaraderie with fellow candidates, and raise funds. That said, I paid more careful attention with these events as to the time and materials required when deciding which to attend.

# Chapter Seven – Special Projects: IACs & Point People

In June, the campaign initiated two special projects to implement my vision of governance and our targeted precinct strategy. The first involved developing Issue Advisory Committees based on the three pillars of my message. The second focused on identifying point people for each of my targeted precincts who could serve to personalize my efforts in their respective communities.

## *Issue Advisory Committees (IACs)*

After the Primary in May, while on a road trip with Harry, I was discussing the campaign and my ideas on how to govern in a more grassroots fashion. In listening to my thoughts, Harry grasped the concept and articulated it as follows:

> ***Concept in Brief***: *For each of the three Gerry Bowles 06 primary campaign issues, an Issue Advisory Committee (IAC) will be formed. Each IAC will have a chairperson appointed by the Campaign Committee. Other IAC members are to be volunteers, with diverse backgrounds being welcomed. The primary focus of each IAC is to research in detail the relevant history, facts, figures, etc. applicable to that IAC's issue. A summary of the research activities' key facts related to the IAC issue and concise position papers are to be drafted for use by Mrs. Bowles during the campaign and, if elected, during her term in the Senate.*
>
> ***Additional Background***
> *\* The campaign should publicize the formation of the IACs extensively, including use of local news media to request IAC volunteers.*
> *\* The campaign should emphasize the fact that this concept can serve as a viable alternative to the lobbyist industry in terms of where legislators obtain their facts, figures, and legislative initiatives. At the state level, legislators cannot afford large staffs to perform this function, so this concept fills a void that otherwise has been, and will continue to be, filled by lobbyists.*
> *\* The campaign should communicate that the initial three IACs*

154

*are to be a pilot phase, and that over time, if elected, Mrs. Bowles would expect to form other IACs.*
*\* Each IAC should consist of a minimum of four members and a maximum of twelve. Exceptions to this rule may be allowed on a case-by-case basis.*

Upon my return, excited by this plan of action, Andrea and I enlisted help from our supporters in our June 3$^{rd}$ Campaign Update as described below:

**"Working together to make things work"**
*As part of her promise to make people the special interest of her campaign, Gerry is launching an Issue Advisory Committee (IAC) initiative to assemble "citizen lobbyists" for each of Gerry's 3 key issues of Education, Transportation, and Representation. Each IAC will be tasked with identifying key points within the particular issue of senatorial/legislative relevance, gathering information to further educate committee members and Gerry, and putting forward legislative proposals that can be taken forward by Gerry upon election. Those interested in learning more about participating in this initiative may contact Gerry, Dan or Andrea (see contact information below).*

**Recruiting Volunteers**

Recruiting for these committees was not an easy undertaking. It was clear it would require much time and commitment by those volunteering. We sent email inquiries to targeted volunteers based on interests they had expressed in our previous encounters. Also, when new supporters sent questions related to my message, we gauged their interest in joining one of the 3 committees. The following sample email shows our approach to recruitment:

*Subject: A different kind of volunteer opportunity*

*Good Evening [volunteer name],*

*I am e-mailing you to see if you might be interested in participating in a different kind of volunteer opportunity with Gerry Bowles' campaign.*

*Gerry is looking to create an Issue Advisory Committee (IAC) for each of her 3 key issues of Education, Transportation, and Representation and is seeking "citizen lobbyists" to chair/co-chair and/or work within these groups with a view to being proactive, current and connected in her approach to ramping up for the election season in September. By Labor Day, each task force would produce a report based on a 3 fold directive: 1) Identify key points within the particular issue of senatorial/legislative relevance; 2) Gather information to further educate task force members and Gerry; 3) Put forward legislative proposals that can be taken forward by Gerry upon election.*

*While the 3 committees would be free to liaise with Gerry over the summer, she envisions each of these groups largely meeting and working independently on their mandate.*

*Gerry has identified a number of people who she feels could take an effective leading role in chairing a committee and your name came to mind. Gerry would welcome your involvement in a chair/co-chair capacity for any of the 3 groups.*

*In seeking working members of each task force, we will be advertising their launch in our forthcoming update, on the Wake County Democratic Party events listing, at an upcoming Campaign meeting mid June, and in other news media. We would love to list you as one of the point people for an IAC in these communications. We would also welcome the involvement of others in your circle of friends who may be interested in participating.*

*Please do let me know if this opportunity is of interest to you.*

*Thanks,*
*Andrea*

Andrea's email on the 2nd of June captured our delight at some of the early replies:

*Here's our first yes to the IAC! Yeah! Chris' enthusiasm is wonderful too!*

*From Chris Lizak
Sent: Friday, June 02 10:12 AM
Subject: RE: Gerry Bowles' Campaign for NC State Senate & a different kind of volunteer opportunity*

*Thanks for the invitation, it's very flattering to be so highly considered.*

*I am very interested in Gerry's Representation IAC, as it does provide a practical application for a lot of the election protection work that we have done lately, as well as for the initiatives that have come out of my work with NC Voters for Clean Elections. I would like to participate in that IAC, and believe that I can make contributions in the areas of Verified Voting, increased scrutiny of DRE's. Public financing of elections, and straightening out the manner in which SBOE members are appointed.*

*However, I must say that I am concerned about the amount of time that I can actually devote to the project. I am already seeing my political schedule this election cycle expand to the point where I worry about the time it is taking from my day job, as well as from previous political commitments. As President of the Wake Progressives, in a critical election year, with important legislation being rolled out on an almost daily basis, I do not believe that I could successfully chair that IAC.*

*So please sign me up as a member of the Representation IAC, but not as a chair.*

*Chris Lizak*

This additional response on June 6 was gratifying:

*Hello Andrea and Gerry,*

*I am honored by your offer. My only worry is that I may not have enough time to devote to this. If you do not find someone with more time, I would be happy to help.
All three topics are important to me, but I have the least knowledge in Education.*

*I was undecided on the 540 tolls until Gerry spoke on it the other night. I agree with her comments about needing to use the current surplus to restore the highway fund rather than add tolls. I already avoid taking 540 because of the congestion at certain times. Toll booths would only add to that congestion. Gerry's "follow the money" story also struck home with me. There seems to be an agenda to dismantle the government and replace it with privatized operations. I am opposed to that agenda. It does not strike me as being efficient and I am seeing too many ways that private companies are sucking up all of the government funds. Our son Tim works for the FAA and is seeing a lot of push from the federal government to privatize there also.*

As the above two emails illustrate, time concerns stood as a road block for a number of possible volunteers with this undertaking. For all of the difficulty in recruiting IAC Chairs, we felt grateful that by our June 25$^{th}$ Update, we were able to celebrate the following:

**Sign On to the Declaration of Citizen Involvement:**
*We are excited to announce the appointment of the Chairs for Gerry's Issue Advisory Committees (IACs) on her 3 key issues of Education, Transportation, and Representation!*

*Education IAC*
*Chair: Pam Green [phone and email contact info provided]*

*Transportation IAC*
*Chair: Herbert Reichlin [phone and email contact info provided]*

*Representation IAC*
*Co-chair: Sam Brewer [phone and email contact info provided]*
*Co-chair: René Martin [phone and email contact info provided]*

*We are pleased to have the leadership of our Chairs as well as the involvement of some early members in pursuing the short term committee goals to identify key points within the particular issue of senatorial/legislative relevance, research in detail the relevant history, facts, figures, applicable to the particular IAC, and to put forward legislative proposals that can be taken forward by Gerry upon election. In the long term these IACs will serve as pilots for "making people the special interest" by creating viable alternatives to lobbyists for generating research and legislative proposals. Once elected, other IACs will be formed for other important issues identified.*

*We invite you to build on the ideas, energy and enthusiasm of our chairs and early members of these committees – to participate in one of the IACs or to recommend other interested community members, please contact the IAC Chairs (see contact info above) or myself (Andrea Bertole – see contact info below).*

### *Goals of Each IAC*

With chairs for the three committees identified, we provided each with the contact information of confirmed and potential volunteers and a description of their role and goals. In response to their questions regarding the field of research, we narrowed the scope for each issue to the following suggestions:

**Role of Chair**
- Liaise with Gerry
- Be responsible for the report
- Organize the meetings
- Be the point person for new members

**Education IAC: Specific areas to focus on**
As a legislator, how to implement the Leandro Decision?
(1997 NC Supreme Court decision that the State of NC has a constitutional obligation to deliver to all children residing in NC a sound basic education).
    How to fund construction of new schools
    How to attract & retain teachers
    How to decrease drop-out rates
    How did distribution of Lottery Funds get decided
    e.g. Mecklenburg's share vs. Wake County's
[Possible resources: FORUM Binder, NPRs The State of Things; Wake Up Wake County at wakeupwakecounty.com]

**Transportation IAC: Specific areas to focus on:**
The Highway Transportation Fund
    When was it established
    When was it "raided"
    What exactly is happening with it
    How does that play into the "Toll Road" suggestions for I-540
    What exactly is the situation with the NC gasoline tax, as of today.

[Possible resources: News and Observer articles such as: http://www.newsobserver.com/243/story/448848.html; N&O's Crosstown Traffic by Bruce Siceloff Blog at http://blogs.newsobserver.com/crosstown/index.php (e.g. May 19th and June 8th; www.stop540toll.com article links; Wake Up Wake County at wakeupwakecounty.com]

**Representation IAC: Initial Specific areas to focus on:**
1) Look at the process of making people the special interest i.e. involving citizens and reducing the influence of special interest groups e.g. the IACs are one vehicle;
2) What other key issues are citizens identifying as needing attention e.g. mental health

[Possible resources: Progressive Democrats of WC, Wake Up Wake County]

Narrowed scope for Representation IAC:
Looking at representation from the perspective of
- Who are our current representatives:
  * Demographics (age, race, gender, profession)

- What are the difficulties in having a "citizen legislature"
  * Numbers re the costs of campaigning – costs can be daunting.
  * How do these costs relate to average income for District 15 or Wake County etc.
  * How much is the average legislator paid once in office.

- Current ethical landscape in holding office:

* Undue influence of lobbyists (perhaps look at the voting records to see if this influence can be evidenced numerically here)
* Recent response to making the ethical reforms e.g. July 19$^{th}$'s article by Dan Kane on "Senators rebuff fundraising ban - But Senate bill would keep lobbyists from giving to campaigns of lawmakers, statewide officials"
(http://www.newsobserver.com/114/story/462036.html)

Andrea forwarded these "nice words from Sam Brewer" after receiving clarification of expectations of research.

*Date: July 21, 2006*
*Subject: Re: Narrowing the scope for the Representation IAC*

*Your bullets provide, for me, an excellent starting/focal point. I personally feel that these are exactly the type of questions I want a candidate for office to be asking and once again shows me that Gerry is what the district needs. I'll be in touch with the other IAC members beginning next week to start thrashing out research needs and specific goals and I'll bounce whatever we come up with back to you in email updates that you can share with Gerry. Thanks,*

*Sam*

*ps, congratulations on the successful event this week [Dellinger/ Mayor Meeker event]!*

### Pros and Cons of the IAC Special Project:

Looking back on this project, it was a great idea, but one hard to implement well in the short time frame of our campaign. A definite benefit was that of engaging people in the process of researching potential policy issues. I was delighted by the enthusiasm apparent in the following suggestions for "electioneering" contained in the email about toll road research from one of the chairs:

*A Mr. Schwartz from the Transportation Actuary office telephoned this morning. He had been assigned to check on the questions I had raised. "They were very interesting." He hadn't found anything but he offered, and I accepted, [for] him to send me some web sites that might provide answers. I offered to send him copies of what I had discovered and he said he would like to see it. I don't know if that was a truthful statement.*

*In terms of electioneering, the questions I have raised are all valid and all sensitive. Can't you see Gerry on the stump. "YOUR CAR INSURANCE WILL GO UP!" "THERE WILL BE MORE HIGHWAY ACCIDENTS, THE SECOND MOST DANGEROUS KIND!" "WE WILL HAVE TO TAKE STATE TROOPERS OFF THE HIGHWAY AND STATION THEM NEAR TOLL BOOTHS TO PREVENT TRAFFIC TIE UPS FROM THE BACK END ACCIDENTS THAT ARE CAUSED BY TOLL BOOTHS!" THE PEOPLE WHO WANT TOLL BOOTHS HAVE NEVER ASKED ABOUT OTHER STATE'S EXPERIENCE WITH TOLL BOOTHS BECAUSE THEY DON'T WANT TO KNOW THE ANSWERS!" VOTE FOR GERRY BOWLES. SHE FINDS THE FACTS THAT THE NC STATE SENATE NEEDS TO MAKE THE RIGHT DECISIONS.*

Two of the committees provided findings that we were able to use in our final election materials/mailings. However, the project required much more of our valuable time resource than anticipated. We had hoped that the media would pick up this undertaking and help generate interest in volunteering, yet despite our efforts to get coverage, none was forthcoming. Even when we sent a request to one of the papers considered most liberal in the area, asking if the *Independent* had a place it could publicize our IAC initiative, we were politely refused with the following explanation:

*From: Bob Geary*
*To: Andrea Bertole*
*Sent: Thursday, June 22, 2006 2:24 PM*
*Subject: Re: Inquiry re Gerry Bowles' Issue Advisory Committee Initiative*

*Andrea --*

*Since you asked so nicely :)*

*I'm printing out your note, and I'll try to find a way to put some good thought about Gerry in the paper. We send questionnaires to the candidates prior to our endorsement issue, which comes out two weeks before the election, and the fruits of this issue effort should be apparently in Gerry's answers, at least.*

*Gerry knows how fond I am of her, and so I'll be inclined to try to help. But, just as a cautionary note, I made a list earlier today of elections I will be chiefly responsible for, and there are exactly 25 of them, including yours. I'll do stories on a few, but I won't get to most of them until the endorsements. I had a brief exchange with Nell Whitlock the other day about the fact that I don't run campaign event announcements in Act Now, mainly because there are so many of them, but also because, until we actually endorse somebody, I think we need to at least look like we're open to the possibility of supporting either candidate. That's not a hard & fast rule, because pretty clearly, e.g., we aren't to endorse Jessie Helms over Harvey Gantt. But what does it say to Neal Hunt about the questionnaire we send him when, prior to that, we're listing Gerry Bowles' events in our do-this Act Now column?*

*That's maybe more than you needed to know. Gerry's on my list, and I'll do my best. Feel free to write or call Jen Strom, our managing editor, or Richard Hart, our editor, with any thoughts you might have for them. I'm not the only person writing about politics for the Indy. But in Wake County, I do most of it.*

*Best regards,*
*Bob*

We had hoped to have committee sizes ranging from 4-12 members, but ended up having 3-4 for Education, 3 for Transportation, and 4-5 for Representation. In reality, those involved in the final report production numbered 1, 1, and 1 respectively. The IACs required more time than even the interested volunteers were able to contribute and the Chairs encountered difficulty in actually getting members to participate. Consequently, more work fell to fewer individuals and more coordination was needed by Andrea than was ideal as indicated by the follow-up email reminders she sent in August and September:

*1) Sent:* Tuesday, August 01, 2006 11:48 AM
*Subject:* IAC Check In - Gerry Bowles for NC Senate

*Dear IAC Committee Members,*

*Happy August 1st! With a month left to go until Labor Day and 97 days until the election, I just thought I would touch base to see how the committee work is faring and to check whether Gerry, Dan or I can be of any assistance in helping your research process and report production. I know it can be challenging to meet and coordinate with various summer holidays and schedules, and we do appreciate your agreement to take part in the committees and work on this project.*

*As you know we are looking at these committees in part as serving as a pilot for citizen participation and an alternative to lobbyists for generating research and legislative proposals. It is a learning process to see the challenges and benefits of the IACs so if you are encountering difficulties, we would welcome your input and ideas regarding how to improve this process.*

*As a refresher, here are the particular areas of research for each of the committees: [details provided as summarized above]*

*2) Sent:* September 2006
*Subject:*
*Dear IAC Committee Chairs & Members,*

*Happy Labor Day! Hope you have some relaxing plans for this long weekend. I just wanted to check in regarding two questions:*

*We had set Labor Day as the initial reporting time marker for the IACs – IAC Chairs, are you ready to pass along your findings on the particular areas of research for your respective committees and additional points of interest you think important?*

*As you hopefully have noted in the Campaign Update sent*

164

> *August 30th, we have a campaign update meeting from 7:00pm to 8:30pm on Thursday, September 7th at Gerry's home – would you be available and/or feel comfortable providing a 5 minute highlight of your committee's findings during this meeting?*
>
> *More generally, I would welcome your input regarding the pilot nature of the IACs (e.g. in continuing with the structure of Issue Advisory Committees upon Gerry's election as a way to involve citizens in their government, are there strengths to build on or problem areas to tackle).*
>
> *Thanks so much again for your involvement in this process.*
>
> *Andrea*

Finally, while Committee findings were indeed reported at our Campaign Update Meeting on September 7th, the reports themselves did not come in until late September/early October, at which point we still needed to take time to assess how to best use the material. Despite these challenges, I felt the IACs provided a good example of how I would govern if elected by avoiding the influence of special interest groups. This project also proved a good learning experience in highlighting potential obstacles to making this approach work, particularly in regards to the hours required of volunteers who were juggling multiple demands on their "free" time.

## *Point People/Precinct Organization*

The second special project the campaign undertook was intended to further our stated goal of winning the election one precinct at a time. In a perfect world, the Wake County Democratic Party would have organized all of our 52 precincts, which in 2006 meant having an identified precinct chair, vice chair, treasurer and a minimum of 5 registered Democratic voters who had attended the annual Precinct Meeting in March of that year. In order to be considered a precinct in good standing, an organized precinct needed to have also paid "its dues," an amount determined by the percentage of its voting Democrats in the previous election. With the challenges of getting people involved in the political arena, not surprisingly, precinct organization took some work. In my district, in particular, where people were not as inclined to be part of a party structure, it was less common still to find precincts functioning in this manner. I had firsthand experience with this challenge as I had served as the precinct chair for 02-01 after I ran for the House in 2000. Having worked hard to generate excitement and interest in the political process, I found it troublesome to then request monetary contributions to meet the financial requirement set forth by the party. In 2006, though there were some shining exceptions, many of the precincts in my district were not organized in a way that allowed me to tap into a pre-existing team of volunteers to help with my campaign.

When initially looking to implement my precinct focus, I started by trying to contact the recognized precinct chairs in my district, but few responded. In the list of precinct officials we received from the Wake County Democratic Party, indeed only 20 of the 52 precincts had met the threshold, at least on paper, of having identified members in the three positions noted above. In truth, many of those listed were no longer involved in the capacity cited, and one, in fact, had died. While many identified on this precinct officials' list were wonderful volunteers in my campaign, they tended to be so on an individual basis and not as a representative of their precinct. In reality, during my campaign only about half a dozen of my "organized" precincts were active in a structured way. Acknowledging this situation, Dan and I attempted to set-up our own organization of precinct point people. We hoped these people might mobilize the voters in my precincts to be sure my campaign needs were addressed. The thought was that after helping organize these point people, they would then further locate their own group of volunteers to help carry out the requested tasks.

By June 25th we had assembled names of potential point people based on lists of voting and active Democrats, our door-to-door recruitment, and willing volunteers already involved in our campaign. In early July we began by contacting roughly 20 possible volunteers. Ideally, we wanted to match our point people with our 3 tiers of key precincts, but, in fact, we were only able to identify potential contacts in 13 of the 28 targeted precincts, and only in 5 of the top 9.

### *Support Materials for Precinct Point People*
At the end of July, Andrea and I had prepared kits to assist the precinct

point people in continuing to implement the process. We began distributing them at that time and throughout the rest of the summer and early fall. A list of the kit contents follows below, but notably each included a welcome letter from Dan outlining the numbers needed to win, a guide to the Point Person role (including a description of what was hoped for from them, and precinct specific information which included campaign contacts, precinct officials where available, other candidates running in the precinct and the voter numbers specific to the particular precinct.

### *Point Person Kit:*

Dan's Introductory and Thank You Letter (sample included below)
Guide for Point Person (sample included below)
Campaign Contacts & Precinct Specific Information (sample for precinct 01-11 below)
Contact List for the Precinct
Guide for Precinct Call List (variation of call scripts used for Phone Canvassing-see samples in that section)
Web Site & Current Calendar of Events
Recent Campaign Update
District Map –precinct highlighted & Precinct Map
10 Palm cards
5 "Why vote Gerry" Talking Points
3 Gerry Bowles Stickers
5 "No Toll" Stickers
5 Business Cards
Voter Registration Form
2 WCDP Get out the vote cards
Early Voting Schedule

<u>*Dan's Introductory and Thank You Letter*</u>

*Dear Precinct Point Person Volunteer,*

*Thank you for volunteering to be the point person in your precinct for Gerry Bowles in her run as the Democrat for District 15's North Carolina State Senate. Your support is a vital part of our "One Precinct at a Time" strategy. As the point person you will be able to not only give out information in your precinct to other*

*Democrats for us, but also to help us get the word out through your assistance in informing us of events that are happening in your precinct and your community.*

*This packet of information will further explain the variety of activities that Gerry hopes you will be able to assist us with. Your time and participation are greatly appreciated by everyone on the Campaign Committee and your continued efforts will help us get Gerry elected. To give you and your neighbors an understanding of what we are looking at, the numbers of Democrats, Republicans and Unaffiliated voters in the district should tell you just how good of a chance we have.*

*In District 15 there are 45,589 registered Democrats, 51,777 registered Republicans and 29,410 registered Unaffiliateds for a total of 126,776 voters. Based on a number of predictions the turnout for the election should be between 36% and 42%. In other words we expect approximately 50,000 total voters in the district. This means that to ensure victory we need 26,000 votes. Spread across all of the precincts in our district, this is certainly achievable. If we can get 60% of registered Democrats in the district to vote, we would win. If 40% of Democrats turnout then we need 50% of the Unaffiliated turnout to reach the margin of victory.*

*Your help is a crucial part of our plan. Your volunteer work will be geared to increasing Democratic turnout in your precinct and your neighborhood. There are other volunteers doing the same thing in other precincts across the district, coordinated with Gerry, Andrea Bertole (volunteer coordinator) and myself to ensure the maximum efficiency and effort of the plan. Thank you so much for volunteering your time and effort. If you have any questions please feel free to contact Gerry, Andrea, or myself. With your help, we WILL send Gerry Bowles to the North Carolina Legislature as our State Senator.*

*Best Regards,*
*Dan Williams*
*Campaign Manager*

## Guide for Point Person

### *Gerry Bowles for District 15's NC Senate Precinct Campaign Point Person Guide*

*Thank you so much for volunteering to be your precinct's point person for Gerry Bowles' campaign! With our grassroots strategy, your assistance in connecting us with your community is invaluable.*

### *What does this role involve?*
*We have identified people in your precinct who have stated interest in or should be predisposed to supporting Gerry in her run this November $7^{th}$. Our list comes from 3 sources:*

- *The record for Democrats & Unaffiliated voters who voted as Democrats in the May $2^{nd}$ primary;*
- *Wake county's active Democrats listing;*
- *Our contacts from campaign undertakings (Democrats, Unaffiliateds, Republicans).*

*As the precinct point person, we ask that you help build & mobilize our network of supporters in your neighborhood by:*

- *Contacting all those on the list we provide to seek their involvement in the campaign.*
  - *Please recruit volunteers of friends, family, neighbors, and interested folks from the call lists to help in finding telephone numbers where needed, contacting all those listed on the call list and helping with other activities.*
- *Coordinating our lawn sign distribution and set-up.*
- *Organizing our "Get Out the Vote" efforts for your precinct (e.g. help organize a mailing to and additional canvass of your precinct)*
- *Organizing volunteers from your precinct to distribute Gerry's literature at your precinct's polling station on November $7^{th}$.*
- *Identifying opportunities for Meet & Greets in your precinct for Gerry to introduce herself to community members.*

*Support Available to Point Person:*
This role is a key component of our "winning one precinct at a time" strategy. We will support you in every way possible.

- Please feel free to work with the volunteer coordinator, Andrea Bertole, in organizing and coordinating your precinct.
- Please communicate your findings back to us e.g. contact information of new volunteers, e-mail addresses to include interested neighbors in campaign updates, community needs requiring attention by the campaign.

*Additional Points:*
- Please know that while we would consider you our campaign's point person, we are happy to work with other campaigns in your precinct (e.g. with the House Candidate)
- Your precinct may have an existing organization – our network is not intended to replace this organization but to dovetail with it when possible, while giving us our personal contact to connect with in our precinct mobilization efforts.

Sample of Precinct Info included in kit for 01-11

*Campaign Contacts & Precinct 01-11 Information*

*Campaign Contact Information:*
Gerry Bowles: visit www.GerryBowles06.com * e-mail: gerry@gerrybowles06.com or gerrybowles@yahoo.com * call: 919-847-9901

Dan Williams (campaign manager): e-mail: ax4782@wayne.edu * call: 919-271-5845

Andrea Bertole (volunteer coordinator): e-mail: andreabertole@hotmail.com or abertole@nc.rr.com * call: 919-793-0160

**Precinct 01-11 Officials**
Maria Kiser – Chair (782-1469)
Sylvia Holtzman - Secretary/Treasurer (787-2494)

**North Carolina State Board of Elections**
For voter registration information or electoral questions contact the NC State Board of Elections via (919) 733-7173 or www.sboe.state.nc.us.

**Where to Vote? Polling Place for 01-11:**
Root Elementary School at 3202 Northampton Rd, Raleigh, NC 27608

**Other Precinct 01-11 Candidates Running for Office**
US Congress District 13 – Incumbent Brad Miller
NC House District 34 – Incumbent Grier Martin

Wake County Commissioner (voters may support all 4 candidates)
  District 1 - Don Mial
  District 2 - Lindy Brown
  District 3 - Martha Brock
  District 7 - Rodger Koopman

Clerk of Court – Lorrin Freeman

Wake County District Court Judge (voters will need to choose between these 2 candidates)
  Aida Havel & Vince Rozier

Contact information for the above candidates and additional candidate listings can be found at www.wakedems.org/candidates

**Party Statistics for Precinct 01-11**
Total registered voters = 2,125
  897 Democrats * 972 Republicans * 256 Unaffiliateds

By mobilizing Democrats and Unaffiliateds, we can win this precinct for Gerry!

***Pros and Cons of the Precinct Point People Special Project:***

Not unlike the experience with the IAC project, the precinct point people undertaking was a good idea, but required more time to implement well than we had available. It demonstrated our commitment to involving all interested people, regardless of party affiliation and offered a flexible approach to schedules that we tried to show to all volunteers. No financial contribution was required of organizers. However, to be successful, this approach needed more time to foster relationships with volunteers as it did require a great commitment from them. Furthermore, while we outlined in our guide to them our willingness to work with other candidates and to be a support to existing precinct structures where applicable, many of those who were willing to take on this role were also involved in helping other voting efforts. Of the approximately 20 point people recruited, few took on the role as envisioned, though many contributed their time in the ways they could. Given the launch of this endeavor coincided with that of the IAC undertaking, much of our valuable time resource went to implementing these projects with little immediate benefit, though with the potential for longer term advantages.

# Chapter Eight – Communication

Canvassing, events, and special projects provided important avenues for sharing and demonstrating the message of my campaign. In addition, I used a number of other means and opportunities to communicate with the electorate. While less direct, responding to questionnaires sent by groups and organizations offered different ways to reach voters I may not have otherwise. Media outlets such as newspapers, radio and television gave me the potential to speak to large numbers of people about issues. The internet provided a relatively new way, at that time, to connect with interested parties, yet I did not ignore the more traditional approach of sending mailings. Finally, I chose from a large list of campaign products ranging from yard signs, to stickers, buttons and magnets to select additional items I hoped would gain the attention of potential supporters.

## *Questionnaires*

As early as March 22$^{nd}$ in the 2006 campaign, I started receiving requests to complete questionnaires by various interest groups. The hope in answering these questions is that the particular group will endorse your candidacy, perhaps give money, and that you will gain the recognition of their membership. My perspective in completing questionnaires was to be candid in sharing my views as people in my district deserved to know what I believed. There are a wide variety of groups that organize around particular concerns in order to influence the Legislature. The following lists a sample of the groups who contacted me in 2006:

- Called 2 Action (group mentioned in Chapter One's "Motivation" section)
- Democratic Women of Wake County
- Equality North Carolina
- The *Independent* (newspaper)
- Lillian's List
- NFIB (National Federation of Independent Business)
- National Organization of Women
- The *News and Observer* (newspaper)
- North Carolina Association of Educators
- North Carolina Assisted Living Association
- North Carolina Police Benevolent Association

- North Carolina State A.F.L.- C.I.O. (Triangle Labor Council)
- N.C. Voters for Clean Elections
- NC Go (advocate for transportation)
- Raleigh Regional Association of Realtors (Wake County Board of Realtors)
- Raleigh Wake Citizen's Association of North Carolina
- State Employees' Association of North Carolina (SEANC)
- Votesmart.org
- Wake Weekly (newspaper)

I could have spent every waking moment responding to these questionnaires. They ranged from being short and straightforward to answer, to being lengthy and requiring more detail to complete. Some were followed up by an interview. I wondered how much depth was needed to be responsible when answering these inquiries. In receiving questionnaires from groups throughout the state who had specific interests, I questioned how to weigh a group's concerns against those pertinent to my community.

In my 2000 campaign, I struggled with balancing the interests of a group with those of my church and my own personal beliefs. The *News and Observer* was preparing their usual campaign guide that featured a profile of each of the candidates including their church affiliation. I had received a questionnaire that asked my views on "crimes against nature," that is, sodomy with animals and humans. So, what did I think of that? I was worried that my views might not represent my church's and I did not want to reflect badly on the church, knowing that others might not necessarily share my views. I had the opportunity to share my concerns over coffee with our church's new minister from out of state. I introduced myself and let him know I was running for a seat in the State Legislature. I explained the position and district and let him know he could vote for me. He was excited. I mentioned I was in the process of filling out questionnaires, some of which were explicit, and that in responding honestly according to my beliefs, I was worried I would be seen as a spokesperson for our church and felt awkward about the situation.

> "What kind of questions?" he asked.
> "Well, for instance, crimes against nature" I replied.
> The minister inquired "is that some kind of environmental law?"
> "No, that's sodomy."

*"Oh." was his response.*

I explained my responses and views on abortion, homosexuality and my more liberal thinking. To my great relief, my minister responded that everything I had stated so far was what the Presbyterian Church believed. For example, while no one was pro-abortion, the church felt this was a decision that ought to be left to a woman and her God, a private matter not for the state.

I had not anticipated this type of conversation when I signed up to run for office! But I thought, well, in for a penny, in for a pound. I will go to all groups who ask me to speak and respond to all questionnaires. Consequently, the process was time consuming but I found it informative and helpful in framing my beliefs.

When time is one of the precious resources you have, completing questionnaires is expensive. In the larger campaigns, policy papers are written on the key issues of the day such as the death penalty moratorium, abortion, illegal immigrations etc. What I discovered on a local level was that many candidates did not fill them out.

In my 2006 election campaign, with time a premium, I needed to carefully select which questionnaires to answer. For example, I made a strategic decision not so seek the endorsement of Lillian's List, an organization that aims to elect Democratic pro-choice women to the Legislature. In 2000, I had spent much time answering their comprehensive questionnaire and participating in a follow-up interview. In selecting key races where they thought the candidates would be most successful, Lillian's List, unfortunately, did not choose to help me. It put me in a bit of an awkward position as their membership and supporters assumed I said something that contradicted their pro-choice platform. As a result, I did not gain support of those in favor of Lillian's List and I also potentially alienated the support of those whose views were not in line with this group. In 2006, I declined to complete their questionnaire with the following explanation:

> *From: "Gerry Bowles" <gerrybowles@yahoo.com>*
> *To: "Carol Teal" <cteal@nc.rr.com>*
> *Sent: Wednesday, March 22, 2006 10:30 AM*
> *Subject: Re: Lillian's List*

*Good morning Carol,*

*I wanted to explain that even though I am a strong believer in a woman's right to choose that I would not be asking for an endorsement from Lillian's List.*

*I appreciate the wonderful work that "Lillian's" does, but realize that given my opponent and his views that it might be best not to stir up the hornet's nest and give him any information that he could use to discredit my views.*

*Thanks for understanding!*

*Gerry Bowles*

Another organization that I declined to respond to via their questionnaire was the group, Called 2 Action. My opponent's being a board member was not the reason for my reluctance to answer the questionnaire but rather the black and white responses required for their controversial questions:

*Marriage Amendment Vote - Would you vote to force the Marriage Amendment bill out of committee to the legislative floor for a full vote? Yes or No*

*Domestic Partner Benefits - Should the state of NC provide benefits to unmarried "domestic partners" of state employees? Yes or No*

*Abstinence-Only Sex Education - Would you vote to keep abstinence from sexual activity until marriage as the expected standard for school-aged children? Yes or No*

*Vouchers - Would you vote for the state to provide vouchers or tax credits for children to attend private schools? Yes or No*

*Charter Schools - Would you vote to remove the limit on charter schools in NC? Yes or No*

When I encountered someone from an organization whose questionnaire I did not complete, I would address any of their specific questions and refer them to my website for additional information about me and the issues on which I was focusing.

In balancing the demands on my time, I realized my answers to a questionnaire were primarily a litmus test on an issue and would not necessarily win me votes. Furthermore, I had discovered in the 2000 election that being the Republican candidate and having an "R" by your name was the key to winning votes, regardless of any answer given on a questionnaire. Folks at the polls were in and out quickly which seemed to reflect straight ticket voting. Questionnaires certainly offered an education on the diversity of interests and concerns throughout the state about which a candidate needed to be familiar if elected. Overall, as a tool to communicate my message, it offered some value and I was always candid but selective.

## *Media*

Even though I fully recognized the value of newspapers, radio and television in reaching a larger audience with my message, I had to weigh this benefit against the financial costs of using these outlets, particularly given our limited budget.

### *Newspapers*

I was disappointed in the role newspapers played in covering my campaign. It seemed to always come down to money. I was welcome to buy ad space anytime, but could not be assured of getting a mention of events or other activities planned by my campaign. For instance, *Triangle Politics,* a weekly column in the *News and Observer* devoted to covering local political events was inconsistent in what they chose to publish. We regularly sent notices of upcoming events to the contact person for this column but could not count on their making it to print. The following two emails illustrate the uncertainty and complexity of getting something published:

> *From: Holly Stepp <hstepp@newsobserver.com>*
> *To: andrea bertole <andreabertole@hotmail.com>*
> *Subject: Re: Follow-up re Gerry Bowles Events for Triangle Politics*

Date: Sun, 18 Jun 2006 16:57:14 -0400

Thanks for your email. Because of space limitations, we don't publish events that happen outside of the Triangle as is the case with the June 20 event [High School Reunion Event in Williamsburg, VA]. For the same reasons, we also only publish items on the Saturday before the event. The pre-Independence Day item will appear in June 24 edition of Triangle Politics.

However, the June 27 event will be posted this week on our Wake Politics blog which often includes information about political fundraisers.

- H

From: Holly Stepp <hstepp@newsobserver.com>
To: andrea bertole <andreabertole@hotmail.com>
Subject: Re: July 2006 Web Posting of Gerry Bowles Events for Triangle Politics & Question
Date: Mon, 3 Jul 2006 15:38:07 -0400

Thanks for your email, Andrea.

Our general rule is to publish items in the print edition a week out and the items online on Wake Pol no more than two weeks out. While we try to get every item into the print edition, we sometimes have to edit for space, taking care to consider political parity. That's why we believe Wake Pol offers a reasonable back-up to our free listings.

For clarity's sake and to provide the most information for our readers, we generally try to include the candidates' opponent. In the case of forums and groups events, we occasionally omit them for space reasons as was the case on Saturday.

It may also help to know that Triangle Politics varies by geographic area - a separate one for the Western Triangle and one for the eastern half. On July 1, we had a combined edition to accommodate some holiday press schedules. That affected the

178

*space we had in Saturday's edition.*

*That said, the Political Trail is only one component of Triangle Politics, and we try to make sure that we leave adequate space for the other content. We always try to accommodate as many listings as possible within that framework. The free listings are imperfect system, and certainly don't take the place of other options such as paid advertising.*

*Thanks again,*

*- H*

While I appreciated that the *News and Observer* did have some avenues to publish my activities, be it in print or through their online blog, the inconsistency with which they did so made it hard to plan around. Furthermore, I felt my chances of getting my events publicized shouldn't depend on the activity level of my opponent's campaign. We had lots going on that we wanted people to know about. If my opponent didn't, why should I be penalized? Being a grassroots campaign, the more "perfect" options suggested by Holly were not financially available. As you may recall from the chapter on Special Projects, I had a similar response from my contact at the *Independent* who suggested it would be unfair to my opponent to publish my activities. My thinking was that there was nothing stopping Neal Hunt from requesting his activities be conveyed but he was running a different type of campaign from mine. The *Independent* also mirrored the response from the *News and Observer* in pushing paid "advertising" over news reporting as illustrated by the email I received below on June 2$^{nd}$ from an account executive, despite having sent my email to the political reporter.

*Hi Gerry,*

*Thank you for providing information about the proposed I 540 tolls. I'm glad that I checked out your web site http://www.stop540toll.com/*

*I didn't have a clue about the tolls.*

*I sell advertising for the INDY and I think you would get some great feedback and support if you advertised with us.*

*We have our Best of the Triangle Issue coming out on June 14th. If you are unfamiliar, this is the issue where we announce all of our Reader's Choice winners.*

*A few other issues of note in the near future...*

*June 21- Gay Pride*
*June 28- Summer reading*
*July 12-Indies Arts Awards*
*July 19- Casa: Home and Garden*

*Good luck. You have a very nice campaign theme.*

*Best,*

*Tommy Fowler*
*Account Executive*
*The Independent Weekly*
*919-832-8774 (p) (press 5 to bypass greeting)*
*919-832-8668 (f)*
*http://www.indyweek.com/*

Instead of "We Report, You Decide" coined by Fox News, I felt like the motto was "you pay, we report."

The campaign tried a variety of print news services in attempting to get our message to our voters. My son, Hal, was hopeful of getting our Transportation message to the business community through his contact at *The Triangle Business Journal*, as his June 9th email to me indicates. Unfortunately, this effort did not produce the hoped for results showing once again that it is difficult to get noticed in the media unless you pay or break the law.

*I have contacted the editor of the Triangle Business Journal and have mailed him some stickers. Since we have a subscription here at the office, I'll keep an eye out for any mention. I have a feeling*

180

that Dale Gibson (the editor) will make a reference to your 540 stickers in his Biz section. That should get you some good publicity here in the business community.

Hal
------ Forwarded Message
From: Dale Gibson <dgibson@bizjournals.com>
Date: Fri, 09 Jun 2006 12:43:31 -0400
To: Hal Bowles <hal@hardin-bowles.com>
Subject: Re: Stop 540 Toll

OK, thanks,
Dg.

From: Hal Bowles <hal@hardin-bowles.com>
Date: Fri, 09 Jun 2006 12:29:59 -0400
To: <dgibson@bizjournals.com>
Subject: Stop 540 Toll

Hey Dale,

With all the excitement heating up about the proposed I-540 toll, I wanted to make you aware of a website that has been developed by Gerry Bowles (full disclosure – my mother), a democrat running for senate in district 15. The website is www.stop540toll.com.

I will mail you some stickers.

Thanks,

Hal

One of the services offered by the *News and Observer* is a Voter's Guide that is included in the Saturday edition prior to the Tuesday election. This compilation of candidate profiles whose names will appear on the ballot in November provides a biographical sketch and allows the candidates to specify their issues. This tool offers voters the chance to compare candidates side-by-side. The following is the ***2006 General Election***

***Voters Guide Candidates' Questionnaire*** from the *News and Observer*.

- *Name: (As it appears on ballot)*
- *Home address: (Street address, city or town)*
- *Date of birth (00/00/00)*
- *Family: (Spouse, children)*
- *Education:(Example" B.A. English, Meredith College)*
- *Occupation/Employer:*
- *Political Experience: (Include previous offices held or runs for office)*
- *Political Affiliation:*
- *Community Involvement: (Civic groups, religious affiliations, volunteer work- Please limit to 5 organizations.*
- *Name your top priorities if elected: (Limit 250 words, please)*
- *If you could solve one problem in your community and/or district, what would it be (Limit to 250 words, please)*
- *Who is your political hero?*
- *Name a book, movie or piece of art that has inspired you the most and explain why.*
- *How to contact: (e-mail, telephone)*
- *Campaign Web site:*
- *Campaign e-mail*

The timing has struck me as less than ideal. While the paper contends that voters only focus on an election immediately beforehand, I think a better timing would be a couple of weeks out, as done by The *Independent*, to give people a chance to reflect on the content and to personally follow-up with candidates if they have questions. Also, given the early voting options provided, the guide cannot be used as a resource by those wanting to take advantage of the early voting dates. Furthermore, there is no time for a candidate to correct misinformation that may have been published in this guide. An example of this scenario was the paper's use of some of the responses I had made to the publication during the 2000 election as if it were information they had obtained in 2006. Unfortunately, I found what I considered to be lazy and sloppy journalism more frequently than not. Yet another problem with the timing is that the content used is submitted to the paper just after filing (in February), so a candidate's answers to some of the questions may not be current.

The *News and Observer* was not the only newspaper in which my profile was published. In early October, I responded to the following email request from Clair Romaine.

> Dear Ms. Bowles,
>
> The Wakefield Howler Newspaper is conducting a "Know your Candidates" for Wakefield High and we need specific information about each candidate. If possible please email the howler@wcpss.net with the college you attended [the description included more information about me found from other sources].
>
> Thank you!

As an advocate for civic involvement at all levels, I welcomed this opportunity to communicate my message to future voters.

## Radio

As with newspapers, certainly I could have paid to get my message out over the airwaves, but being financially constrained I considered how I could tap into this source without paying. In 2000, I tried to think of which radio stations might provide their listeners political coverage of local races. I looked to the college stations and *National Public Radio*, but the demographics of my district did not include many college students and NPR didn't offer any opportunities that I was aware of for local candidates. Another possibility that crossed my mind was WPTF AM 1480 which had a conservative talk radio format. Jerry Agar owned these airways between 3-6 pm in Raleigh, even outperforming non-talk radio. His show followed 3 hours of Rush Limbaugh and preceded Sean Hannity's so listeners could potentially get 9 hours of "verbal" red meat each day. My then opponent, Russell Capps, ran many ads on Jerry's show.

As I have mentioned before in relation to my 2000 campaign, I availed myself to all groups who showed an interest in my campaign. In that spirit, I attended a meeting hosted by Citizens for Tax Reform and turned a few heads when I walked in. As I was signing in and trying to get the "lay of the land," I realized that it was not my land! I was most certainly the only candidate present who was not on the far right of the political spectrum. Jerry Agar was the moderator for the evening, and afterwards I introduced myself and let him know how much I enjoyed listening to his show. Even though his views were far to the right of mine, he had always seemed somewhat fair to me and smart as a whip. He seemed surprised when I shared that I would love to be a guest on his show. My thinking was that I had nothing to lose by appearing (as most of the listeners were probably not a part of my natural constituency) and much to gain if I could hold my own and thereby possibly gain a few converts. It was arranged that I would go on Jerry's live call-in show during the last hour to debate my opponent and answer questions. To this day, I feel that appearing on Jerry's show was the gutsiest thing I did as a candidate.

On the day of the airing, Nell, my media volunteer extraordinaire, and I arrived at the station early and sat in our car in the parking lot listening to the first part of the show and announcements promoting my upcoming debate. Just before the third hour, Nell and I went inside to get set up for my on-air debut. Little did I know that I was stepping into my opponent's "sanctuary" with a target on my chest. We were directed to the waiting room outside the studio where we could listen to Jerry live on the air. With the clock ticking down and only five minutes remaining until "air time," I was anxiously awaiting being prepped for my live appearance. The receptionist confirmed that Jerry knew I was present and waiting. On the hour, during a commercial break between segments, he finally came out and ushered me into the studio.

I walked in and who should I see, smirking and already sitting on his stool with his head set on, Russell Capps! Can you say set-up? Sorry suckers sandbagged me! My first thought was *"this is not right – we should have come in together."* During the remaining minute of the commercial, I was seated forming a close triangle with Russell and Jerry while the sound technician struggled to get my head set operational. The red light flashed and we were "live."

Jerry introduced us both and went straight for my jugular. No more mister nice guy. I remember trying to respond to a question that was less a question than an accusation. Russell chimed in and I had the overwhelming sense that the "debate" had all been staged. Russell, in a belittling fashion, cited Thomas Jefferson and the Declaration of Independence as though it was the Bible. I thought *"don't preach the Declaration to a Williamsburg, Virginia history teacher"* and during the next commercial break I pulled out a copy of the US Constitution I kept in my purse. When back on the air, I quoted Jefferson and the preamble to the constitution "We the People" and with that turned the conversation on its head. Nell, who had been sitting in the sound booth next to the technician reported that he remarked, "no one else has ever got the best of him [referring to Jerry]" and the phones lit up. At this point I felt a sense of relief and was able to just be myself. My goal was to hold my own. I left with my head high and a sense of victory in having survived such a hostile environment. You would be amazed how many people, from different walks of life, later stopped me to say *"I heard you on the radio."*

The following week, I sent Jerry Agar a thank you note for having me on and he later served as a moderator for a candidates' forum sponsored by the group that we started after the election, the *Wake County Citizens for Effective Government*. Prior to the forum he thanked me for that thank you note and shared that he could count on one hand the number of such notes he had received in his career. He was gracious in his praise for me and for the agreeable atmosphere that our group had promoted.

In 2006, I opted not to seek out a repeat of this radio exposure. My email response to one of my volunteers sums up the situation:

> *Gerry - Have you had a radio interview on [W]PTF? Henry Strong called me today at 5:10 to tell me that Neal Hunt was in an interview and that your name was mentioned. I didn't hear the interview because I needed to help my mom. Are you allowed equal air time just before the election?*
>
> *Hey Diana,*
>
> *Yes, I had an opportunity to go on the show, and decided that it would not be in our best interest. We have been manning the polls at early voting at Shelly Lake...and have had a positive response from the voters. We will indeed win this one vote at a time...just need to get our folks out! Thanks for getting all your crew to the polls.*
>
> *Thanks again,*
> *Gerry*

In declining this radio appearance, I considered that Jerry Agar was no longer the host for WPTF and I had no relationship with the new host. I perceived the station had become more conservative still. Knowing that I would be walking into the lion's den, I felt the time needed to prepare well for such an undertaking wasn't a good use of this limited resource. After all, borrowing from the quote made infamous by George "W" Bush, "fool me once, shame on you, fool me twice, shame on me."

## *TV*

I was lucky to have a few supporters offer their time and talents to produce a television spot for my campaign, as indicated by this email exchange:

> *Greetings,*
>
> *Just wanted to make you aware in case you didn't already know that your opponent, Neal Hunt, is preparing to air TV ads.*
> *By trade I am a commercial producer. If you wanted I'd be willing to produce a spot for you for free to put more money to an air schedule (if this is something you were considering or if campaign funds allowed)*
>
> *Although my personal access to equipment is limited since I couldn't use my company's equipment for free for a political candidate I could create some things at home where I have some editing capabilities.*
>
> *A fellow Democratic*
> *[name withheld for privacy]*

Unfortunately, we never had enough funds to air one, hence my reply:

> *Dear [name withheld for privacy],*
>
> *Thank you so much for your kind offer to help my campaign by working on a TV ad. Unfortunately, our budget does not allow for paid TV spots. We will be on TV 12 and Time Warner via The League of Women Voters the last week before the election.*

*We would love for you to be able to display a yard sign for us...if that works for you...and to take part as a poll worker (if that works with your schedule). Will forward our newsletter to you...please join us for any of the activities.*

Fortunately for candidates such as myself with limited economic resources the federal government who has control of the airwaves had recognized the value in having an informed citizenry and had required that stations provide political candidates a certain amount of airtime as a public service. The stations could choose how they were going to provide this public service. In the case of one of our local networks (the NBC affiliate) candidates were provided up to 5 minutes for a taped message that aired at numerous times during the last weeks of the election.

My taping was scheduled for October $11^{th}$. I arrived at the studio at my appointed time and was provided a 15-minute period in which to "set up" and deliver my remarks. There was no monitor or prompter, just a single cameraman and sound technicians to make sure the mike was recording properly. Candidates were allotted three minutes for our prepared remarks. We were allowed the use of note cards, but delivering a memorized message was preferred. The extra time allotted was provided in case a candidate required more than one "take." It all sounds straightforward, but was more difficult than it seemed. It was not easy to look natural and deliver a message while operating under a time constraint. Many candidates felt stressed. Having had some experience in the early 90's with this technology while taping a pilot for a television show, I had some comfort with being on camera. The taping took place in a board room where I was seated at the head of the table. We did the first take without a stumble but decided to do a second, as we had enough time to correct a pause that I had taken in the first taping. The following is the message I delivered:

*Good morning, I am Gerry Bowles and I am running for the North Carolina State Senate to represent District 15.*

*I believe that government is a relationship between "We the People" and our representatives. We suffer when the people's interest is superseded by our representatives taking care of special interests.*

*My campaign has been about putting people's interests first. We have knocked on over 5000 doors in the district. Many citizens some of whom have never been approached by anyone in government before, have shared their concerns with me.*

*Education tops the list. At a time when our children need to be competitive in a global economy, only 6 of 10 incoming high school freshmen currently graduate.*

*Education is a serious matter for the Senate comprising 40% of the State's annual budget. As a former teacher of Economics, Law and Politics at Millbrook High School, I will bring first-hand classroom experience to the decision-making process.*

*I will fight to ensure that 100% of the monies promised from the Education Lottery are spent on education and that we in Wake County receive our fair share of the education pie. Furthermore, I will work to raise teacher's salaries to the national level, allowing us to recruit and retain great educators to prepare our students to compete strongly in a global economy.*

On the 23$^{rd}$ of October, I was provided another opportunity to "air" my remarks by the League of Women Voters and Time Warner Cable as explained in the following invitation:

*"...to participate in a Citizen's Choice Program. Each candidate will be provided three minutes to address an issue or question submitted from the LWV-Wake as well as issues of your choosing.*

*Production and taping of this program will be done at the Time Warner Production facility at 708 E. Club Blvd., Durham, NC. It will take place over a period of three days with fifteen minute sessions available. The dates* [a list of dates and times were provided]

*This is not an interview, but an opportunity to speak on issues provided by the League of Women Voters, or to say whatever you like as you campaign for the November election. Your presentation should last no longer than three minutes and you may tape it as many times as you like in your 15 minute session. There will be no editing, and due to time restraints you will not be able to view your presentations afterward. Please do not bring any campaign props or signs. "Citizens Choice" will be cablecast on Time Warner Cable's Channel 24 on the following dates and times:*

*Monday, October 30$^{th}$ 7:00 PM*
*Wednesday, November 1$^{st}$ 7:30 PM*
*Thursday, November 2$^{nd}$ 12 NOON*
*Saturday, November 4$^{th}$ 12 NOON*
*Monday, November 6$^{th}$ 7:00 PM*

*The LWV has teamed with Time Warner in order to provide information to the general public regarding upcoming elections. We urge you to respond positively to this invitation in order to get your message to the voting public.*

While my presence on TV was limited, my opponent had more than enough funds to "take to the airwaves," as evidenced by Jim Morrill's October 18$^{th}$ online reporting in the *Charlotte Observer* that was forwarded by one of my supporters:

*TV ad features a photo of embattled Democratic House Speaker Jim Black, along with a montage of headlines about the scandals and controversies that have hounded him for a year.*

*The ad isn't for his Republican opponent in Mecklenburg County. It's for Neal Hunt, a state senator from North Raleigh.*

*It's an example of how some Republicans are trying to use Black and his problems to boost their own campaigns, by linking their opponents to the speaker or by pointing out what they see as a pattern of Democratic corruption.*

*Skeptics say the link may be hard to make.*

*"My personal belief is voters don't make that connection". Says*

*John Davis, executive director of NCFREE, a pro-business group that tracks legislative politics. "They're not going to punish their legislator, who they know well, because they're in the same party as a leader who has been implicated in some kind of wrongdoing."*

*A Superior Court judge in Wake County ruled that Black's campaign violated campaign finance laws, and ordered it to forfeit $6,800. Though Black has denied any wrongdoing, a parade of legal setbacks to associates has cast a long shadow over him.*

*However, a poll for NCFREE found that N.C. Voters confuse federal and state corruption and aren't sure who to blame. Asked which party was most likely to be corrupted, 72 percent said both.*

*"The average North Carolina voter probably listens more to news about what's going on in Washington than Raleigh", Davis says. "The issue for Republicans this year has been neutralized by problems with their own party in Washington."*

*Missed chance for GOP?*

*But last month Jack Hawke, a former state GOP chairman and president of the Raleigh-based Civitas Institute, said state Republicans weren't using the corruption issue as much as they could and may be running out of time. Bill Peaslee, chief of staff for the state Republican Party, says there's a reason.*

*"It's easy to say, 'Gee, you should have made an issue of it earlier," Peaslee says, "But if you don't have the money, it's difficult to communicate with the voters."*

*Though Republicans have mounted no statewide effort to use the issue, some candidates are using it.*

*"My point is really that we're focusing on the wrong issues," says Hunt, the senator from Raleigh. "We need to be focusing on the big issues, not these sideshows."*

*Strategy failed in '98*

*Guilt by association didn't work for Republicans in 1998, when many GOP candidates tried to tie their opponents to Democratic President Clinton, who was fighting his own scandal controversies.*

*"Not enough was done to make Clinton relevant to everyday lives", says Dee Stewart, a GOP consultant from Raleigh. "We need to make everything we do come back around to improving the lives (of people)."*

*Stewart who represents 10 Republican candidates, advises clients to address other issues. Because corruption diverts attention, he says, it's really good to use a backdrop issue".*

*Former House Speaker Joe Mavretic, a Democrat, says if Black himself is not directly implicated in wrongdoing by this weekend, it will have no effect on the election.*

*Hawke, the former GOP chairman, says it's too early to tell. "Things are looking a little better for Republicans", he says. "But every time I think that, something like (the former GOP Rep Mark) Foley (page scandal) comes along and knocks them back down."*

Unfortunately for me, and for Speaker Black, he plead guilty the weekend before the election and it did indeed have a negative effect on my election.

## *Internet*

The internet was the key to our campaign's communication. It was the glue that kept us together and provided the means to disseminate our message to a larger audience. It allowed Andrea and me to easily interact with our committee and volunteers and served as a vehicle to communicate with the public at large. We tried to be both transparent and accessible to our volunteers and their ideas. If we were not successful in implementing some of their suggestions it was usually because of a financial or time constraint, not that the ideas were unsound. At all times we tried to keep the lines of communication open so that we could publish our message to a broad spectrum of the public. The numerous social media tools we take for granted today were less widely in use in 2006, but we found email, blogs and websites to be of great value in keeping us connected.

## *E-mail as an Avenue for Ideas*

Unlike the many campaigns that fail to respond to individual concerns of a personal nature or the offered suggestions on how to run the campaign, we tried our best to be as responsive to these emails as our time would allow. The following gives an insight into the variety of issues that "traveled the net."

Many of my supporters sent me information they thought would be helpful regarding my education platform. As early as March, Nell Whitlock sent the following discussion she found in the *Independent* regarding school funding:

> *Here's the election issue in a nutshell. Growth in Wake County is not paying for itself. Not in taxes, anyway. (Better restaurants maybe) And why is that? It's simple. We rely disproportionately on property taxes for our revenues; and in Raleigh especially, where the two biggest industries are government and higher education, a huge portion of our income producing property is tax-exempt. So the faster we grow, the farther behind we fall in school construction, road construction, mass transit, mental-health service, you name it, but the issue this year is schools and how to pay for them.*

Education was indeed on the mind of the electorate as indicated by this next email exchange with a gentleman I met "on the trail:"

> *We met today at Cruisers. Thanks for your time.*
>
> *Quick question...what is your opinion of the lottery and the use of its proceeds?*
>
> *Thanks!*
> *[Name and contact information withheld for privacy]*
>
> *From: Gerry Bowles*

192

> Re:   Hello
> Sent:   Saturday, May 13, 2006 4:36 PM
>
> Hi [Name withheld for privacy],
>
> I was not in favor of the lottery. I believe that it is bad public policy, and that education is important enough to be funded in our "regular" state budget.
>
> However, now that it is law, I want to make sure that the monies received do indeed go to public education, as intended. In fact, I would like to see the majority of the money going to provide the facilities that are sorely needed.
>
> Thanks,
> Gerry@GerryBowles06
>
>
> Subject: Re Hello!
> Date: Saturday May 13, 2006 5:54 PM
>
> Great stand. Good luck. That will be a difficult battle given the leanings of the governor's mansion and leaders in the legislature. You are taking the wise position and the one that is right!
>
> Good luck! You have my vote and support.
>
> [Name withheld for privacy]

Still more news about funding education was directed to Andrea, which she forwarded to me, in response to one of our newsletters.

> Andrea-you may be interested in a new group that is gaining momentum in Wake County called Wake Up. You may be able to tap volunteers for the IAC committee through this group as some of the issues they are fighting for are similar to Gerry's. Check them out www.wakeupwakecounty.com.
>
> Jennifer Tisdale

> Subject: Jennifer Tisdale information referral
> From: Andrea Bertole
> To: GerryBowles@yahoo.com
> Date: Monday, June 5, 2006 3:36 PM
>
> Hi Gerry- Jennifer Tisdale passed along this information and I thought it looks interesting. Have you heard of Wake Up Wake County before? I checked out the web site and on the surface there seems to be a great mesh with your campaign issues.
>
> Have signed up for their announcements and thought perhaps we might be able to check them out if they have some upcoming events.

Some suggestions for campaign issues, while well intentioned, were clearly out of left field and were not so easily incorporated. This forwarded message from the Funeral Consumers Alliance of the Triangle spoke to disparate pricing in funeral costs in which full service funerals for $4,000 were promoted in lieu of cremation services for $1,200:

> Subject: Fwd: Why maybe this is a good campaign item
> Date: Friday March 17, 2006
>
> Dear Gerry,
>
> Folks I know who have worked with the [funeral] industry describe them as sharks out to make a buck. That is why state laws are so important. The funeral homes try to sell the FULL SERVICE to the family.

In addition to issue related email, I received advice on useful tools for the campaign. Nell Whitlock had numerous suggestions for the use of "new" technology. I thought that they were all spot on, but unfortunately, we did not have one computer guru within our campaign organization who was able to devote the time to these endeavors. I do think that had we been able to implement any of these measures our campaign would have been helped immensely.

*Gerry-*

*I have an idea for your website that might be very useful as well as very-up-to the- minute. Have you heard of YouTube.com? It is a fascinating internet phenom-people can upload their own videos to be available online for anyone to see. Some people have developed quite a habit of watching the videos. Many are using this to promote things widely. When one catches on, it spreads virally. Anyway, the idea I have is for you to create your own video and have it linked at your website. I am sure Hal can do the mechanics. All you have to do is make a digital video and open an account on YT and then put a link to it on your campaign website. You could give a stump speech or do it conversationally- ie re-design the traditional delivery of a campaign speech. You could practice and revise until you were satisfied with it. It could be an improvement over the one shot deal you had at Channel 14 in previous campaigns. Also, you could discuss key points of your platform. Possibly, consider a video on each topic and/or a general overview discussion. The possibilities are endless. I think this could make your website more interesting. Every time I check it, I haven't seen anything new except the calendar. I plan to suggest to Holly at TriPol to do an article about local candidates' websites with addresses listed – a public service, etc. But I want to make sure yours is up to date. I think a video could be very effective, especially because you can control its production, instead of depend[ing] on a cable TV station. You can change it, you can have several eg. one showing you on the campaign trail, one about your yard signs and how people can get one, etc. You want people to come back to your site. Anyway, think about it. Talk it over with your staff. But, I think it would be very modern and progressive of you.*

*www.youtube.com/signup*

*Nell*
*8/14/06*

*ps-you could then notify your email list about the video(s) and ask that they let their friends know about it, if they are so inclined, etc.*

A week later, Nell sent another message encouraging the use of this technology. Part of that message is as follows

> Subject: more thoughts on YouTube
> Date: Monday, August 21, 2006 9:50 PM.
>
> Gerry--
> After today's exchange with Bob Geary- I think it would be great if you could be the first in the area to incorporate youtube.com in your website/campaign. It would be news and it would certainly attract a buzz for a bit.
>
> Be sure that whatever you do in a video cannot be misused by the opponent, that is the only caveat.
>
> You may have heard already how it has done in George Allen, at least set him back a lot for a while – Webb is now just three points behind—last week Allen called a Webb supporter assigned to attend Allen's speeches and record them for the Webb campaign— as is common practice. And Allen called him a most derogatory name and by doing so, sabotaged his own campaign and future run for pres. It was YouTubed and spread all over the net.
>
> Nell

### Campaign Updates via Email

As a means to keep us all on the same page, Andrea's Campaign Updates became important in their own right as entertainment and energy builders. It was her vehicle as volunteer coordinator to keep the volunteers current with the campaign. From the get-go it was obvious that her updates were something special. They were meant to be a metaphor for how I would serve my constituents as their representative. More than a catalogue of events they were meant to pique interest in the campaign. Our goal was to educate, entertain and inform. In so doing we hoped to model transparency and show that our campaign was an open book and that we never felt the need to be less than candid with our supporters. The use of different themes for each update was employed so our followers would want to read the entire update, especially as they could be repetitious with the same events being mentioned more than once. Andrea's creativity and sense of humor had our supporters anticipating the next installment.

We have shared some content of the updates throughout the book. As a refresher, the following is an example of the format that we followed from an edition sent toward the end of the campaign:

### Gerry Bowles for NC Senate Campaign Update... 16-Oct-06

Just 23 days or 3 weeks and a day until the Election! A huge thank you to the many of you who have heightened your already wonderful volunteer contributions by calling voters and connecting with neighbors at the doors to inform them of Gerry's campaign and encourage them to go to the polls November 7th! A warm welcome to those of you new to the update. The enthusiasm, interest and support of you all continue to be tremendous sources of motivation. With November just around the corner, we feel excited, encouraged and energized! Join us in celebrating the end of October by taking part in our upcoming activities and events.

### October 18th "Scare Up the Vote" – BOO!
You know how the plot begins ... you are innocently riding your horse to your polling station on November 7th when suddenly a headless horseman comes out of nowhere and chases you miles out of your way. Don't let the unexpected distract you from voting ... you are invited to defy predictions for low voter turnout & celebrate the start of early voting.

Howl at this<br>
"Blue Moon" Election Rally.

Wednesday, October 18th<br>
from 7:00-8:30 p.m.<br>
405 Amelia Avenue (Gerry's home)

Costumes optional but welcome!
RSVP appreciated
(847-9901 or Gerry@GerryBowles06.com)

One stop voting begins October 19th 8:30-5:00p.m.
Wake County Board of Elections
337 S. Salisbury Street.

A cackle of thanks to one of our superb campaign members for suggesting a special call to our college supporters – don't let the fearsome workload of school frighten you from voting ... embrace the reprieve of Fall Break and come home to join the party and vote early!

**Trick or treat?**
With the final push to November 7th and campaign mailers set to go out to targeted district voters, the treasury is looking skeletal. If you have some spare candy, please help plumpen campaign coffers. All offerings are gratefully received. Our Representation Issues Advisory Committee has reported that usually only a small number of people fund the bulk of campaigns, which can create pressure on candidates to please these few donors. Gerry's campaign has been financed in small amounts by many donors. The "trick" to keeping people the priority is receiving "treats" from many. Your check would be most appreciated and can be made payable to "Gerry Bowles NC Senate" and sent to 405 Amelia Ave, Raleigh, NC 27615.

**October 28th Early voting North Raleigh Rally – Ahhhhh!**
Between your nightmares on Elm Street, your neighbor Jason running his chainsaw non stop, and ghosts speaking to your family through the T.V., you just never know what may disrupt your plans to vote on November 7th. Remove the suspense by voting early! Join us at "campaign headquarters" for our North Raleigh Rally located at the
BP on Newton Rd and Six Forks Rd

Saturday, October 28th from 10 a.m. to 12 p.m.

Festivities include shuttle rides to the Sertoma Arts Center at 1400 W. Millbrook Road where One Stop voting begins from 10 a.m to 6 p.m. Other 2006 One Stop Voting Locations and Hours can be found at:
http://www.wakegov.com/elections/1stopvoting/default.htm.

**October 25$^{th}$ & November 2$^{nd}$ - If you're all alone, pick up the phone ... And call...**
*Question: What happens when a ghost gets lost in the fog? Answer: He is mist.* We don't want to miss any district members. Join us in calling voters to tell them of Gerry's campaign and include them in the election process. Solidify votes in the district at two phone canvassing evenings on Wednesday, October 25$^{th}$ & Thursday, November 2$^{nd}$ from 6:00 – 8:30pm at Hardin & Bowles located at 1514 Glenwood Avenue, Suite 201 (look for the 2-story yellow building on Glenwood between the Wade Avenue underpass and the Rialto Theatre at Five Points). No need to limit your efforts to these two nights – connect with district members from home - scripts and phone lists supplied happily by the campaign.

**Disappearing Voters – Search Door-to-Door**
Something is amiss this blue moon election in the sleepy area of Wake County – without races for the president, governor or U.S. Senate it is feared that the local citizenry will vanish from the polling stations this November 7$^{th}$. Join Gerry in knocking on doors to raise a mob of voters to voice their choice and make their presence visible. Contact Andrea or Gerry to coordinate times.

**Bowles Blue Invasion**
The outbreak of Bowles Blue yard signs has received rave reviews in spreading the word of Gerry's campaign. Be it at the coffee shop, at the door of a newly canvassed street, or in

discussion with supporters, we are hearing that Gerry's signs have made their mark. Have we missed your yard? Contact Andrea or Gerry and speak volumes through this powerful form of communication.

**Sightings**
Less elusive than a ghost, you can spot Gerry at the following events:
*October 17 Meredith College "Meet the Candidates" Forum*
Gerry will be participating in a political forum at Meredith College on October 17 from from 5:30 p.m. – 7 p.m

*October 17 Wake County Town Hall Meeting on Senior Issues*
Gerry will be present at this Town Hall sponsored by the North Carolina Assisted Living Association and open to the public at the McKimmon Center on the NC State University Campus from 7:30-9:00 p.m.

*October 19 Triangle Community Coalition Political Pig Picking*
Gerry will be attending the TCC's fourth-annual Political Pig Picking on Thursday, October 19 from 5:30 to 8:30 p.m. at the Brier Creek Country Club at 9400 Club Hill Dr. in Raleigh.

*October 21 Picnic & Democratic Rally*
Gerry will take part in this event sponsored by Steve Wilder and Jim Mettrey from 4-8 pm for volunteers, elected officials, candidates and voters at the home of Steve Wilder, 4424 Clifton Road, Knightdale, NC, 27545

*October 23 North Raleigh Meet and Greet for Wake County Democratic Candidates*
Gerry will be joining other candidates at this meet and greet for Wake County Board of Commissioners and other county office Democrats on Monday, October 23 from 7 to 9 p.m. at Sertoma Park on Shelley Lake, 1400 W. Millbrook, Raleigh.

**Carving out good times!**
A long and loud scream of thanks for your help in connecting with and mobilizing large numbers of district members through phone and foot canvasses, meet and greets, fundraisers, and other community gatherings. Your time and energy have been vital in tackling the monstrously large number of tasks important to electing Gerry and in keeping spirits high. There is no masking our gratitude!
A particular word of appreciation to:
* Katherine Morgan for supporting Gerry through numerous volunteer contributions and most recently a stimulating meet & greet evening with friends.
* Alison Donnelly, Jennifer Tisdale and Patti Pilarinos for providing a great venue at Coachman's Trail for energetic discussion on education and other issues.

With undisguised thanks to all,

Andrea Bertole

**Need More Details? No cause for fright - Contact:**
Gerry Bowles: visit www.GerryBowles06.com * call: 919-847-9901 * e-mail: gerry@gerrybowles06.com or gerrybowles@yahoo.com

Andrea Bertole (volunteer coordinator & acting campaign manager): call: 919-793-0160 * e-mail: andreabertole@hotmail.com or abertole@nc.rr.com

Dan Williams (campaign manager - telecommuting now from Michigan with his return to law school): e-mail: ax4782@wayne.edu * call: 919-271-5845

**Summary of New and Ongoing Areas for Action:**
1) October 17$^{th}$ - Meet Gerry at the political forum at Meredith College from 5:30 - 7:00 p.m.

2) October 17 - Join Gerry at the Wake County Town Hall Meeting on Senior Issues at the McKimmon Center from 7:30 - 9 p.m.

3) October 18th - Come "Scare up the Vote" with a pre Halloween North Raleigh kick-off to early voting from 7:00-8:30 p.m at 405 Amelia Avenue (Gerry's home).

4) October 19th onwards - Cast your vote for Gerry as "One Stop" early voting begins.

5) October 19 - Attend the Triangle Community Coalition Political Pig Picking with Gerry from 5:30 to 8:30 p.m. at the Brier Creek Country Club at 9400 Club Hill Dr. in Raleigh.

6) October 21 - Join Gerry at this Picnic & Democratic Rally at the home of Steve Wilder from 4-8 pm, 4424 Clifton Road, Knightdale, NC, 27545

7) October 23 - Take part in the North Raleigh Meet and Greet for Wake County Democratic Candidates on Monday, October 23 from 7 to 9 p.m. at Sertoma Park on Shelley Lake, 1400 W. Millbrook, Raleigh.

8) October 25$^{th}$ & November 2$^{nd}$ - Participate in our Phone Canvass evenings from 6:00 to 8:30pm at Hardin & Bowles, 1514 Glenwood Avenue, Suite 201.

9) October 28th - Participate in our early voting North Raleigh Rally on Saturday, October 28th from 10 a.m. to 12 p.m. at the BP on Newton Rd and Six Forks Rd & voice your choice for Gerry as various satellite "One Stop" voting locations open their doors.

10) Find 15 for Gerry by pledging $5, phoning 5 district members and e-mailing 5 friends. Direct newly interested community members to Gerry or Andrea. Checks can be made payable to "Gerry Bowles NC Senate" and sent to 405 Amelia Ave, Raleigh, NC 27615.

11) Canvass door-to-door with Gerry - to coordinate canvassing times contact Gerry or Andrea.

12) Request, pick-up and place your Gerry Bowles yard signs.

13) Contact Gerry to join you in attending your community's gatherings.

14) Visit www.GerryBowles06.com to refresh on Gerry's campaign and keep up-to-date on events.

15) Volunteer to help with future events, lawn signs, mailings, phoning, working the polls, canvassing or other areas of interest.

(If you do not wish to receive future updates just let me know and I will remove your name from our list)

We were careful not to overwhelm our volunteers by filling up their mailboxes with too much information. We tried to limit the amount of news from the campaign and always (as stated at the end of the letter) gave our folks the means to remove themselves from our mailing list.

We had a handful of folks that asked to have their names removed from our mailing list but there were many more who asked to be added to our list so that they could see what theme Andrea was using to communicate our activities for the upcoming week. We found our updates to be a good tool to use with new email recruits. We hoped to "hook" them with the multitude of activities that we were involved in.

Our newsletters throughout the summer would comment on the vacations of our staff and the "human events" that we were all involved with. It was our belief that professional did not mean impersonal and it was in keeping with the grass roots approach that was the key to our campaign.

As mentioned in Chapter Four's discussion of updates, we did receive cautions about our candor in these communications. The concern raised was that my opponent's supporters could be receiving these updates or have access to them. We chose to continue to include the markers for our success in the updates, most notably the number of doors that we had knocked on and the growing list of supporters. We saw it as a testament to the fact that our campaign was not just about money, and our transparency revealed that our campaign had no secrets or hidden agendas.

### Campaign Web Pages

Web pages are a great tool to communicate your issues so that folks can educate themselves about you in the privacy of their own homes. As novices in the use of this technology, it was definitely not one of our strong suits. Indeed, it was one of the shortcomings of our campaign. That said, we were constantly improving our sites, trying to keep them up to date and always striving to be user friendly and interactive. For this campaign, I actually monitored two web sites.

### GerryBowles06.com

The first was my main campaign web page, GerryBowles06.com. In terms of content, this site contained my personal bio and the issues that engaged me. It also contained a list of upcoming events and a map of the district. I did not have a designated person from the campaign to maintain the two sites, so this job was filled by me. I hired one of my son's colleagues to build and manage our "pages" but I needed to supply him with the current information and the images that I wanted to portray.

Many campaigns had sites that allowed for online contributions. At first blush this seemed to be a useful tool for fund raising but when we ran the numbers it seemed that the expense of collecting contributions outweighed the amount of money that we anticipated raising. My site did list ways to contribute such as displaying a yard sign, helping with phoning, helping with campaigning door-to-door, coordinating volunteers in a supporter's neighborhood, helping work the polls on Election Day, or sending a financial contribution. As the campaign progressed we were able to add a little pizzazz to the site with repeating/flashing images. I recognize that today, this feature would be considered passé.

As was the case with so many facets of the campaign, the logistics surrounding the websites were time consuming. As I was responsible for the material to be contributed, it took a while to get our site up and running. The capability of the main site grew from its conception in April to its close post-election. On April 16$^{th}$, six weeks into the campaign, I was able to email the website copy to my web master, Michael Chase. On the 29$^{th}$ of that month, he informed me that the site was "live." Two weeks later we got our first comment from a volunteer regarding a typo mistake on the site. The correction was quickly made and thanks offered for keeping us informed. One of the benefits to employing this technology was the ability to be linked to other media sites. By May 17$^{th}$, we were informed that the North Carolina Democratic Party was "now getting Gerry's link." As of the 24$^{th}$ of July, we were adding events to the web (prior to this time, the site was more static) and enriching the site further with photos by mid-September. Acting on a suggestion from Nell Whitlock, we further included the remarks that I delivered to the folks at Westinghouse to a bit of critical acclaim. The last email from our web master on the 13$^{th}$ of November was to ask if we wanted to include a thank you to our supporters prior to taking the web site down. We enthusiastically responded "yes!"

## Stop540toll.com

My second website, Stop540toll.com, was devoted to my transportation issue and my opposition to the proposal that the 540 belt line, which ran through our district, impose a toll to raise the funds to complete the road. This website stated the following:

> How do we pay for new roads? How do we fund unprecedented local growth without burdening property owners? Are toll roads the answer or another financial burden.
>
> First Step: Be a Road Worrier,
>
> In recent months, the prospect of Triangle toll roads has become front page news. While there are strong arguments on both sides

> *of the issue, the real question has to be raised: Why are we in this mess in the first place? The answer is ineffective government. The need to balance the state budget has gutted the Highway Trust Fund. Instead of using our transportation tax dollars to adequately fund our roadside needs, they have been expropriated to make up for mismanaged revenues in other areas. This, along with the proposed toll road solution, is unacceptable.*
>
> *Gerry will fight any toll road that unduly burdens selected citizens or does not completely cover the cost of its own construction. Typically, 30 percent of a toll road's construction costs are never recouped from the tolls. These funding shortfalls are often made up from local sources. As a result, toll roads do no reduce taxes and often lead to increases.*
>
> *As a resident of this district for over three decades, Gerry Bowles has experienced the disappointment that we all feel from our local transportation shortfalls. Many of the so-called solutions seem tantamount to putting band-aids on broken limbs. With Gerry as your senator, you can rest assured that when the road tolls, it won't be for thee.*

In addition to using this website, I also advertised with "No Toll" stickers and signage on the doors of bathroom stalls in local restaurants, as discussed further below under "Political Campaign Products." Of further note, I was able to mention this website in a published letter to the editor which I had written in response to a June 18$^{th}$ letter in the *News and Observer*.

> *Regarding: Responding to June 18$^{th}$ Letter to the Editor on the Proposed I-540 Toll Road*
>
> *In June 18ths letters to the editor titled "Free up the roads by charging by the mile?" regarding the proposed I-540 toll, Kurt Bienis asked what politician will have the courage to say "no" to tolls? I am moved to respond with a resounding "I have!" As a long time North Raleigh resident, I have experienced the pressures that unprecedented local growth has placed on our transportation system. As a candidate for District 15's North*

206

*Carolina State Senate, I have identified Transportation as a key area of focus, with a specific eye to the effective management of state monies dedicated to highway construction rather than a reliance on toll band-aids. I invite those wishing to read more on my position on the toll roads to visit my website at www.Gerry Bowles 06.com. To link to additional articles on the proposed toll, I welcome a visit to my www.stop540toll.com website, and ask you to join me in my visible stand by ordering your "No Toll" car sticker from this site.*

*Regards,*
*(Dorothy) Gerry Bowles*
*Candidate, NC State Senate – District 15*

## *Blogs*

While we never had our own campaign blog, we were mentioned in a few others. Most notable was a shout out to two of our campaign volunteers who had met the blogger, Bill Scher, author of "Wait Don't Move to Canada" at a book signing and was forwarded to me by Andrea on October 20th:

> *Monday, October 16th*
> *"...Special thanks to Rene at Quail Ridge Books for arranging the event, as well as to the Wake County Progressive Democrats for co- sponsoring it. ...also thanks to the two passionate Volunteers for NC State Senate candidate, **Gerry Bowles** who generously took me out to dinner afterwards."*
>
> *www.liberaloasis.com/2006/10/thanks-north-carolina.php*

In addition, Nell Whitlock was our eyes and ears to the greater national websites and blogs. In the following, her attention was directed towards the Huffington Post:

> *Gerry--*
>
> *I just discovered via the huffingtonpost.com this great website that lists Dem candidates nationally, all levels—you can get listed with*

*a link to your website, etc. IT is a national clearinghouse for donations, etc. ActBlue.*

*I almost sent in your name, because they don't know about you—think there isn't any candidate for dist. 15. See below. So I think you should send link to website, photo if you want to, etc. Check it out. At least you can be on the list. It is very easy to do. Who knows—you might get a few donations!*

*Nell 9/19/06*

*http://www.actblue.com/directory/search?q=state-senate&state=NC*

That afternoon Nell emailed me this follow up:

*Gerry-- I couldn't wait for your reply. I went ahead and sent your name to ActBlue. I couldn't stand the idea they didn't think we had a candidate in Dist.15! Below is what I sent to the site. Nell 9/19/06*

*> http://www.actblue.com/contact   text of message I sent to the page above:*

*We do have a candidate for NC Senate District 15- Gerry Bowles, an outstanding Wake County/Raleigh public interest activist who is courageously challenging the Repub. incumbent in a very red district . Her website is: http://www.gerrybowles06.com/*

Nell forwarded this reply from Beth Sievert and ActBlue the following day:

*Hi,*

*Thanks for your email and for the information on Gerry! I've just updated our records to feature the Bowles campaign in our North Carolina directory;*

*https://secure.actblue.com/directory/search?q=state-senate&state=NC#12105*

*Unfortunately, we cannot yet do what would be truly helpful to*

*Gerry-enable online contributions- because we're not yet legally set up to help candidates for state office in North Carolina.*

*One of our major projects this cycle is to expand our fund raising capacity beyond the federal level to candidates for state executive and legislative office in as many states as we can. As you can imagine, each state has its own campaign finance laws to be navigated and the process is quite costly at approximately $10,000 in staff time and legal work.*

Our No Toll campaign got a mention on the Crosstown Traffic blog by reporter, Bruce Siceloff, the self-described, Road Worrier:

*Friday, May 19, 2006*
*Toll Worrier*

*Looks like toll roads will be a campaign issue this fall for sure. A Wake County senate candidate has made it official by launching a website that takes an anti-slant on the subject: www.stop540toll.com. This is the work of Gerry Bowles, a Democrat challenging first-term Republican Sen. Neal Hunt in District 15.*

*But wait a sec: District 15 is in northern Wake County, slicing across a broad arc of I-540 that is already built and filled with toll-free traffic. (Here's a pdf map.) It's in western and southern Wake that the N.C. Turnpike Authority is considering building a big new stretch of I-540 as a toll road.*

*It'll be interesting to see how the Western Wake Freeway toll issue plays in the Falls watershed.*

*Meanwhile, on a separate web page where she discusses transportation issues, I notice that Bowles made a campaign promise she may not be able to keep: to "Be a Road Worrier." Sorry, Gerry, That job is taken.*

In June the campaign was featured online in the Political Trail blog of the *News & Observer*:

> NC Senate District 15
> Supporters of Democratic challenger Gerry Bowles will host a Pre-Independence Day celebration campaign fundraiser Tuesday at 6 p.m. The event will be held at 405 Amelia Ave., and the suggested contribution is $10.
>
> Senate District 15 represents much of North Raleigh and northeast Wake County. Bowles will face Republican incumbent Neal Hunt in the November General Election.
>
> Bowles also is launching Issue Advisory Committees (IACs) to assemble citizen groups for each of her three key issues-education, transportation, and representation. Those interested in learning more or joining her committees should contact her volunteer coordinator, Andrea Bertole, for more information (919) 793-0160 or andreabertole@hotmail.com

And, though not predictable in its timing, we were mentioned a couple of times on the *News & Observer's Wake Politics* blog site regarding our events.

In the final weeks of the election, fellow candidate, Grier Martin, sent us a link to Blue NC that gave a nod to our campaign:

> *Finally, there's the long shot race where the wonderful Gerry Bowles is taking it to the incumbent Neal Hunt, yet ANOTHER person who wants to shred public services. Insiders give the edge to Hunt, but at least one observer says BOWLES is creating her own "Kissell Effect" and building some powerful grass-roots momentum.*

### *Liaisons to Active Democrats: Julia Lee & Blaise Strenn*

One of the beneficial things that the Wake County Democratic Party did to assist our campaign was to post our activities on their web site. Julia Lee, the Executive Director, was supportive in responding in a timely and attentive manner to our requests to add our events to the Party's webpage. Given the value we placed on our events, this advertising was most appreciated as a way to reach the active Democrats likely to check the WCDP's calendar of events.

Blaise Strenn was one of the heroes of our campaign. He volunteered his time to organize and email a weekly list of Democratic events to active Democrats. His steadfastness to detail, attention to our activities and technical wizardry allowed our grassroots campaign to flourish by keeping our campaign linked to the greater Democratic Party

The following email exchange exemplifies his "work ethic."

> *From Blaise Strenn*
> *To Andrea Bertole*
> *Sent Saturday June 03, 2006 7:16 PM*
> *Subject: RE: Gerry Bowles for NC Senate Campaign Update...*
> *3-June-06*
>
> *Andrea- This is quite the list. You are doing a great job! But could you please provide additional info for the following:*
>
> *\*\* Education Excellence: A Common Goal - With her key issue focus on Education, on Monday, June $12^{th}$ from 1:00-4:00 pm Gerry will be participating in an education briefing provided by the FORUM. Public School Forum of NC, whose membership is "working together to make North Carolina schools second to none". Wonder where this will be? Any other details? I could not find anything else out online.*
>
> *\*\*Participate in Gerry's Neighborhood Pre Independence Day celebration and meet & greet/fundraiser at 405 Amelia Ave on June 27th-donate food or funds and enjoy the fun. Wonder what the time is for this?*

Blaise kept our campaign and others in the spotlight by posting an ever changing catalogue of events. Sharing space with all the various campaigns helped to bolster a feeling of camaraderie or esprit de corps. It helped our campaign to build momentum and created a buzz regarding our activity level. It was also successful in reaching folks that we may not have encountered otherwise.

Being a part of a team, a candidate among candidates, lent credibility to the campaign and provided comfort to those who were "looking for the union label." It captured the attention of others that we may not have connected with otherwise.

## *Political Campaign Products*

One of the questions I had for veteran office holders was how to manage the plethora of interest that is generated once one files for office. My mailbox was filled with fliers advertising deals for election paraphernalia (bunting, buttons, stickers, yard signs, and much more) and solicitations from the print media to advertise. I chose to order palm cards and stickers and created self-generated products when need arose. Also of importance and of budgetary significance were mailings and yard signs which I will discuss in separate sections following this one.

### *Palm Cards*

In addition to the advice described in earlier sections, Senator Gunter recommended the use of palm cards when campaigning. This product served me well in my 2000 campaign and proved to be the most important communication tool in this campaign. We left them at thousands of doors, offered them at all events, and relied on them to promote my campaign throughout the district.

For this campaign, I consulted with professionals. I was fortunate to have the help of my son, Hal, who was the owner of a marketing, advertising and design agency, *Hardin-Bowles*, that specialized in brand identification, and his assistant, Carly, whose expertise was graphic design. The process to create this card was complex as I needed to make numerous decisions before placing an order. Initial work went into deciding the look of my yard sign (see a more detailed discussion under "Yard Signs" below) which became my campaign logo and was used for these palm cards and throughout the campaign in various forms such as on my website, stickers, and self-generated literature. In addition, I had to have my message synthesized, slogans (effective.government.now), website set-up, and my campaign photo selected. As noted in the "Message" section of Chapter Two, Hal, and I distilled my message to fit the 8"x4" format. As financial limitations were always uppermost in my decision making, rather than sending a series of glossy mailers to introduce myself to the voters, I opted for palm cards figuring I would distribute them personally to the doors. They fit easily into voters' hands, could be tucked into a purse without difficulty, and were a rich source of information. I ordered 10,000 for $1,045 and, as noted earlier, ran short in the final weeks of the campaign.

## *No Toll Stickers*

front                                                                back

In lieu of car bumper stickers that campaigns often purchase, I ordered "No Toll" stickers. I hoped that the novelty of the stickers might create a buzz of its own and some coverage by the media. While the stickers were popular and we sent out hundreds of them to folks as far away as California and Wyoming, the connection to my campaign was obscure and therefore my name recognition was not enhanced.

They did hit a nerve with those folks who felt passionately about the toll and my stance on the 540 Toll resonated with the public. My web master received this email in early March from a Raleigh native who grew up in my district but currently lived in a part of Wake County that would be directly impacted by the toll. It read in part:

> *Any idea how many stickers have been requested and how often you get a request for them? We would certainly appreciate the mention of our site, and possibly a link from her page if willing? We hope at notollson540.org that we are creating a good, interactive online environment for the public to get involved, any feedback is welcome. Certainly as we get more up to speed and have more activity on the site, we plan to make formal announcements of its existence to a variety of media resources including the 3 major local news networks, local papers, NPR and others. If you have any suggestions on how we might spread the word about our site, I'd love to hear them.*
>
> *Thank you,*
> *[name removed for privacy]*
> *www.notollson540.org.*

214

In June, this email gave proof to our web-site/sticker connection.

> Gerry,
>
> *I came across your website after seeing the bumper sticker on someone's car. I requested some because I strongly oppose this toll road. I moved here from Tampa, FL where I have [seen] toll roads built and the tolls never lifted as promised. I'm very disappointed and disillusioned with NC government at this point. I agree with your view that it's poor financial planning and misappropriation of government spending, but there's other issues. I think we should be looking at both sides of the problem here-no money AND the exorbinant (sic) cost of building the road. If we don't have as much money, maybe we can fix the other side of the problem. NCDOT has a contract with prisons to do road repairs, clean up, etc. Why can we not utilize a drastically discounted workforce at our disposal? I want our government officials to think of alternative ways to get the job done instead of passing the cost around. I'm glad you are considering this issue, and I see that you are opposed to a toll road, but how far are you taking this.... I sincerely hope you are wanting to push this issue and not just use it as a forum to make yourself know[n] to be elected. I applaud your efforts, and I am more than willing to participate in the fight on this issue. Please let me know if you need help, and what your plan is for this important issue.*
>
> *[name & address removed for privacy]*

When we received a request for a sticker, my standard response was:

> *Dear....*
>
> *Your "No Toll stickers" are in the mail...thanks for the interest. I do hope that you will let others know about this issue.*
>
> *How did you hear about the stickers?*
>
> *Thanks*

*Gerry*

A sampling of replies follows:

- *August 2, 2006 - A sign in the bathroom at Longview Grill off hwy 70 in Raleigh. [See discussion below about indoor advertising based on this sticker]*

- *August 23, 2006 - I met you at the Rally and was excited that you are doing such great work for a NO Toll on 1 540. I took one of the no toll [sticker] and visited your website. I have told several friends.....*

- *August 23, 2006 - Another Friend informed me so I checked out the website. I've spread the word also.*

Some sticker request emails received in September were proof that our campaign had come full circle. They were a validation of the interconnection between our door-to-door canvassing, web sites, toll stickers and yard signs. The first read as follows:

> *THANKS! I need to get a yard sign...where can I pick one up? I live off Lynn Road, (Summerland /Nikole Ct) I doubt you remember, but we met when you were pressing the flesh in my area. I was concerned about full State Employee Status for Community College personnel(l).*
>
> *[name and contact information removed for privacy]*

I received another email just after midnight after I had spent that day greeting folks at Shelly Lake while they were early voting.

> *Thank you so much for your stand on NOTOLL. The very idea! We pay one of the highest gas tax rates in the country and someone has the gall to even suggest toll roads. You have my vote.*
> *PS I am a retired employee of the NCDOT*
>
> *[name and contact information removed for privacy]*

This supporter's subsequent reply to having received his stickers was:

> *I'm already committed election day. I would like to display a yard sign. Let me know how I can get one. I got the NO TOLL stickers and put them on both vehicles. Thanks.*

In addition to being popular in our area, our No Toll sticker was a national and international hit! The issue had resonance in six other states - California, Pennsylvania, Missouri, Wyoming, Vermont, and Michigan – and three Canadian cities - Ottawa, Vancouver and Winnipeg. Post-election requests followed into March of 2007. By the end of October, I had received 32 requests and had sent out 113 stickers.

To further publicize my stand in opposition to the 540 toll I made the decision to take part in some indoor advertising based on this sticker. The following exchange between my son Hal, and the owner of *All Over Media Raleigh*, Bill Garrity, and myself describes our plan:

> *From: Hal Bowles [mail to:hal@hardin-bowles.com]*
> *Sent: Sunday, April 16, 2006 3:36 PM*
> *To. Bill Garrity*
> *Subject : Indoor For Mom's Senate Campaign*
>
> *Hey Bill,*
>
> *My mom is running for NC Senate in District 15. I think it would be a great thing for her to advertise via indoor. This won't be a direct campaign ad for her but will be a reference to a separate non-partisan website that we are constructing called www.Stop540toll.com.*
>
> *I wanted to check with you to see if we might be able to do indoor for her at some locations in her district. I have enclosed a PDF outlining the district so that you can see where you might have locations.*
>
> *The election is in November but we would probably want to see if we could have the indoor displays up between May and November (I'm not sure on this yet).*

*If you could put together a location list and pricing for each month, that would be great. I'm not sure of her budget yet as it depends on some matching funds from the Democratic party, but at least we can get the ball rolling.*

*Thanks! Hal*

From: Bill Garrity <bgarrity@allovermedia.com>
Date: Mon, 17 Apr 2006 08.14.29
Subject: EW: Indoor for Mom's Senate Campaigning
Hey Hal

*We can definitely do some indoor throughout District 15 and in other Districts without a problem. We can for sure place one ad in every women's room throughout N Raleigh and we will float a men's room ad also. We can also target specific high traffic venues outside of her District such as the NC State Fairgrounds, Koka Booth, and Alltel Pavilion if she's open to advertising outside her district.*

*As far as pricing goes once you get her budget set allocate an amount of money for indoor that makes sense to her budget. Don't worry about basing it off of key account packages or other deals. We may need to move some ads in the men's rooms from time to time but we'll make sure all of the locations in District 15 have ads in them. If it's $50/month then that's what it is...hopefully we'll reach younger voters in her District and help make a difference and if that happens we'll look to get a testimonial from the NC Senator of District 15!*

*Talk soon,*
*Bill Garrity*


*From: Hal Bowles (hal@hardin-bowles.com)*
*To:      gerrybowles@yahoo.;com*
*Date: Monday, April 17, 2006 9:25 AM*

*Bill is going to give you a great deal on indoor. You'll just need*

*to figure out a monthly budget that you can afford and he'll get your No Toll message out to District 15 and beyond!*
*I think that whenever you begin your campaign would be a great time for the No Toll message to begin the buzz. When will you officially begin to kick-off your campaign? We don't have to run indoor from now until November-but it would be a good idea to start as early as possible.*

*Hal*

The following restaurants and spas are some of the locations in which we displayed our No Toll advertisements:

- Buffalo's Southwest Café
- Beyond Fitness
- O2 Fitness
- San Carlo Italian Bistro
- Spa Health Club
- Taste of Thai
- Los Tres Magueyes
- D S Parada
- Blinkos
- Hibernian Restaurant and Pub

*Gerry Bowles Stickers v. Magnets*

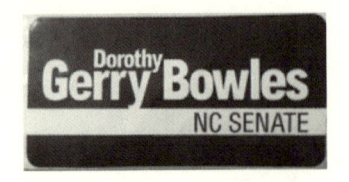

Sticker used in 2006

We also ordered a large supply of Gerry Bowles for Senate "stickers". Our records indicate that we paid $179.00 for 5000 in early August. While I included these stickers in several of our kits and had them available at events, I nonetheless had almost three quarters of this number remaining at the end of the campaign. As a tool to increase name recognition, I would choose to direct funds towards magnets as I did with my 2000 campaign instead of these name stickers. As noted earlier when speaking of the Primary Day event, I discovered that many people still had these on their refrigerators long after the Election.

Magnet used in 2000

*Self-Generated Products*

I did not just rely on commercial products for my communication needs. A handout that became a staple for the campaign was entitled "Why vote Gerry" (see sample below). We created this "cheat sheet" early in the campaign and ended up using it broadly (at events, on Primary Day, in point-person packages, on canvasses, etc) and found it particularly useful in the final weeks of the campaign when our palm card supplies were running low. This self-generated option offered flexibility in that we could print our own copies as needed at little expense.

> **Dorothy**
> **Gerry Bowles**
> NC Senate
>
> WHY VOTE *GERRY BOWLES* FOR NC STATE SENATE, DISTRICT 15?
>
> "effective. government. now."
>
> ♦ Former Wake County public educator & tutorial center director.
>
> ♦ Founder and president of Wake County Citizens for Effective Government.
>
> ♦ Former assistant to 4 North Carolina Senators (both Democrat and Republican).
>
> ♦ Wife, mother, community volunteer, and Raleigh resident for over 30 years.
>
> ♦ Endorsed by: NC Association of Educators, Triangle Labor Council, NC Police Benevolent Association, & The *Independent*.
>
> Support Gerry Bowles to focus attention on *Education, Transportation, & Representation* and:
>
> ♦ Tackle key education problems & scrutinize use of Education Lottery funds.
>
> ♦ Ensure proper road work funding without reliance on toll programs.
>
> ♦ Make people the priority not special interests.
>
> www.GerryBowles06.com
> phone: 919-847-9901 ♦ e-mail: gerry@gerrybowles06.com

## *Mailings*

Having attended any number of campaign workshops that addressed the myriad ways to publish a campaign message, I knew early on that the best and most affordable approach was through direct "targeted" mail. The campaign had determined the registered voters who were to receive this mail. From the workshops, I knew that ideally I needed to send this group a minimum of three mailings. I also knew that I could get the most "bang for the buck" by sending multiple mailers (I had been told that research had shown 6-7 were effective in name recognition) but unfortunately this was not to be the case. We were unable to raise enough funds to do so.

Creating the mailings was uppermost in my mind from the get go. The message was generated from the research accomplished by my IAC's. They gathered the information (facts) that could be used to capture the voter's attention and frame a message that would persuade them to vote for me based on my three key issues: education, transportation and representation.

This email from Andrea on the 29$^{th}$ of September to the chairs of the transportation and representation IACs clarifies our intentions:

> Hi Herb & Sam,
>
> *I am working my way into getting back up to speed with the campaign and wanted to touch base with you both regarding your work on Transportation and Representation. We are going to be pulling together the content for Gerry's mailers and wanted to get your further input. We are going to be working with Gerry's son Hal early this week and anticipate a "Did you know" kind of approach for each of the 3 issues. Your numbers and findings from your research will be of great help. Herb, we have your report to consult for specifics but wanted to tap your mind on the compelling elements you think we should target. Sam, if you could email some of the numbers, findings and key questions that you mentioned at the last update meeting, and likewise the points you think most compelling, that would be fantastic.*
>
> *If you have a chance to send your thoughts by Tuesday that would be super.*
>
> *Thanks so much for your continued insights and input!!*
>
> *Andrea*

This request prompted Herb's response:

> *Dear Andrea.*
>
> *Welcome to your buoyant spirit, it is a delight. My brain may work differently from the norm. What I would respond to is:*

> *They are promoting a Toll Road extension to complete I-540, but do they know the accident facts? If they do, they would want to keep them a secret. Our fact finding showed that 35% to 45% of accidents on toll roads take place at the tolls. Toll stations promote accidents, the bad kind, rear end collisions.*
>
> *We could not find any on record cost/income figures for the proposed Toll Road extension. Was this analysis done? If it was, there is a reason to keep it secret. When you put in the cost of full time toll booth workers, supervisors and the bureaucratic overload, not much money will be left to pay for the road.*

In late September we met with Dave Wilkin at the Millennium Print Group and talked numbers (his and ours) and tried to arrive at a budget that would accomplish our goal of sending three mailers to a targeted group with the hope of being able to add more to our total if we were able to raise more funds. The following email exchange illustrates the costs and decisions involved:

> *Dave Wilkin -dave@mprintgroup.com wrote:*
>
> *Gerry, Thanks so much for thinking of me for printing your postcards. We do have time in [our] schedule for this project and would be able to meet your mailing date.*
>
> *The price is based on running 5,000 each of 3 versions at the same time at 6" x 9" as four color process two sides on 100# Gloss or Dull cover, trimmed, packed and delivered to Triangle Mailing Services.*
>
> *15,000 cards at 5,000 each of three versions for $ 1,622.00.*
>
> *Please let me know if you want me to reserve schedule time for you and we'll get the files here and in production.*
>
> *Thanks, and keep knocking on those doors.*

My reply:
> *Sent Tuesday, September 26, 2006*

Subject: Re Postcard Mailing

*This sounds good...could you tell me how much it would cost to do 7500 of each!*

*Gerry*

Dave Wilkin wrote:

*7,500 each of three versions [to] run at same time for a total of 22,500 cards is $2,214.00. Let me know and we'll get file transfer started. Thanks, Dave.*

My reply on the 29th

*Dave,*
*This sounds good...haven't gotten back sooner because we are checking our budget to try and get as many as we can...checks are coming in daily and we want to make the best estimate...we are getting with Hal this weekend to get the message written and hope to get the project to you by Wednesday. Will that allow for having it ready by Monday (9th) of the following week?*

*Gerry*

His reply:

*Gerry, looks like current schedule would require another day. Either files to us on Tuesday morning or if here on Wednesday, we will have cards ready for delivery to mailer Tuesday the 10th.*

*Please make sure files are prepared with images in cmyk mode, 300 dpi or higher at size used, fonts included. Can supply us with high res print ready pdf file, would like to have native files as backup. We do have a ftp upload site available that I can get Hal info for. Thanks Dave.*

The plan was for the first mailer to be sent on the 18th of October. Knowing that we had three to send and mindful of the dates for early voting, we were hoping to maximize our message by sending to the same universe of folks similarly formatted mailings three times in the period of 10 days. We wanted them to arrive well before the last weekend of early voting so that, heaven forbid, none were delivered after election day. Not trusting bulk mail and its sketchy delivery, we used the postcard pricing for first class mail.

By the $5^{th}$ of October we had the final proofs for the mailings. Between the $5^{th}$ and the $18^{th}$ (the targeted first mailing date) the printer's office was destroyed by fire. Fortunately, they were able to get temporary space in which to complete our work and our goal was met. The second mailer was sent on the $24^{th}$ and the third on the $30^{th}$. Almost all copies of each mailer were sent to our targeted group. Below is a copy of one that got "returned to sender."

## *Clandestine Mailings from the Caucus*

What we didn't know while we were planning our mailings was that the NC Democratic Senate Caucus was also in the process of sending out mailings to our district. Had we known we could have coordinated a message. WE could have worked together to target the same areas that our campaign had identified as being important to our turnout models. None of this happened. Not only was there no coordination, their mailer was neither similar in appearance nor in style. It was dark with a negative message. Whereas we had not identified my opponent on our mailings, they did. I had made every attempt to run a positive campaign against my opponent focusing on issues and not personality. He was never the point but rather the issues that he felt were a priority, and those he ignored that were at the heart of my concerns.

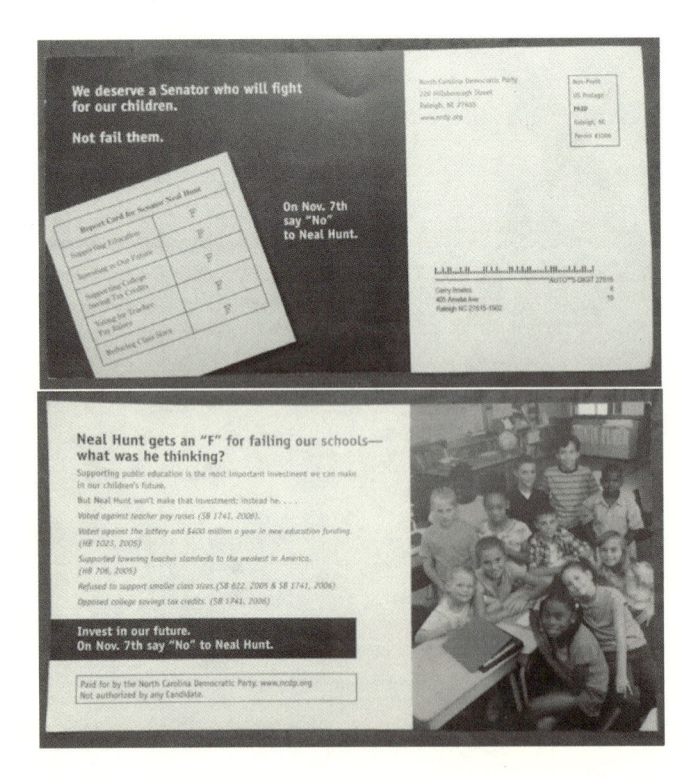

The only bright spot on the mailers that were sent out by the Caucus was

226

that my name was not mentioned and the NC Democratic Party was clearly identified as the sender. Nonetheless, I once again felt that the powers that be at the Goodwin House (party headquarters) had treated my campaign in a patronizing manner.

### *NC Democratic Party Mailers*

What was helpful to our campaign was being included in all the mailers that were sent from the greater NC Democratic Party which listed the names of all the Democrats on the ballot for election day. In an earlier time in North Carolina history, when the Democratic Party reigned supreme, being the Democratic candidate on the ballot would have been enough to assure victory. This scenario was not the case in my district. There were few instances of straight party voting for Democrats, while the opposite was true for Republicans. That said, I was delighted to be identified as one of the team to others who ascribed to the same beliefs.

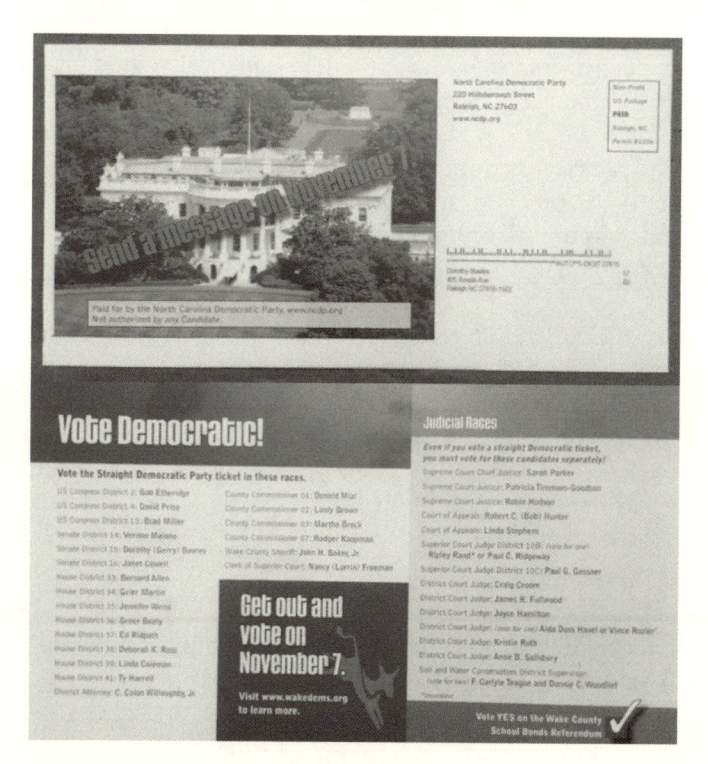

## Yard Signs

There is some disagreement to the value of yard signs in political campaigns. Consultants acknowledge their value in building the morale amongst a candidate's supporters. However, they advocate directing funds to additional mailings in lieu of yard signs when funds are limited. I disagree. The money and effort we spent on yard signs paid dividends.

I did not begin this campaign as a complete novice to the process. I had my earlier experiences as a legislative candidate to inform my beliefs. In the 2000 campaign my opponent for the NC House, Russell Capps, was viewed as outside of the mainstream and extreme even in Republican circles. Consequently, many Republicans were vocal in their support for me. I had the funds available to have a second sign printed to supplement my first. Using the same colors as my primary campaign sign, this second sign, "Another Republican for Democrat Gerry Bowles," was tailor made for these supporters.

There was some confusion with this approach. Some folks thought I was the Republican candidate! It was hard to assess if this strategy was effective overall. In the end, it may just have provided a morale boost to my supporters. Given my opponent in 2006 was viewed more favorably by Republicans (and some Democrats) and recognizing there had been misunderstandings from the second sign approach of 2000, I opted to focus on one sign during the 2006 Election cycle.

From the outset, I knew the importance yard signs would play in having my name recognized by the public. I focused on getting them into our supporters' yards from the moment we began our door-to-door canvassing. It was one of the first questions we asked of interested supporters, "Would you display a yard sign?" When we got a yes to this question it felt the same as getting a financial contribution.

### *Appearance*

Entire industries are devoted to brand identification. Coca Cola has spent billions of dollars on their logo. If branding was not important, would they invest such an amount? I spent a great deal of time on my sign's design and selection as it was to become my logo.

The choices available within each of the key yard sign variables felt

infinite:
- color
- font
- what name to use - first, last or both?
- size
- photo

As mentioned, *Hardin-Bowles* handled all my communication needs. Carly and I spent a good bit of time crafting a sign that fit with the requirements of the state and the vendor. My first decision was to determine what color or colors to use. I reflected on earlier conversations that I had had about sign design with former candidates for the Raleigh City Council. Betty Ann Knudsen shared with me that she chose orange for her signs because it matched the color of her hair. I, too, aimed for something that was personal to me. Julie Shea Graw, another candidate, chose fuchsia signs because they showed best in headlights. I also wanted a color easily seen in the dark. In poring over the color charts, I settled on royal blue. It seemed to reflect the best in low light conditions. Hal's marketing background confirmed these instincts. Furthermore, living in a community that has strong loyalties to its chosen ACC sports teams, I thought that red might be too associated with NC State, sky blue with Carolina and deep blue with Duke. Even though I am an NC State fan, I was prepared to represent all my constituents, even Tar Heels and Blue Devils!

Mindful of economic considerations and knowing that two colors cost more than one, I chose to go with blue and white (white being the absence of blue and not considered another color). I chose block letters as opposed to italics as I felt that they were more easily read and projected a bold image. We designed the sign to include the website address so that interested parties could easily "look me up" and learn more about the campaign.

I had decided to use my full name "Dorothy Gerry Bowles" in the signage as that's how I legally filed and this name would be on the ballot. Another reason for including the name Dorothy was for gender identification. Previously I had just used "Gerry Bowles" which caused some confusion in people thinking I was a man. Supporters told me that numerous neighbors asked, "What does HE stand for?"

In my 2000 campaign, I included a photo on my yard sign which helped with gender identification but which cost more as the sign had to be larger to accommodate it. This time, with my name choice serving that purpose, I could avoid the photo and use the money to order more signs. In terms of the size of the yard sign, I opted for the traditional dimensions to minimize the cost.

## *Numbers*

When deciding on the number of signs to order, I was of the belief, the more the better. That said, I had budget limitations to consider particularly as I was placing my order early in the campaign before much fund raising had occurred. The yard sign packages available offered a range of numbers to work with starting with a basic cost. The more signs ordered, the smaller the individual cost per sign. I knew that on Election Day I needed 2 signs for each of my 52 precinct polling locations (the Democratic Party would place them out for all their candidates the evening before). In addition, I wanted to have enough for identified supporters and was mindful that I might need extras to replace stolen and vandalized signs. In deciding my final number of 1,500, I was limited mostly by the costs which amounted to $2,285 with an additional $545 for shipping for a total of $2,829.

## *Distribution*

Our hard work in canvassing door-to-door yielded tangible results. The seeds we had sown in late May and throughout the summer produced a bumper crop of requests for signs and interest in the campaign.

Our growing database proved to be instrumental in following up on my earlier supporters' offers to place signs in their yards. I took responsibility for this task and made sure the signs were delivered to their doors. As often as possible we arranged for our volunteers to personally deliver my signs and place them where the homeowner requested rather than leaving this task to our supporter. I was ever mindful of how busy people were and while they might be happy to display a sign, requiring them to go out of their way to pick it up from another location could delay the impact of having the signs in their yards.

This response from Andrea to one of our volunteers gives some insight into the "production" of getting signs into yards!

> September 6
> Hi Scott,
>
> Thanks so much again for offering to help with sign distribution!! We definitely will take you up on your offer to place and collect them at the intersections you mention. Would you be willing to drop them off to some of your neighbors in precinct 14-02 as well? In one case the woman is disabled and indicated she would need help placing the sign- is that something you could help with too? If you are willing, we have an additional 12-20 locations in Wake Forest (in other precincts) of folks who have indicated they would like to display a sign. If you could help with these other sign drops that would be amazing-just let me know.
>
> I know you are away on Saturday-would we be able to drop signs to your home (or another location convenient to you) on Friday afternoon or Monday? If you would prefer we could set out a bundle of signs at Gerry's which you could pick up on a day that fits better with your plans-it is our hope to get as many signs up as possible this upcoming week-let us know if this will work for you.
>
> Thanks again,
> Andrea

There were the inevitable kinks in the procedure that led to memorable encounters. One obviously distressed man left a message on my answering machine that the campaign had placed an unwanted and unasked for sign in his front yard. A similar complaint was lodged via email which I found a tad satisfying in that it proved advertising does work - my website address was on the sign allowing this person to contact me. In a true fashion of turning lemons into lemonade, once I sent word that I had removed the signs, I received a reply of "Thank you! BTW, you'll get our votes." In both cases I quickly called the folks and apologized profusely, explaining that mistakes do happen and that we had a geographically large district and relied on an all-volunteer army to distribute our signs.

In past elections, I had used wooden stakes to secure the signs. The stakes were hand-made and donated by P.R. Latta, a living legend in North Carolina Democratic circles, but using these stakes was labor intensive. Volunteers were needed to prepare the signs for distribution (two signs were stapled back to back with the middle left open for the stakes) and I carried a rebar, sledge hammer, and staple gun in the trunk of my car so that I was always ready to help my supporters get the signs in the ground.

Having been cumbersome to assemble and difficult to put into the ground and maintain (for example, if they came down in the rain they were hard to put back up), I opted in 2006 to spend more money for the ready-made signs that just slipped over a preformed wire frame. They were much easier to assemble, to place in the ground and to maintain. Folks could easily pull them out to mow the lawn and place them back in.

*Placement*

There were a myriad of rules and regulations that were dictated by the State Board of Elections and the various local communities that determined where the candidate could place campaign signs. Each of the localities had different rules – Wake Forest was stricter than Raleigh and Raleigh was stricter than Wake County. My district encompassed parts of all these areas! This letter from the City of Raleigh dated September 14 shows the complexity and penalties associated with sign placement:

> *Section 10-2083.3 "prohibits any sign from being placed on any curb, sidewalk, post pole, hydrant, bridge, tree, or other surface located on, over, or across any public street, right-of-way, property or thoroughfare. Right-of-way includes medians, interchanges, and major thoroughfares such as 1-440 and 1-540 which tend to have larger rights-of-way.*
>
> *Violations will subject you to a civil citation of $100 and an administrative fee of $100 for the first offense. Continuing violations are subject to a $500 civil citation for each day that the violation continues.*

We saw my opponent's signs in such illegal locations. As a result, they were presumably subject to fines. Our grassroots campaign operated on a shoe string budget with no line item for fines. In addition, I never wanted to see my name on the front page of the *News and Observer* for misdeeds! The state's right of way extended 15 feet into private yards, so signs had to be placed somewhat back from the street. When we were placing them in the more rural areas, we had to be mindful of state and private mowers who had no regard for our signs and would just run them over. Most businesses were reluctant to display a sign, as they had customers on all sides of the political spectrum. I was fortunate to have a number of businesses buck this custom and display my sign. The "Easy Street" BP at Newton Road, my effective campaign headquarters, was one such business.

The one hazard to our signs that we couldn't find a solution for was mischief. The following email exchange illustrates some of the interest triggered by the signs in addition to highlighting one of the sign placement challenges I encountered:

*Gerry,*

*Couldn't help but notice your campaign signs on Mount Vernon Church Road@ the Kinsdale Drive entrance to Stonebridge.*

*I have several questions that I'd like you to address:*

1. *In the past you ran for the NC House and have now made the grand leap to run for the NC Senate. What prompted this shift? Are the chances of winning looking better here?*

2. *I read some of your comments regarding key issues [on my campaign palm card] and have some comments and questions.*

   *Education- Certainly a key issues especially with the funding needs for new schools. I've written to several Wake County Commissioners on this subject in the past, and received little satisfaction. Here are some of my concerns on the topic.*

> a) It appears that every new school is custom designed and involves huge campuses. More standardization of design with more stories to the building would reduce costs. The savings come from lower architect fees, reduced material costs based on volume purchase and much lower land costs.
>
> b) How many of the new students are legally entitled to an education in North Carolina schools?
>
> c) The incorporation of "Impact Fees" on new home construction is long overdue. The extraordinary student growth is coming from this segment of the population and needs to be addressed accordingly.

His email continued with questions on "illegal immigration" and Voter ID requirements. He ended his correspondence with:

> Finally, on the subject of your campaign signs. Unless you and the other candidates for office have received a special dispensation, I believe you are in violation of N.C. Gen. Stat. 14-145.
>
> Regards, [name withheld for privacy]

I replied to his email that evening, answered his education questions and responded to his inquiry of sign placement in this manner:

> As to our signs and their placement...we do all that is possible to make sure that our signs are on someone's private property and if that is a business we have that owner's permission. I appreciate your alerting me to those you think might be misplaced. I'm afraid to say that putting signs in places where they don't belong is often a part of "dirty politics." It is hard to maintain custody of our property. It is a shame that folks would resort to this type of behavior, but sad to say it is true!
>
> Thanks,
> Gerry

There was always a risk of signs being stolen or vandalized. My signs fared better during this election cycle than they had in previous elections. Having learned from past campaigns, I chose not to place the signs in some of the key vandal areas along the more rural county crossroads.

The most prized position in sign display was the front yard of a supporter. This simple endorsement of the candidate offered an opening into conversation with neighbors who often were reluctant to talk politics. Some believed that one sign of support on each street was enough; however, we were of the "more is better" philosophy and delighted in the Burma Shave effect, a practice in the 1920s and 30s of placing six or seven advertising signs in a row along rural roads. The blanketing effect was positive. There were any number of folks that commented that they had seen my signs all over. I was especially buoyed when one of my peer candidates commented that he also was amazed by and a little envious of the quantity of visible support he had seen while driving through our district.

# Chapter Nine – Financial

Although fully aware that "money is the mother's milk of politics," I had largely focused my attention and the campaign's energy throughout the summer on increasing my name recognition and spreading my message. I had spent time on fund raising, but not nearly the amount of time that the North Carolina Democratic Senate Caucus and Perry, their Deputy Director, and my earlier political compatriot, would have liked. As I described under "Choosing Imbalance" in Chapter Three, this approach was a calculated decision based on what I felt was the best use of my time given the district that I lived in. Furthermore, more energy was being generated by the door-to-door canvassing than by the less than positive financial results of events like the Dessert & Dancing fundraiser. The handwriting was clear to me that fund raising in and of itself wasn't going to be the answer to my winning a seat in the legislature.

## *Money Matters*

I had raised a good bit of money at my key events over the summer. The July Meet and Greet with Mayor Meeker, my August Campaign Kickoff with Congressman Price, and the September Strong Women's Tea had done well in generating funds. That said, the overall financial needs for the campaign were greater than the amount I had in my treasury. Also problematic, because I had not raised enough money according to benchmarks set by the Democratic Senate Caucus, our campaign was not deemed worthy of their much needed financial support.

## *Trying to Play Fund Raising Ball with the Senate Caucus*

When I talked with Perry and agreed to file for office in late February, I felt that we were on the same page about the logistics of my grass roots campaign. As time passed, I was to find that not to be the case, and moreover, I would come to feel slighted and dismissed. The first indication that my assessment of the campaigns' accomplishments was not shared by Perry came in early June.

On June 5th and 6th, Andrea and I canvassed in my first tier 01-43 precinct. We had spent the morning knocking on doors and collecting volunteers. We had left invitations to our upcoming meet and greets and were expecting a positive outcome. At 3:00 in the afternoon of the 6th, Dan, my campaign manager, Andrea, my partner in door-to-door canvassing, and Bill Robinson, a member of my campaign committee, and a veteran of my earlier campaigns, met with Perry at the North Hills (inside the district) Panera Bread.

Prior to our meeting, we were feeling very positive about the direction of the campaign. We had been raising funds and people. Our door-to-door activities were yielding fruit and we were busy organizing precinct point people. We had manned the precincts during the May primary and were in the midst of planning fund raisers in Williamsburg, Virginia, my hometown, and in Raleigh. Andrea had initiated an email newsletter that kept our growing volunteer army updated and enthused. We were excited to update Perry as to the many and myriad accomplishments the campaign had experienced.

Perry's response to our recounting left us all bewildered, surprised and deflated. Perry's only interest was in how much money we could/would raise. I felt like Jerry McGuire when Rod Bartlett was shouting, "Show me the money." This experience was my first notice from Perry indicating a change from what he had led me to believe in our earlier conversations about the value of a pure grassroots campaign. We found him to be tremendously dismissive of our efforts and unimpressed with our canvassing success. The dye was cast; no matter what we said we got a sound bite about the need for me to focus the majority of my time calling folks for contributions, or, in political parlance, "dialing for dollars."

While disagreeing with this allocation of my time and energy, I kept my game face intact during the meeting, and the following day I called the Wake County Board of Elections to follow-up and get the list of names of those who had voted in the May primary so we could invite targeted voters to the David Price Campaign Kickoff event. There had been a delay in getting the names because much of the staff was involved in the investigation of the alleged *fund raising* irregularities of the NC Speaker of the House, Jim Black.

To more directly comply with Perry's directive, on the 29th of June, Andrea and I abandoned the doors for some phone solicitation. We traveled downtown to the Goodwin House (Democratic headquarters) to meet with the Senate Caucus fund raising guru per Perry's request. The idea was that this person would "hold my hand" and instruct me in the ways of "dialing for dollars." Further, he would give us some leads on deep pocket contributors that we could contact. In the back of my mind was a recent phone conversation with Betty Ann Knudsen. She was making calls to solicit sponsorships for my August campaign kickoff. In conversation with one of those "deep pockets" and Democratic party stalwarts, she was informed, "Neal Hunt, was not so bad for a Republican!" Betty Ann's response was pitch perfect. She replied, "When did 'not so bad' ever become good enough for a Democrat?" Despite this discouraging news, and skepticism that these pockets were going to be emptied for me, I was determined to be a team player and follow the guidelines that the Caucus had communicated by way of Perry.

Unfortunately, my worst fears were realized. The young Caucus representative was disrespectful and didn't trust that I knew how to make solicitation calls (even though he knew that I had run for political office before). After monitoring a few of my calls, he stated in a somewhat sarcastic manner, "that went better than I thought." Such condescension. To add insult to injury, he pumped *me* for names that I had as potential contributors, after leading us to believe that the Caucus was going to provide me with contacts for support. The only names that ended up being shared with me were those of prominent, wealthy donors who for the most part had contributed to the Mike Easley Campaign for Governor or to the State Democratic Party. They did not strike me as the type to likely take an interest in my campaign. The end result to this one size fits all fund raising approach was not positive! One of the few promised donations made that morning fell through (another check in the mail that I am still waiting for) and I wasted an entire morning making "generic" calls, many to folks with whom I had no relationship. Additionally, I had taken on the opportunity costs of abandoning my canvassing efforts and depleting my energy and spirit, much valued resources for the people raising side of my campaign strategy.

It was obvious that my attempts at fund raising were feeble in the eyes of the Senate Caucus. They had a plan for a conventional campaign and given that I didn't fit that model they didn't have a way to help me. From a less than tactful email I received the first week in July, it was apparent that our financials were not going to help their $2^{nd}$ quarter numbers look good. At this time, we decided to abandon any pretense of trying to fit the mold that they had established. While I removed myself from this fund raising part of the ballgame, I tried my best to be a team player in all other aspects from attending party gatherings and events to supporting the other candidates on our ticket.

Adding salt to this unhealed wound, when there was an indication close to the election that my campaign was polling well, the Caucus seemed to want to hedge their bets. Mid October, I received an email from Perry sent as a pep talk of sorts presumably to all of the Democratic Senate candidates, though I can only speculate on the recipients apart from me.

> --- *Perry Woods <pwoods@ncdemocraticparty.org> wrote:*
>
> *We know the GOP is shameless in playing to fear. Here is a great column from Kevin Tillman, the Brother of Pat Tillman. Pat was the former NFL player who quit to join the Rangers, was killed in Afghanistan, and the Army covered up that it was Friendly Fire to continue to help sell the war. If you find yourself getting tired over the next three weeks, this should inspire you to stretch for the tape.*
>
> *Perry*
> [column included in original email but omitted here]

I welcomed the emotional support and replied on October $22^{nd}$, including Jerry Meek in this exchange, asking for something tangible in addition, as the following email reveals:

> *From: Gerry Bowles [mailto:gerrybowles@yahoo.com]*
> *Sent: Sun 10/22/2006 3:54 PM*
> *To: Perry Woods*
> *Cc: Jerry Meek*
> *Subject: Gerry Bowles Campaign....SOS*

> Hi Perry,
>
> Thanks for the words of encouragement.
>
> We are indeed stretching for the tape!
>
> We are continuing to canvass door-to-door and by phone. We sent our first direct mail piece last week and if anecdotal conversations count, we have hit a nerve.
>
> We have two additional pieces to be sent out in the next 10 days...and if we could get some financial help from the caucus we can increase the number of households that receive our message.
>
> We have received "pledges" to cover some of the costs of our mailings...but they are late in coming in. We feel that we have done our part in keeping Neal Hunt "on the reservation". He is on tv and the radio, and is appearing at most functions....therefore he and his money are not going elsewhere.
>
> If the caucus has $5,000 to contribute to our cause, it would be well received!
>
> Thanks,
> Gerry

His reply later that night left me hopeful:

> On Sunday, October 22, 2006 7:27 PM, Perry Woods <pwoods@ncdemocraticparty.org> wrote:
>
> Gerry,
> Call me in the AM. [personal phone number omitted for privacy].
>
> Perry

Unfortunately, my expectations were dashed. In my return call to Perry I learned that the Caucus, without my knowledge or input, had already created mailers "in support" of my candidacy. Indeed, as can be seen by the following email, Perry wanted me to include an "In Kind" contribution of $6765.67 from the Caucus on my financial statement. My shock and disdain were evident from my included exchange with Andrea:

> --- Perry Woods <pwoods@ncdemocraticparty.org> wrote:
>
> Subject: In kind Contribution
> Date: Fri, 27 Oct 2006 16:41:54 -0400
> From: "Perry Woods" <pwoods@ncdemocraticparty.org>
> To: "Gerry Bowles" <gerrybowles@yahoo.com>
>
> Gerry,
>
> I've attached an in-kind memo for a contribution to your campaign from the NC Democratic Party for $6765.67. Since we didn't coordinate this, there is question as to if this is an independent expenditure or an in-kind, but to be overly cautious and open, we are sending you an in-kind memo. You should report this as 48 hour report, or you can contact the SBOE and ask them if you need to.
>
> Report would be due Monday AM.
>
> Call me if you have questions.
>
> Perry

North Carolina Senate Committee
220 Hillsborough Street
Raleigh, NC 27603
(919) 821-2777
(919) 828-7960 fax #1
(919) 821-4778 fax #2

Kimberly Reynolds, Director   Ext. 20
Perry Woods, Political Director   Ext. 219
Jared Wiener, Finance Director   Ext. 204

# Memo

**To:** Gerry Bowles
**From:** Perry Woods
**Date:** October 27, 2006
**Re:** In-Kind Contributions

Below is a list of the in-kind contributions made on behalf of the NC Democratic Party to your campaign. You will need to file a 48 hour report to the State Board of Elections. The Democratic Party's ID number at the Board of Elections is STA-C3839N-C-001.

If you have any questions or concerns please do not hesitate to contact us.

Thank you.

| Bowles | 10/27/2006 | Mail | $6765.67 |

From: Gerry Bowles <gerrybowles@yahoo.com>
To: andrea bertole <andreabertole@hotmail.com>
Subject: Fwd: In kind Contribution
Date: Fri, 27 Oct 2006 18:51:09 -0700 (PDT)

*Can you believe this?*
*Gerry*

242

> On Friday, October 27, 2006 10:45 PM, andrea bertole <andreabertole@hotmail.com> wrote:
>
> Unbelievable!!!

Needless to say, I refused.

> From: Gerry Bowles [mailto:gerrybowles@yahoo.com]
> Sent: Tue 10/31/2006 8:19 AM
> To: Perry Woods
> Subject: Re: In kind Contribution
>
> Perry,
>
> We are not listing this independent expenditure in our report. We had no prior knowledge, and did not coordinate in any way.
>
> Thanks,
> Gerry

## *Consequences of Not Playing Ball*

In addition to not receiving funds directly from the NC Democratic Senate Caucus, I also missed out on some support from individuals who had assumed their contributions to the party would be channeled in part to me. During any given election, the positions on the ballot may run the gamut from candidates running for the judiciary to the folks trying to win a seat on the Soil and Water Conservation board to candidates competing for House and Senate races. With so many names and offices to choose from and so many campaigns vying for dollars, many people feel more comfortable sending money to the party with the belief that these funds will get distributed to individual candidates. Most of the folks I met at the doors who claimed Democratic allegiance and who had contributed to the party believed that I was getting a portion of their contribution. I had to tell them that this assumption was not the case and the only way that they could be sure which candidates received their monetary support was to give to them individually.

The harsh reality was that some candidates got left out of the process entirely. In my case this circumstance happened not just with this Senate race, but with 2 previous election bids as well. I could understand an imbalance of monetary support but when the Caucus deemed fit to spend a quarter of a million dollars on one of my peers in Wake County and I didn't receive one red cent, I felt that the system was not only awry but it was broken.

To look at this situation using a sporting metaphor, even the NY Yankees, who have more dollars than sense, know that it is important to have a farm team. You can't just focus on one season. In the same fashion our Caucus seemed to spend an inordinate amount of money on a few "key" races, rather than giving a bit to some of the less strong candidates as determined by their numbers. Not only did I experience this narrow approach, a number of fellow candidates have shared similar stories with me. By contrast, EMILY's LIST, a national interest group that supports Democratic women who are pro-choice, knows how valuable having monetary support early can be to a campaign. Their name, in fact, is an acronym for EARLY MONEY IS LIKE YEAST. This group began in response to the difficulties many female candidates were having raising money for their campaigns. My experience as a woman running for office was not unique in the world of politics as indicated by this email received by a supporter prior to Election Day:

> *I hope you got some help from the **Senate Caucus**! It is still the good ole boys...same thing with lobbying. A person in our office is ranked #47 and never wrote a letter or summary of any bill last session. The bill he was in charge of never got anywhere---not even out of committee! He is a great socializer with all the news people and lobbyists. But, we girls have to fight on!!!!!!!!!! I'm making signs and will email to all the candidates soon today with our plans.*

Another outcome of not receiving funds from the party was that many other organizations (i.e. Sierra Club, State Employees Credit Union, Wake County Board of Realtors) took their cue from this decision and responded similarly. From conversations with friends who served on some of these boards, my impression was that these groups decided that if the party was not going to lend its financial support to me, then why should they? The adage of jumping on the bandwagon was true. I was asked repeatedly "is the party helping you?" The question was really "does the party think you might win?" By not contributing to individual candidates who were on the ballot the party deprived us of credibility. I have learned to contribute my time and treasure to individual candidates that I feel will best represent the issues I care about, rather than to the NC or the Wake Democratic Party.

## *Managing the Money*

We used a variety of vehicles to encourage financial support. In addition to the previously discussed fund raising events, our campaign updates informed supporters of our activities and served to generate enthusiasm from them to donate. The following is an example from the August 30th update of our fund raising efforts:

> ### *Accounting – Fundraising*
> *While no dollar amount can top the value of your involvement in helping Gerry earn voter support, campaign expenses tied to mobilizing voters are upon us. With the arrival of the yard sign invoice and the anticipation of key mailings for September/October, the need for financial contributions is pressing. Can you help?*
>
> *Donate to a Specific Expense – With Gerry's grassroots and cost conscious approach to her campaign, a little goes a long way. Your contribution of $10 toward the specific costs noted above (yard signs & mailings) would make an unquestionable difference. We value greatly and apply carefully any contribution your budget can absorb.*
>
> *Sponsor Gerry's Afternoon Tea for Strong Women Honoring Betty Ann Knudsen – Not only will this event reflect on Betty Ann's contributions and pass the torch to Gerry, it will also feature a number of strong women influenced by Betty Ann who are currently active in politics. Your sponsorship of this event at $100 will contribute significantly to electing Gerry and furthering the participation of strong women in governing North Carolina. Your contribution as a guest at $25 provides a valuable input toward the expenses involved in this final stage of the campaign.*

*Checks can be made payable to "Gerry Bowles NC Senate" and sent to 405 Amelia Ave, Raleigh NC 27615*

We pulled additional stops out a couple weeks before the election and sent the following fund raising letter to my Christmas Card List. The response was more of an emotional boost than a financial windfall.

*Dear____*

*Did you know that Gerry Bowles is running this November for election as the Democrat for the North Carolina State Senate? Dismayed by current representation and motivated by her "we get the government we deserve" outlook to the political process, Gerry has launched a campaign with a strong focus on people to offer her citizen focused inclusive approach to NC's District 15.*

*My name is Andrea Bertole and I am serving as Gerry Bowles' volunteer coordinator and campaign manager* [since Dan had to return to law school at the end of August]. *I am delighted to report the campaign has been going wonderfully well. We have been working solidly over the past half year to mobilize voters in Gerry's district with the most welcome energy of many volunteers and supporters. We are very encouraged by the receptiveness, openness, and enthusiasm we have encountered and feel motivated by the energy we have generated and which continues to grow. While initially thought the underdog, Gerry's campaign is now being described as building some powerful grass-roots momentum.*

*These successes in addition to the national climate and the anticipated low voter turnout for this "blue moon election" (with no race for president, governor or U.S. Senate at the top of the ballot) have set the stage for change.*

*Having polled district members while canvassing over 5000 households, Gerry has heard the call for a return in priority to Education, Transportation & Representation issues. It is time for this former Economics, Law, and Politics teacher to bring her classroom experience, watchdog approach and inclusive manner to the decision-making process at the General Assembly. You know Gerry as a mother, friend, neighbor and community volunteer who will find solutions to problems instead of just pointing fingers. Can you help with this challenge?*

*With the final push to November 7$^{th}$ and campaign mailers recently sent to almost 15,000 targeted district voters, your contribution would be truly appreciated and would have a large impact. Our Representation Issues Advisory Committee has reported that usually only a small number of people fund the bulk of campaigns, which can create pressure on candidates to please these few donors. Gerry's campaign has been financed in small amounts by many donors. Your check can help Gerry keep people the priority. Checks can be made payable to "Gerry Bowles NC Senate and sent to 405 Amelia Ave, Raleigh, NC 27615.*

*With deep gratitude,*

*Andrea Bertole*
*919 793 0160*
*andreabertole@hotmail.com abertole@nc.rr.com*

*PS Please do visit www.GerryBowles06.com to learn about Gerry's campaign and keep up-to date on events.*

Over the course of the campaign, while not generating ideal levels of funds, I did receive a fair amount and needed to be sure these monies were handled properly. As noted before, I was blessed to have Gail Christensen, a person of integrity who was also computer literate, to serve as my treasurer. The increasingly complex financial requirements and online reporting required by the State Board of Elections was mind boggling and technically demanding.

It was necessary for me to "loan" the campaign money in order to open an election banking account. The state regulations were very precise in how to navigate these waters and how to "repay" yourself. This email from Gail on the 10$^{th}$ of August notified me that the campaign had raised enough to pay me back, though I chose not to do so at that time!

> Hi Gerry,
>
> You now have collected $13,941 in monetary contributions! And another $750 in in-kind donations!
>
> Your campaign has paid out only $6613.13 (that's before the yard sign bill is paid).
>
> Is it time yet to repay your $1000 loan to the campaign? Gail

Gail and I both had access to the campaign's bank account. For the most part, I handled all of the banking transactions. All of the contributions were sent to my home, and after making two photocopies of the daily deposits, I would save one for my records and pass on the other to Gail to be used for her quarterly reports to the Board on April 1st, July 2nd, October 3rd, and January 4$^{th}$. She kept intricate records of all the donations (contributors' names, addresses, occupations, and the amount that they contributed) as the Board of Elections had regulations as to how much could be given by any one individual during the primary and the general election.

> A candidate may not accept and a contributor may not give more than four thousand dollars ($4000) per election......A candidate, the candidate's spouse, parents, brothers and sisters may contribute unlimited amounts to the candidate and are not subject to the limitations. Any National, State, district or county executive committee of any political party (recognized under GS 163-96) is exempt from the contribution limitations as well.

Gail kept a running tally for each individual as it was necessary to report the name of any individual that had contributed $100.00 or more to the Board of Elections. This included any in-kind donations.

The time required to follow up on the details of contributors was considerable as Gail's email in early May illustrates:

> Here are the questions I have so far: You photocopied two bills -

a $20 and a $10. There is no identification nearby that I can see. Do you have any records of who gave you these? You have a note in the margin that says Anita Harwood $25. Was this a cash contribution? Do you have an address? You photocopied a volunteer card filled out by David and Melissa Jesser (spelling?), who checked that they enclosed $100. I see no check. Was this a cash contribution? There is a partial photo of a check from someone whose name appears to be Ellen Czenege or something like that. Can you give me the correct spelling and the address, please? It was for $25. You note in the margin that Debby Edgerton gave $50, but there is no check. Was this a cash contribution? The top of the check written by Carol Teal, whom you wrote is the director of Lillian's List, is missing in the photocopy and I'm unsure of the spelling. Help! This month's statement from Wachovia does not include a charge of $11.95 for the account fee. I'm assuming that the account maintained the minimum balance for free checking. Is that your understanding, too? These are the people who have contributed over $100 and for whom I have no information about their employer or their occupation. Can you help me with any of them? Those whom you cannot identify I will call. Meredith Ann Lundy, Bill Robinson, Thomas L. Gipson, Martha Farmer, W.E. Page, Jr. David and Melissa Jessen, Shirley Willett, Diana L. Monroe (Zandt,) Gary Jarvela, Vickie Burns, Herb Reichlin.

In addition, during certain periods of the campaign (two weeks prior to the primary election, and two weeks prior to election day) any contribution of $1000.00 or more had to be reported to the state board within 48 hours. This restriction was to prevent the possibility of a big donor turning the tide on an election without full disclosure. Though I awaited eagerly for such a bountiful last minute contribution, and was fully prepared to make such a report, I never had cause to do so.

Corporate donations were not allowed at any time. While money could be accepted from Political Action Committees, there was a limit to the amount that could be raised. What constituted a corporate entity was open to interpretation. After all, didn't former Presidential Candidate, Mitt Romney, say, "Corporations are people, my friend?" One of my supporters had the same mentality! When Gail asked one of our donors to write a check from her personal checking account instead of from her business account this was her email reply:

> *May 18, 2006*
> 
> *[The donor] returned my call. She says she IS [her company], that she doesn't want to send a personal check because her husband's name is on that account, that she has given hundreds of campaign contributions over the last 20 years from that account without any problem. So I said I would simply put it through as is, and if they give me any problem, I will contact her and we'd see what we had to do to comply. Gail*

It was not enough to have someone commit to contribute to the campaign, we had to collect! Additional time was required to "bring home the bacon." By the end of the campaign while most contributions had been collected, a few of the promised higher dollar donations were still outstanding. A Table summarizing my receipts and expenditures ("Gerry Bowles' 2006 Campaign Finance Summary by Reporting Quarter") can be found under "Funds raised & Expenses" in the "Numbers" portion of Section Four's "Conclusion."

## *Expenses*

We were responsible for keeping our records up to date within seven days of any financial activity (donations or expenditures) in case a state auditor wanted to check the books. Not only did Gail keep me apprised of funds coming in, she spent much time monitoring the campaign's expenditures. A receipt was required for every payment made by the campaign.

*May 26, 2006*

> *Hi Gerry and Dan,*
> 
> *I deposited $820 in checks in our RBC Centura bank account today. The May bank statement should be mailed next week. The total of monetary **contributions** (not in-kind gifts) deposited to date is $3900! Way to go, Gerry! The total of **expenditures** that have been paid to date is $2806.57. I wrote checks to the following today:*

*$1500 to Cool Cat Creative for Web design, contribution form, and database.*

*$1045 to Carter Printing for 10, 000 palm cards*

*$125 for "indoor advertising" production and space rental (for the toilet ads)*

*$482.22 to reimburse Gerry for campaign supplies (stamps, envelopes, printer ink, etc.) that she paid for with her credit card.*

*This leaves us with a total in the bank TO DATE of $1093.43. However, several checks (for a total of $375) have been received but have not been deposited. So we actually have **$1468.43 remaining funds**.*

*Not a bad place to be...*

As the campaign progressed through the summer and into the fall, we were always able to stay just ahead of our expenses. For example, our June 30th report showed that we had $7,285 in contributions but only $4,309.41 in expenses. Closer to the election, costs linked with yard signs and mailers added to the "outs" side of the equation. We were hoping to have an economic windfall the final weeks before the election, but this was not to be. Even close to Election Day with tight funds and incoming invoices, we were able to keep our sense of humor despite our less than stellar economic situation.

*From: info@trianglemailingservice.com*
*Subject: Final Invoice*
*Date: Thu, 01 Nov 2006 15:56:22*

*Good Afternoon Andrea,*

*I hope that the campaign is going well as it comes down to crunch time. When will John Kerry be stumping and telling jokes for Gerry this weekend? Just kidding. I just wanted to notify you that we had your final invoice prepared for the additional labor and postage required to mail the extra pieces from postcards #2 and #3. The labor balance comes to $108.00. The postage totals $496.71. Let me know if you'd like to come by or have me put these in the mail. Again, best of luck. Thank you for the business.*

*Regards,*

*Bill Seymour
Triangle Mailing Service*

*Date: Friday, November 3, 2006 8:13 AM
Subject: RE: Final Invoice*

*Hi Bill*

*If you could put the invoice in the mail that would be great! These last days are packed but really exciting (so far Kerry hasn't contacted us though...)*

*Thanks for the note,
Andrea*

Before all the votes had been tallied on election day, Gail sent an email detailing the campaign's economic status.

*Subject: Finances as of Election Day, November 7
Date: Tuesday, November 7, 2006 4:42 PM*

*Hi Gerry
Tomorrow I will deposit **$1575** in check contributions to your campaign, for a total of **$21,086** in contributions towards your campaign to date.*

*Our expenses now total **$20,555.09**. That means we have **$530.91** left to spend.
Two bills remain to be paid to Triangle Mailing Service, for a total of **$604.71** which will put us **$73.81** in the red.*

*Gail*

Unfortunately, I ended my campaign in the red. I had made an "executive" decision to over spend the last weeks of the campaign as it had been my experience during my previous runs for state office that a lot of money came in during the final days. In fact, when I ran for a seat in the NC House

I received a lot of money the week after the election that I could not put to good use. When told by the State Board of Elections that by law I could keep that money, I felt that it was unseemly to do so, and gave it to charity. Looking back, I would make the same choice regarding these final costs. The spending was strategic, not reckless.

## *"Certification to Close Committee"*

The adage *"It ain't over til it's over"* so often quoted on the sports page, is apropos of political financial accounting as evidenced by this July 12, 2007 email exchange between Gail and myself:

> *Hi Gerry,*
> *I updated the campaign reporting software and printed out a bunch of reports: Loan Proceeds Statement (CRO-6100) Forgiven Loan Statement (CRO-6200) Loan Proceeds (CRO-1410) Forgiven Loans (CRO-1440) Disclosure Report Cover (CRO-1000) Only the last one can be done electronically. We'll have to fill out the others manually, and you and I must sign them and mail them snail mail. I notice that the software references our "fourth quarter" report, wherein it says that we went only $562.76 in debt, whereas my accounting (and Alfred checked every single line item against the checks, etc.) says expenses outpaced contributions by $3988.88. (It may be that "in-kind contributions" - that is, food - counts as income in monetary terms, which makes no sense to us.) Will you be willing to write the loan off for $562.76, even though you went into debt for a LOT more than that? Tomorrow morning, I will call the SBOE and speak again to Ralph Gable and make SURE we have done everything correctly, because I won't have a chance to amend my ways before the filing deadline of July 27, 2007, since I won't be here. When I am done filling in the forms, I will bring them to your house for your signature (probably in late afternoon). If you are not home, I will leave them in your mailbox, and you can just sign them and mail them. I will address everything. But you may have to take them to the Post Office when you get back from Katherine's (but before 7/27). Let's hope this is the LAST time we will have to do anything about campaign finances.*

*To gailc@nc.rr.com*

*Jul 9, 2007*

*Hey Girl,*

*I am willing to have the report "read" whatever makes it work for you! I am so sorry that this keeps coming up...I never intended to cause so much grief. Good Grief!!*

*I will be here all tomorrow...will do whatever you need!*

*Gerry*

And so, at last, it was over!

## *Wrap Up*

It is an understatement that fund raising was a weakness in my campaign. I wasn't able to identify members for a finance committee or designate a person to be in charge of raising money. What I did have was a dedicated campaign committee that tried as best they could to schedule a number of fund raisers and to generate interest in the campaign and to develop relationships with voters. What we could have used was a few large dollar contributions, but the costs of panning for that gold seemed too high given the odds of payoff. With the total of $23, 487 in contributions from my fourth quarter campaign finance report, I did my best to navigate the election highway on my horse instead of the Cadillac and Pinto vehicles Dan had planned for at $100,000 and $35,000 budgets respectively. In comparison to my opponent's rocket ship $490,122 receipts amount from his fourth quarter report the financial race was far from even. For a striking visual presentation of the disparity, refer to the Table "Bowles versus Hunt: 2006 Campaign Finance Summary by Quarter" which can be found under "Funds raised & Expenses" in the "Numbers" portion of Section Four's "Conclusion."

# Chapter Ten - Special Interest/Endorsements

As described earlier in the questionnaire section of Chapter Eight – Communication, once a candidate files for office her mailbox is flooded with information, invitations and surveys from any number of "special interests."

## *Explosion of Interest – Questionnaires and Interviews*

The following partial chronology of events illustrates this phenomenon:

| February 28 | File for office |
|---|---|
| March 2 | Attend a candidate's meeting |
| March 4 | Met with Bill Robinson to discuss campaign messaging |
| March 13 | Interviewed by Triangle Labor Council (received endorsement soon after) |
| March 15 | Met with some of the leadership of the NC Association of Educators (NCAE) |
| Week of March 22 | Conversation with Carol Teal, the president of Lillian's List explaining why I would not be seeking their endorsement (discussed more fully in Chapter Eight). |
| Early June | Learned of Wake Up Wake County (a pro public education group) |
| June 12 | Attended a Institute for Education Policymakers' Forum |
| June 30 | Contacted by the local chapter National Organization for Women (NOW) |
| July | Responded to questionnaires from the Wake County Board of Realtors and the Raleigh Wake Citizens Association. |
| August 1 | Interviewed by the state employees SEANC |
| August 2 | Met with the Police Benevolent Association. |
| Mid-August | Met with the Wake County Board of Realtors. |

As you can imagine, with such a short time between filing and addressing questions from a variety of groups about my positions, I needed to have my ideas and messages prepared as quickly as possible. I was lucky to have had prior experience as a candidate given the eleventh hour nature of my filing.

## *Endorsements*

Getting the backing of a group can mean different things. Not only can it bolster support within what is deemed to be your natural constituency (i.e. a Democratic candidate might expect endorsements from union groups but not the National Rifle Association), but it can also add money, volunteers, as well as further exposure to the campaign. The following illustrates some of my experience with endorsements.

### *Triangle Labor Council*

In early spring, I received the endorsement of the Triangle Labor Council which initially brought with it a financial contribution. The week before the election, I received a letter from them with a sample of the political literature that they had distributed to affiliated union members prior to the general election and with wishes for good luck on Election Day.

### *North Carolina Police Benevolent Association*

Mid-summer, I met with the North Carolina Police Benevolent Association and soon after received written notice that I had received their endorsement.

> *Our endorsement carries with it our permission for you to use the association's endorsement, should you wish. If you wish to discuss the ways in which the PBA can support your campaign, please call Randy Byrd at [contact information removed for privacy]*

> *We will ask our members, their friends and families, and all citizens who respect the strong and efficient enforcement of our laws to cast their ballots in the upcoming election in your favor.*

A follow up email gave further details as to what an endorsement could mean for our campaign.

> *By now you should have received our endorsement letter. We would like to get a short paragraph of what this endorsement means to you. You can intertwine this statement with your own words. Also attached please find our logos that you can use in*

*your advertisements along with our caption "The Voice of Law Enforcement." This logo and caption serve as a positive force in your campaign. On a final note if you could send me all the addresses, fax numbers, and email addresses of all the newspapers where we can write letters to the editor and send a press release. Thanks. Good luck. Looking forward to working with you in the next legislative session. NC PBA represents sworn law enforcement officers and support personnel by providing legal services and advocating changes to improve the quality of work life for people employed in all aspects of criminal justice.*

*Randy Byrd State Division Legislative Chairperson North Carolina Police Benevolent Association*

I happily replied:

*Dear Randy,*
*Thank you for sending the logos that may be used in campaign updates. Please feel free to include my comments in any of your literature. "I am honored and delighted that the men and women who serve and protect the citizens of North Carolina have chosen to endorse my candidacy. I am proud to announce the endorsement of the North Carolina Police Benevolent Association."*
*Gerry Bowles, NC Senate District 15*

The following email came in response to my request to this group for volunteers to canvass door-to-door or to make phone calls. I appreciated his candor in explaining where the comforts of his membership lay:

*Gerry,*

*Got your message. Sorry for the delay. In ref. to your question about canvassing and phone calls. Not an area we are going to be able to help you with...Cops by in large hate politics and especially the old time politics. We have always been successful in influencing our members and their families who are solid voters. Can even work to get some signs out. Where we can help is with our logo on your website and advertising (trust me when I*

257

> say this holds tremendous weight with voters, especially with our caption (the voice of law enforcement)...a press release at a good time for your campaign...I can show up at any appearance you would like and speak on behalf of the PBA...letters to the editor...and last but not least...PAC money...I am in the process of making a PAC requests for funds...and last but not least we will be doing a mailing to our members showing your endorsement. Hope this helps...
>
> Randy Byrd

Indeed, the Police Benevolent Association honored the commitments they made both financially and in a volunteer capacity, always of such importance to our grassroots campaign.

### North Carolina Association of Educators

On the 7th of September I received a $750.00 contribution from the NCAE Fund for Children and Public Education, the political arm of the NC Association of Educators, and this note of assistance:

> "We are in the process of notifying our members of NCAE's recommendations subject to the November General Election. We are asking them to volunteer to be actively involved in our endorsed candidates' campaigns. In the meantime, if you need assistance in other ways please contact our Government Relations office. We can supply you with names of key NCAE leaders in your area."

Whereas I was appreciative of their financial support, I never felt a personal relationship with any one person in the association. I was unable to identify a strong supporter among them. I was just one candidate amongst many. Their support was of a more generic nature. This experience was in contrast to the support that I felt from the Firefighters Association as described next.

### Raleigh Professional Fire Fighters Association

I was notified of my endorsement by the Raleigh Professional Fire Fighters

Association on September 8th by Trey Mayo. I had met him while canvassing door-to-door in the early summer. When I introduced myself at his door, we started a lengthy conversation about the issues that engaged me and he shared the concerns he had as a firefighter. That was the start "of a beautiful friendship". He told me that he was involved in his professional organization and would like to pass on their literature to me. I was supportive of the group's legislative concerns and was pleased to hear of their endorsement. Enhancing the sense of a personal connection with this group, in the early morning of September 25th, Rodger Koopman, candidate for Wake County Commissioner, and I were the guests of the volunteer fire fighters at the local IHOP. I was a little unsure what I should expect of this venue. As there were several tables filled with fire fighters, some coming off of a shift and others preparing to go on, it was difficult to "give a speech" in the proverbial manner. I visited each table and then midway through our eggs and bacon, Roger and I stood to offer a few remarks. On the 26th I had a repeat of the breakfast with the next shift of volunteer fire fighters. In addition to a financial contribution, the firefighters helped in manning the polls on election day.

### *Raleigh Wake Citizens Association*

The evening of September 27th, from 7:37-7:44 (I kid you not), I was interviewed by the Raleigh Wake Citizens Association, a nonpartisan, political advocacy organization whose goal is to empower minorities in Raleigh and Wake County. I arrived early as I was not sure of the location and found Representative Grier Martin, a fellow candidate, who was scheduled to be interviewed following me. The location was a church and lacking signage, it wasn't clear from the outside which door to enter into. With such an unusual designated time I was afraid to miss any of my 7 minutes. As I sat in my car waiting for the appointed moment, I observed folks leaving the building that I believed to be interviewing panelists. It felt awkward. Should I go in at 7:20 and perhaps steal valuable minutes from an interview or should I sit in the parking lot until the last possible moment? Finally, at 7:35 someone appeared and directed me to an ante room. The 15th district that I was hoping to represent did not have a heavy African American population so I was not on their radar screen. I was never officially notified of an endorsement but Lindy Brown, candidate for Wake County Commissioner, told me she had to ask them about the status of her endorsement, and that she thought that I had been endorsed.

We never got an answer to Andrea's follow up with the group. Though not dismissed by them, they clearly never embraced me. They did keep to the time allotment.

## *Newspaper Endorsements*

The most coveted endorsements are those given by the newspapers. Even though they are less influential than they were in the past, for a large part of the population, those who don't follow politics on a daily basis, they have importance.

### *Independent Weekly*

The *Independent Weekly (now the Indy Week)*, a newspaper with a progressive, liberal political perspective, published their political endorsements in their October 25th edition.

I received the endorsement for NC Senate 15 which included my picture and the following statement:

> *We hoped that Sen. Neal Hunt, the incumbent Republican, would take a centrist path when he was elected two years ago, based on his pretty good record as a Raleigh City council member. Unfortunately, he's aligned himself with the Called2Action crowd- the Christian conservatives- and spent his time getting their favorite bill passed, the one that requires every student to say the Pledge of Allegiance every day. He was a "no" vote on the budget and on raising the minimum wage to $6.15 an hour. He signed the conservatives' so-called Taxpayers Protection Pledge, which would bar any tax increase unless approved by a legislative super-majority or in a public referendum. And he co-sponsored the amendment to ban gay marriage.*
> 
> *Hunt's Democratic opponent, Dorothy (Gerry) Bowles, will be familiar to Independent readers as the organizer of Wake Citizens for Effective Government, a nonpartisan forum on public issues in North Raleigh. Bowles, who used to be a high school history teacher, has run an energetic, door-knocking campaign emphasizing her support for mental-health insurance parity and*

*opposition to corporate tax loopholes and lobbyists raising campaign funds for legislators. She promises, if elected, to hold her own monthly issues forums a la the now-defunct WCEG. Good idea.*

### The News and Observer

In contrast to the emotional boost from the *Independent Weekly's* endorsement, I felt disappointment at the decision by *The News and Observer* to give their editorial endorsement to my opponent. There was a time that this endorsement was valued especially for Democratic candidates because the paper was seen by many as the mouthpiece of the Democratic Party. While this was no longer the case, their opinion still held sway with a large swath of the population. I wasn't entirely surprised by their choice as I had wondered if they might select Neal Hunt as a way to demonstrate balance to a public that viewed them as biased toward Democrats. My real frustration came with the paper's inattention to my campaign as I mentioned in Chapter Eight. I was not called in for a personal interview as I had been in 2000 for the NC House seat. When they printed personal information about me in their 2006 Voter Guide, some of the information was incorrect, based on answers that I had given them in 2000 when I ran for the State House. I had received their endorsement at that time! I understood that Neal Hunt was a different opponent than I faced in the previous race, but I was different as well. I had six years of accomplishments and experiences to shape my thinking. In my mind the paper was lazy in its reporting and was delinquent in not interviewing me personally.

The following is the *News and Observer's* endorsement for District 15:

> *This northwest Wake district is represented by Neal Hunt, a 64 year old Raleigh businessman (property management is one specialty). A former Raleigh City Council member, he has been a predictably conservative vote in the Senate, where the simple truth is that majority Democrats rule with an iron hand, not always to the good. Republicans such as Hunt simply don't have much clout.*
>
> *But on the City Council, Hunt showed an ability to forge compromise and a willingness to listen to those with whom he*

*disagreed. We'd like to see him move a little to the moderate center and become more of a consensus-builder in the Senate in his second term.*

*He is an advocate for opening up the legislative process in a place where too many decisions are made by too few people, essentially in secret. He also wants to cut pork barrel spending, which still exists to some degree. Hunt believes that proposals from the minority just wind up buried in committees and the like. Perhaps that's where some of them belong, but open debate in which ideas rise or fall after public scrutiny is a cornerstone of our system of government.*

*Hunt's opponent is energetic Gerry Bowles, 59, also of Raleigh, who has previously run twice for the legislature. She's a long time community activist who sees and deplores the influence wielded by special interest on Jones Street. Bowles is clear in her views, and passionate about them. But experience at two different levels of government, coupled with his potential as a constructive centrist, gives the nod in this race to Neal Hunt.*

Perhaps if the *N&O* had only read the concerns voiced by the *Independent's* editorial staff as to the decidedly far right groups Neal Hunt had aligned himself with, they would have been prepared for his subsequent stances. Instead of viewing Neal Hunt from the point of view of "past as prologue" as to his City Council voting record, they should have focused more on his present actions and influences.

## *Further Disappointments –Expected and Not*

When it came to groups not as aligned with my party, I did not harbor much hope of endorsements. That said, I did choose to interview with the Raleigh Regional Association of Realtors and felt I had performed well. They represented my opponent's bailiwick and I knew that he was the darling of their group. I was ushered into a conference room for the interview and seated at the head of a large table surrounded by close to 20 people. I was given the opportunity to introduce myself and to offer a few remarks about my campaign.

I was immediately verbally assaulted by one fellow who questioned my position against the proposed 540 toll. He rather flippantly questioned my concerns as the proposed toll would not impact the district that I was hoping to represent. My reply to him was to take a more macro rather than a micro view. It was my opinion that we should all care about the inequity of having a portion of the road being financed by a toll. I noted that folks "in my neck of the woods" would drive on 540 to get to other areas of the county. Did he suggest that they would exit the road prior to paying the toll? I also noted that we had all paid taxes into the transportation fund and why then should some people on one side of the belt line pay extra to access the road.

It became clear that most of the folks who were questioning me had not read all the material that I had submitted for the interview. I responded to questions that had been answered in my literature. I was able to respond to all their questions even those delivered with an air of skepticism and doubt. Given that I had entered a metaphorical lion's den, I left feeling more positive about my message. There was a definite shift in body language and more than a few nods of the head to some of the comments that I made. Still, my expectations were affirmed when on the 22$^{nd}$ of September I received the following email notification from them. The remarks were somewhat boilerplate. It read in part:

> ....'*I want to extend our sincere thanks for meeting with us in August and sharing your vision and views on important issues in Wake County. Our interview committee thoroughly enjoyed meeting with you, however, at this time we are unable to endorse your campaign....*" *We wish you the best of luck in the election and all your future endeavors."*

Though disappointing, this notice from the Realtors was not surprising. By contrast, when groups considered to be within your natural constituency fail to endorse your candidacy, the emotional impact is more stinging. At the end of September, the political action committee of the State Employee Association sent me the following notice by mail:

> "*Thank you for taking time to interview with representatives of Area 10 EMPAC. They enjoyed hearing your views and ideas on some of the issues important to the state employees of North Carolina. After careful consideration, Area 10 EMPAC voted not*

*to make any endorsements in your Senate race. This was a difficult decision, but we felt it was in the best interest of our members.*

I interpreted this lack of endorsement approach as more of the "Neal's not so bad" thinking. I suspect they thought that if I was elected as a Democrat I would still support them but if they endorsed me and my opponent was re-elected, it might be difficult to move their agenda forward. I understood the political expediency of their decision but also felt that those voters not as attuned to the political nuances of endorsement decisions, would question my credibility and not this group's political decision making.

## *Conclusion*

We often view special interest groups negatively. In fact, a key tenet of my campaign was to make people and not groups the "special interest." However, these groups can serve a valuable role in the election process. The key is to not be beholden to or lose sight of what or who your allegiance is to: an issue or a group. For example, with my strong focus on education, I was happy for the endorsement of the NCAE. That being said, if elected, I was not willing to blindly rubber stamp their legislative agenda in its entirety without balancing other identified needs of my constituency. These groups offer a way for voters to identify common ground with candidates and offer candidates much needed financial, volunteer and moral support. Nonetheless, the costs associated with the endorsement process need to be recognized. Considerable time may be spent engaging with various groups in search of their support and misperceptions may arise when endorsements are not made.

# Section 3: The Election

## Chapter Eleven – Early Voting

In 2006, Wake County allowed for voting ahead of the November 7$^{th}$ election date. At that time, the General Assembly's rules for one-stop absentee voting allowed ballots to be cast beginning on the third Thursday before the election and ending on the Saturday before the election. Counties had the option to add evenings and weekends in the 18 days leading up to the election. As early as August 1$^{st}$, our campaign was sent a list of 7 "One Stop" voting locations that had been approved by the Wake County Board of Elections. Voting began on Thursday, October 19$^{th}$ at 8:30 am and continued until 5:00 pm on Saturday, November 4$^{th}$. While fewer locations were available for early voting, people could cast their ballots at locations other than at their usual polling place.

To focus attention on early voting, our campaign had planned for a "Scare up the Vote Rally" to be held on Saturday the 28th of October at the BP (campaign headquarters). Our goal was to engage folks at the BP and send others out canvassing to let people at the doors know about early voting. We also had directions to the voting sites and were prepared to "shuttle" those that needed transportation to the Shelley Lake site. With Halloween candy in hand we were ready for a large party. Unfortunately, the crowds never came. They were already at Shelly Lake!!

Flexibility is key to any endeavor. Andrea and Harry went to Shelly Lake to check out the situation and reported back how energized the crowd was. We quickly took our party to the polling place and discovered a festive atmosphere. It was like coming home for me. After having canvassed at more than 5,000 doors I recognized dozens of faces. Many would acknowledge they met me at their door or had received our information. The voters were always polite. I never heard a discouraging word and more than a few offered a discreet "thumbs up" to indicate their support for me.

We caught our opponent unawares on that Saturday. Supporters for myself and other Democratic candidates outnumbered the Republicans considerably. They mobilized and so did our campaign. We sought volunteers to help from that day on to cover the two early voting sights in my district. We focused less of our time on door-to-door lit drops as our potential voters were actually at the voting sites. Had we unlimited volunteer support, we would have covered the doors more fully, but having to make choices, we changed the strategy and directed more energy to the party in progress. We had little sense at that time how much of a positive impact early voting would have on our campaign. What we were experiencing was a trend that would continue. When speaking of later elections, Robert Joyce, of the UNC School of Government reported on his webpage (http://canons.sog.unc.edu/?p=3301):

> *Of the 2.6 million absentee votes cast in the 2008 general election, all but 200,000 of them were cast at early-voting sites. This popularity no doubt derives from the convenience that early voting provides: voters have a choice of many days (including at least one Saturday) to vote and a choice of several locations (not just their one assigned election-day precinct voting place).*

I covered the Shelly Lake location as it was within District 15. I was aware that voters in my district might be voting where they worked or played, but my thinking was that the majority would be voting near their homes.

At the northern site located at Police Substation # 22 in the Litchford Village Shopping Plaza, Andrea got quick exposure to the faith vote. There was more of a Republican feel out there but Democrats were present and Andrea felt she offered visibility for our campaign. I continued to "man" the Shelly Lake location. It was also the location chosen by my opponent. He and I were "stationed" on either side of the sidewalk where the voters traveled to get into the polling place. I would introduce myself to the voter as they came up the walk with "Hi, I'm Gerry Bowles and I'm the Democrat running for the State Senate to represent District 15 - this is my opponent, Neal Hunt!" This opening always got a smile. Neal and I rarely conversed, we just greeted individual voters.

I was joined at the Shelley Lake location by several volunteers who "worked" the rather large parking lot to identify voters. Their enthusiasm was contagious. Indeed, at times it seemed we had an army of support. On Saturday the 4th of November I left at noon as Harry and I were to attend the wedding of a family friend. I had arranged for a number of volunteers to remain behind. As I was preparing to leave, Neal asked *"are you going...and are your people leaving?"* I jokingly asked why he cared and he admitted that he couldn't go unless I did! It was a compliment to our team that he saw us as a formidable group. There was such an overwhelmingly positive feeling that I had for the process of voting there. As a citizen it felt good to see folks voting and as a candidate it seemed like a positive sign of support. I also thought Neal and I modeled how campaigns can be civil as we were often at the polling station together. Neal was pulling out all the stops. He had two cars with large Neal Hunt signs that he parked in the lot. He was always on his cell phone and from what I could hear on my end, he seemed to be giving feedback to his manager (e.g. "Yes, she's still here.")

The affirmation of support came in written word as well as through body language during this early voting period. This positive response to Andrea's October 16th campaign update had us all feeling good.

> *From: Lois Shirley*
> *To: Andrea Bertole*
> *Sent: Monday, October 16, 2006 12:15 PM*
> *Subject: Re: Gerry Bowles for NC Senate Campaign Update... 16-Oct-06*
>
> *Andrea, Just want to tell you that I thoroughly enjoyed your creativity and originality in this email. Gerry knows, I'm sure, how fortunate she is to have you. It's been great to keep up with the campaign through your emails. And we'll be at the polls. We are so glad we had that pleasant time with you all at lunch at Shorty's in Meet in the Street in Wake Forest.*
>
> *Lois Shirley*

On Saturday the 29th I received this boost from a new supporter:

> *I am a register[ed] Republican and very tired of misleadings [sic] and lies by all Republicans in office. I will vote for you. But I will not for other Democrats that don't have the fortitude to say they are Democrats or Republicans, they just won't say. Where do they stand? Good luck. Allan*

On October 30th ten days prior to election day, I sent the following email to my campaign volunteers and followers:

*Subject: Personal Note from Gerry Bowles*

*Trick or Treat ... Victory Not Defeat!*

*First of all, thank you for all that you have contributed to our campaign. We are poised for victory, and I have your generous efforts to credit.*

*It's the fourth quarter, the score is tied, we're on the goal line, it's third and one...*

*In order to win we need a team effort...the quarterback can't score on her own. She needs someone to block and someone to catch her pass...*

*I have been your quarterback for the past eight months...the end of the season is here and we are playing for the championship.*

*I need your help to get us over the goal line in order to claim victory on November 7th!*

*We have been informed by many sources that our race is too close to call! The Republicans have sent out an SOS to help my opponent raise funds to win.*

*But, "when the going gets tough, the tough get going!" And we are tough!! Though we have gotten to the goal line, we can't rest on our laurels (and they are substantial). We must not let up our intensity. Here's the game plan....*

*\* I need you to tell everyone that you meet about my campaign, and to ask for their vote.*

*\* I need you to pledge to call or e-mail 5 of your friends to recommend they vote for me, then ask them to contact five of their friends to do the same.*

*\* I need you to volunteer a couple of hours to greet voters at the polls for early voting at the Sertoma Center at Shelly Lake and/or the Raleigh Police Substation at 8320 Litchford Road (Saturday, November 4th 10:00-4:00) and on Election Day, November 7th at a convenient polling station.*

*\* Last but not least...I need your vote!*

*Words cannot express how much I have appreciated our journey together in this championship season. I am looking forward to sharing the victory cup with each of you on Election Night!*

*Thanks,*
*Gerry*

During this last week my opponent was continuously on the airwaves, both on radio and television. On this front my voice was silent as our funds did not allow for this type of exposure. His blitz campaign seemed to support our sense that his polling indicated that our race was tight. His opponent in these ads continued to be the NC Speaker of the House, Jim Black and not me! He was helped tremendously on Thursday, November $2^{nd}$ when the front page of the *News and Observer* screamed in ¾ inch bold type: "Decker: I conspired with Black." The article continued "Former state Rep. Michael Decker testified in federal court Wednesday that House Speaker Jim Black was a co-conspirator in a criminal case in which Decker has admitted receiving $50,000 in campaign checks and cash in exchange for supporting Black for a third term as speaker." Just ahead of this announcement, Perry called and informed me that the Caucus was going to send out 3 mailings from headquarters against Neal that might help in my campaign (see samples under "Clandestine Mailings from the Caucus" under "Mailings" in Chapter Eight). As has been described in more detail under "Trying to Play Fund Raising Ball with the Senate Caucus" in Chapter Nine, Perry had the gall to ask me to designate in my financial report these mailing expenditures as "in kind" contributions from the Senate Caucus! I told him in no uncertain terms that that was not going to happen. I had never been informed about the mailers. They focused on Neal's record and I was never mentioned. We were ultimately relieved at the content but frustrated that we had no control over the message or the distribution, particularly so close to the Election.

My overall experience with the early voting process was invigorating. My instincts proved to be correct regarding the supportive feeling at the voting sites.

# Chapter Twelve – Election Day

To paraphrase Charles Shultz's famous quote of "it was a dark and stormy night," November 7th was a cold and rainy day. Had I not been a candidate for public office, I would have stayed in bed until noon! As it was, I was up early and en route to the polls. It was my plan to visit all of the "go to" precinct polling places to "meet the voters" and thank our volunteers who were handing out my literature. It was a testament to the dedication of my volunteers that they not only showed up to support me in this inclement weather but stayed throughout their long shifts in the rain. Their loyalty to me had an impact on the voters many of whom commented to me that they were impressed by their visible support of me in less than ideal circumstances. One of my friends and supporters, Kelly Perrin, described her experience volunteering to Andrea that day as follows:

> *Hi Andrea, we didn't get a sitter, so I think we will bail on tonight [for the "Victory Party"] —to be honest, after a few hours in some pretty cold rain, I am happy to just be sitting here in my sweats and looking out at the weather (not that I wasn't happy to do it, don't get me wrong!). To be honest, I think the rain showed off our dedication—we kept telling everyone that we must feel really strongly about our candidates to be out in that kind of weather! I don't know if the Republicans had more of a presence either earlier or later in the day, but they certainly weren't around when I was at the poll on Ray Road...mostly it was me and a guy named Mark who was campaigning for Ty Harrell, a Democrat running for the NC House of Representatives. So the Democrats were the strong presence in the crappy weather...Mark told one guy that the weather "couldn't have been any worse," and I said, "Don't say that! You'll jinx us! It will start sleeting in a minute!" and then we all laughed. There was one very nice older woman who was campaigning for Neil (sic) Hunt (Gerry's opponent) who showed up, but she couldn't find a sign to hold, for whatever reason did not choose to hand out the Republican lists, and was not dressed for the weather—thin cardigan, no coat, although she did have an umbrella. She stayed and chatted with Mark and me for about a half hour and then left. HA! We ran off the opposition! But anyway, we will be watching the poll results on the TV and keeping our fingers crossed. Good luck! Tell Gerry to have a*

*glass of wine on my behalf!*

The culmination to any political campaign is Election Day! From the get go we had treated November the 7th as our D Day, and had planned accordingly. From the start, one of the first things we asked our supporters was to identify their precinct so that we could potentially cover the polling stations on Election Day. Ultimately, we simply did not have enough volunteers to cover all of the 52 precincts so we did our best to make sure we had someone at the heavily trafficked areas. We were also aware that the Democratic Party was going to have a presence at many of our precincts and so too, the special interest groups such as the Association of Educators who had their own volunteers. We tried as best we could to coordinate with these folks so that there was less duplication of effort and we could spread our resources further. A downside to this generic coverage was the lack of personal interaction with the voters.

One way the Democratic Party helps candidates, is by ensuring yard signs are placed at the relevant polling places for each candidate on Election Day. On the 3rd of November we took enough signs to the selected Democratic Party location so that two signs could be placed at each polling location in which I was on the ballot. When placing my order for yard signs in the summer, I had factored this need into the number I purchased and reserved them for this purpose. But as the demand for our signs grew, I was prepared to take some from supporters' homes to cover the polling needs come Election Day. On Sunday afternoon of November 5th, Andrea and I took any extra signs that we had along with a package of materials to the homes of those folks who were going to cover the early morning shift at the individual polls. There were instructions as to how to pass on the information to subsequent volunteers and how to gather whatever materials remained when the polls closed.

In reflecting on Election Day, I recall feeling a bit surreal and detached from the experience. Though fully aware of what was happening all around me, I felt like a spectator and not a participant. In contrast to the months leading up to the election when I was coordinating many activities, I was without real direction on Election Day and the weeks to follow. I felt vulnerable because the outcome was out of my hands and yet I needed to "do something." I was conflicted in how much to be involved on Election Day. Part of me thought, if they don't know who they are going to vote for by now, then there's nothing more I can do. The other part thought not being involved indicated that I was taking the election for granted. My compromise was to support my team that day. I circulated throughout the polls and tried to bolster the spirits of my volunteers.

This experience stood in contrast to early voting in its finality. At day's end, the campaign would be over. In judicial parlance: the case had been made and now the jury was out. Awaiting the verdict was difficult. Between lunch and the after work/early evening voter "rush" I took a break to prepare chili and to get ready for the election night gathering at my home.

Our committee had decided to have the "Victory Party" at my house. This decision was based on my earlier experience as a candidate for the NC House in 2000. It being a presidential election year with the governor and many of the council of state candidates on the ballot, the entire North Raleigh Hilton was "the place" for most of the Democratic candidates to "watch the returns" and celebrate. In my race for the NC House, I had found camaraderie with Jim Crew, a candidate for the NC Senate whose district overlapped my own. Neither he nor I had gotten any financial support from the NC Democratic Party, not unique to us as I was to later learn. Prior to the election all the candidates received a flier asking if we wanted to sign up for a room at the Hilton in which our campaign could gather. The ballroom was to be used for the "big" races – the governor and council of state. For activists who supported numerous campaigns, this evening could be great fun, affording them a chance to rub elbows with some of the local political elite. Jim and my campaigns' supporters were different. Neither of us was flush with funds on Election Night and our supporters were not political in that way. They were there for us and were more interested in an intimate gathering. Thus, we decided to share the expense of "renting" a suite at the Hilton within which our supporters could celebrate. After reading the small print we discovered that there would be an additional charge to have the beds removed and of course, more money for food. Always mindful of keeping within our budget, we decided to "cater" our own party.

After the polls had closed I went to find our room which was on an upper floor, tucked down a hall and around a corner, not at all easy to locate. Our Election Night was filled with drama. We had the TV set to WRAL, our local affiliate, so that we could all watch as the returns came in. Every time the House races were listed our district would be skipped! I was watching the results come in in real time, surrounded by friends and supporters who were asking me if I knew anything. Rumors were abounding. Someone came to the door and said "Gerry, I think the press wanted to know where you were" which made me think that they knew something that I didn't and to feel hopeful that I might have won. Jim's numbers had been broadcast and he had lost. Betty Lou Ward, our Wake County Commissioner came in and made some well-placed calls to her sources in the media to find out what was going on. She reported that I had lost - no explanation for the many times that my race was passed over in reporting. At least we knew!! Shortly thereafter the ticker tape on the TV popped up confirming the information she had shared with us.

In 2006, even though we decided to celebrate Election Night at my home, the evening was not without drama. Once again the TV news folks let us down. Well into the evening after most races had been called, WRAL gave us all false hope when their numbers were displayed, showing me in the lead even though all precincts had not been counted (in fact, as of November 16$^{th}$, over a week after the election, we were still sorting out the media results with WRAL). But other stations were reporting different numbers, which had us all concerned. Not being privy to which precincts had been counted, I was in the dark about the confusion. Being a grass roots campaign without consultants and number crunchers was telling in this circumstance. I'm sure that members of the Senate Caucus were aware of the numbers but they sure weren't sharing that information with us!

Most of the folks at our gathering had gone home and were in bed before the final numbers were reported. Andrea's email to our supporters the day after the election detailed the unfolding events.

### *Gerry Bowles Election Results – The Picture BIG and small*

*To our wonderful team of friends, family, volunteers, and interested community members:*

*Well, after a very late night first awaiting numbers for District 15's Senate race to be posted, and then riding the rollercoaster of conflicting results with WRAL's coverage showing Gerry in the lead and TimeWarner 14 reporting she was behind, we offer you the "Unofficial 2006 General Election Results" presented on the State Board of Elections site (http://www.sboe.state.nc.us/voterweb/elections.htm):*

*Dorothy (Gerry) Bowles (DEM) 25,277 – 45%*
*Neal Hunt (REP) 30,990 – 55%*

*As a number of calls and e-mails have indicated it seems many of you have been taking this ride with us. We apologize for the continuing confusion. WRAL is still reporting on its website the results as:*

*Gerry Bowles (D) 29,262 - 49%*
*Neal Hunt (i) (R) 30,990 - 51%*

*We have contacted the station and they indicate their results come from the Associated Press. A member of the AP has explained their numbers come from non staff reporters who provide the information from the individual board of elections. The State Board of Elections indicated that it has sent out its unofficial results to media. It would seem that we will have to wait for the official results to be sure of the final breakdown. In the meantime, we are taking some time today to feel the disappointment at the small picture of receiving fewer votes than Neal Hunt.*

*However, leading up to and carrying on from today we are celebrating the many big picture victories of this past election year:*

*1) People*
*Without a doubt, connecting with all of you has been the best outcome of this election process. Whether newer to the campaign or here from the start, your work, supportiveness, and enthusiasm offered continuous and appreciated charges of energy and motivation to the campaign. It is our sincere wish to maintain this wonderful network of supporters who share an interest in helping affect change in their communities. Do keep in touch with us and offer your suggestions on remaining connected with one another.*

*2) Process*
*In a district with a republican voting history, running against an incumbent, and with a truly modest campaign budget, Gerry was separated from her opponent by only 5,713 votes!! This success came from you and others who responded to her call for a people*

focused campaign. Though told her run would not be viable with the budget she was anticipating and in absence of priority being placed on fundraising, Gerry persisted with her grassroots approach of going door-to-door, connecting with voters through all varieties of meet and greets and forums, and involving all she encountered in the process. While a peek at the campaign finance reports posted by the State Board of Elections on their web site shows the difference in monetary resources between the campaigns, the large energy resource of people involved in Gerry's run led to a huge step forward in voter support in the District. You all importantly helped us show that prioritizing citizen involvement can produce competitive outcomes. We hope our campaign serves as inspiration to others to consider in approaching future runs for office.

3) Priorities
With the campaign's large canvassing undertaking connecting with neighbors (Republican, Democrat, and Unaffiliated) at the doors, Gerry has had many discussions regarding her focus on Representation and the need to reprioritize where our District's government should place its energy and focus. We have been heartened by receptiveness of fellow community members and encouraged that party politics need not divide us from one another – we can come together on issues of importance to our community and work to move things forward.

On a final note, though words cannot express the tremendous feeling of gratitude we wish to send you all, we shall try to write them anyway – without your energy, interest, participation and vote we would not have made such fabulous progress on our election journey, nor enjoyed the trip so well. The slide show of memories is rich thanks to you. A particular word of thanks to the many hardy volunteers who stood in the downpour yesterday to be sure that voters knew about Gerry – to paraphrase one great volunteer's words, what stronger endorsement could be given than to be out in that kind of weather!

Our deepest thanks,

*Gerry & Andrea*

<u>Contact Information:</u>
Gerry Bowles
847-9901; Gerry@GerryBowles06.com

Andrea Bertole
793-0160 (home); 741-8690 (cell)
abertole@nc.rr.com or andreabertole@hotmail.com

P.S. It's time to return the Bowles' Blue yard art collection to its originating site. Gerry and I will be taking down signs from the streets over the next few days. Feel free to join in and remove signs from your neighborhood. If you wish, you are welcome to drop off signs to Gerry's (405 Amelia Ave) or remake them into new art – I hear they work well for garage sale advertising.

# Chapter Thirteen - Post Election

So, the results were finalized and I had lost. When all was said and done, the *official* vote count from the State Board of Elections was a 54.9 to 45.1% split of the vote:

| NC STATE SENATE DISTRICT 15 | | |
|---|---|---|
| Name on Ballot | Party | Ballot Count |
| Neal Hunt | REP | 31,478 |
| Dorothy (Gerry) Bowles | DEM | 25,854 |

I never felt that I suffered this loss as much as my friends and family because I knew from the start that I was facing an uphill battle that could be won only if the right circumstances prevailed. Optimistic by nature, my view going in was *"you never know, that's why you have elections!"* So there was disappointment, but the loss while humbling was not life altering. Those things that are really important in life (family, friends, health, integrity, faith and freedom) were still with me the morning after the election. It was not like a natural disaster where I had lost my family or my property. What I had lost was the ability to represent my district in the legislature. I did not have an ambition to build a dynasty or climb a political ladder.

That said, in recalling my feelings after losing the election, awkwardness seems to top the list. I no longer could start the day by initiating conversations with "Hi, I am Gerry Bowles, I am running for a seat in the North Carolina Senate." And there was discomfort in meeting people and wondering if their condolences as to my loss were sincere. The reality is that the morning after, especially following the uncertainty of the results, the question that came to my mind was "now what?"

Personally I found that some doors were open to me whereas others remained shut. I was not a lawmaker, but I didn't exactly fit in where I had "lived" before. Often there was an assumption that I would run for office again. In fact, almost everyone I met after the results were in asked the same question, "Will you run again?" Honestly, it is hard to answer that question so soon after a defeat. My candid answer was, "I try to never say never."

For the previous 8 months, I had been building momentum and excitement, interacting with a growing group of supporters and with this election loss my chance to harness this energy into further action was ended. My disappointment came from not being able to be a part of the legislative process and the perceived loss of the community I had built and shared leading up to the election. The next phase would be a tough transition for me and for others as reflected in Andrea's note to her family in Canada the day after the election:

> *I am resurfacing a bit now with the election done - so strange to go from having every waking moment spoken for to having the election over.*
>
> *Election Day was something else. It poured rain here the entire day so our poor volunteers and Gerry and I got soaked through and through standing at the polling stations - here you not only are allowed but it is common to have candidate greeters at the polling places to make a final pitch for their candidate.*
>
> *In terms of the election results, after a very late night Tuesday first awaiting numbers for District 15's Senate race to be posted, and then riding the rollercoaster of conflicting results with one news station showing Gerry in the lead and another reporting she was behind, the "Unofficial 2006 General Election Results" presented by the State Board of Elections are:*
>
> Dorothy (Gerry) Bowles (DEM) 25,277 – 45%
> Neal Hunt (REP) 30,990 – 55%
>
> *Although one news station is still showing the results as:*
>
> Gerry Bowles (D) 29,262 - 49%
> Neal Hunt (i) (R) 30,990 - 51%
>
> *We have contacted the station and they indicate their results come from the Associated Press. A member of the AP has explained their numbers come from non staff reporters who provide the information from the individual board of elections. The State Board of Elections indicated that it has sent out its unofficial*

*results to media. It would seem that we will have to wait for the official results to be sure of the final breakdown.*

*So bummer! I did so want Gerry to win, but we knew it was going to be quite a challenge to unseat her opponent. Given we live in a district with a republican voting history, running against an incumbent, and with a truly modest campaign budget, the fact that Gerry was separated from her opponent by only 5,713 votes is quite a success. Many in our own party were dismissive of Gerry's chances at the start so I really think we surprised a lot of people with the success of the campaign. We are feeling really good about how we ran the campaign and the people who came to be involved. So while the immediacy of the results still weighs a bit heavily there is lots to feel great about. And of course for me personally, I got so much from the whole process completely separate from the final count.*

*We are so relieved at the national level results with the Dems regaining the House and Senate – whew! Long overdue for some accountability and balance.*

*Chat soon,*
*Andrea*

Communications that came in response to Andrea's email to our supporters about the victories big and small (presented in Chapter Twelve) were reaffirming and a cause for celebration that we had indeed succeeded in engaging people in the political process. Here are a sampling:

- *Gerry and Andrea -- Let me extend to you my deepest appreciation for the leadership you have BOTH exhibited throughout this challenging campaign. Given the circumstances and the relative monetary positions of the candidates, I think the election results are a tremendous victory for Gerry, and a resounding affirmation of your dedication, hard work and solid values. The outcome of the election is binary: either you win or you don't. But the aftermath of the campaign lives on in the hearts and minds of all who have been touched by your true demonstration of democracy in action. We won't forget. And there will be MORE of us next time...My greatest respect to both of you for a battle well-fought and just.*

- *You and Gerry have enriched my life and I am so proud to know you. I think you 2 are a "class act!!" Your grassroots efforts have been an inspiration to many. I really really hope Gerry runs again! If she does, count on me to host a fund raiser! And this time I'll do more for the campaign. I think Gerry is so sweet and kind and genuine. I hope she runs again in the future!*

- *... your door-to-door work made people in your district feel they were an active part of political life. That is a lasting contribution. Thanks for working so hard and doing so well.*

- *Andrea, I know that you are very disappointed, you worked so hard. I do believe that the race was as close as it was because of all the time you and Gerry spent out in the neighborhoods. The positive attitude you both have will serve you well now and in the future. It is a great pleasure to have gotten to know you and I hope that we can continue to build a friendship outside of politics. All my best wishes to you.*

- *Gerry and Andrea -- Even though the election did not turn out like we had hoped, I want to offer you congratulations on running an honest, grassroots campaign. Your enthusiasm and dedication were evident every time I met you and would have been an asset to the people of North Carolina. Also, thank you for allowing me to be a part of your journey; it was the first time that I have been actively involved in a local campaign, and, although I wish I could have given more time, I really enjoyed seeing the process at work. Working on Gerry's campaign rekindled my belief that there is integrity to be found in the current political climate. Yesterday at the polls, several people walked past me with their umbrellas and raincoats and commented that it was a horrible day to be campaigning. I just laughed and said, "Well, I have a great candidate that I believe in!" And, you know what, I really meant it. Thanks again, and please keep me informed of any events or organizations that might be of interest. Here's to a Bowles candidacy in 2008!*

- *You worked very hard for a good candidate who would have made a great senator. You also did a great job for her and I know she is pleased. This is a very tough district for a Democrat to win in any election year.*

- *Meeting and advocating for Gerry was tremendously rewarding for me. In time, we will need to regroup and figure out how to make changes for our future. Gerry represented herself, our party and our community extremely well. Campaign funding needs to be addressed.*

- *Ya'll, It was definitely one of the most exciting, exhilarating, educational times of my life! So many new friends met and so many more to go! Please know how much I love you, Gerry Bowles, and how much you have inspired me as well as countless others who were engaged by your presence. You are truly an inspiring, amazing leader and my personal hero forever. Andrea, I truly feel I have made a new best friend, just when I needed one most. I'll see you real soon and we'll get on with this relationship building and politic talking to get everyone we know on the right track for future success in changing our neighborhoods, towns, and country one person at a time! We don't even have to say we can do it any more -- we really did it! I don't believe our supporters will be surprised when we show back up at their doors. I don't know about you, but I'm having canvassing withdrawals! Let's go again soon!*

- *I am so sorry! The website you mentioned is the one I was using, and so I spent the day in uncertainty. I am disappointed, as I know you are, and I know from talking to other people that we were all surprised and saddened by those results. (One lady at work said she couldn't believe it; everybody, including herself, had Gerry's signs in their yards!) However, you and Gerry ran a clean, organized, energetic campaign, and I think you should be proud of the way you've handled yourselves. I'll talk to you soon*

- *Andrea & Gerry, I know you are disappointed in the election results after you had worked so hard. My wife and I are disappointed too as we think there should be a clean sweep downtown. We do appreciate you coming and talking to the Westinghouse retirees.*

- *Thanks Andrea. Without a doubt, the strong campaign you ran helped me. You ran a textbook grassroots campaign. At some point, I'd like to sit down with you and Gerry and get your advice on how I can duplicate your effort. – Grier Martin, [NC House Representative]*

My treasurer, Gail, and her husband, Alfred, helped provide a first step toward closure by hosting a party for me in December, inviting many of those actively involved in my campaign. This evening gave a wonderful chance to reflect on and celebrate the victories we shared. Three months later, I took a moment to touch base with the many people involved in my campaign with the following email:

*From: abertole@nc.rr.com*
*CC: gerrybowles@yahoo.com*
*To:*
*Subject: A Word from Gerry Bowles*
*Date: Wed, 7 Mar 2007 16:08:50 -0500*

*A little over a year has passed since I filed to run for the NC State Senate Seat in District 15. Over the past 4 months, so many of you have inquired about life after the election. In reflecting on the experience of a political campaign, I want to take a moment again to express how much your involvement meant and how positive the process was.*

*Even though I did not win, I feel great joy that so many people, a number of whom had not considered themselves "political animals," became engaged in the campaign. Whether I met you at one of the 7000 doors the campaign visited, or at the BP over coffee, at your neighbor's home, or at one of the forums I was privileged to be a part of, your support was invaluable and appreciated.*

*Many have asked if my plans for the future include campaigning for political office again. I have learned never to close any door, but have no immediate plans to run.*

*I still remain committed to involving people in the political process and recognize that communities are strengthened when there is a greater intimacy between the people and their government.*

*To that end, I am writing a book to share my campaign experiences in the hopes this will encourage, educate and inform others who are interested in running for office. In addition, I am involved in supporting candidates with a grassroots focus. I have been working with my friend Doris Weaver (www.DorisForChair.org) in her run for the Chair of the Wake County Democratic Party and am following with interest the candidates for the '08 presidential election.*

*Thank you once again for all that you did to make my campaign a success. I hope our paths will cross again.*

*Gerry*

I received many positive replies to this notice ranging from those I met on the trail, friends who were supportive of the campaign and those who were not, leaders of special interest groups, and others like me who had sought office under the Democratic banner. Many of these emails served as a validation that one can make an impact trying to include people in the process. First, four months after the election I was gratified that the relationships I had built in my grassroots campaign were strong enough that folks still felt interested enough to respond. I was particularly honored by an email from Hunter Tapscott, a gentleman with whom I connected early in the campaign with a simple knock at the door and who subsequently invited me to speak at his retirement group, then finally continued with a politically observant reply that showed he was still invested in his government. A note from a friend appreciating the service component of running for office cheered me in its affirmation that not every citizen views everyone in the political arena with a cynical eye:

> *...The people of Wake County owe you a huge thank you for your willingness to stand up and be counted. Your dedication, insight into what needs to happen within government, and between government and people...your integrity, your sense of humor, your capacity to connect with people...and on and on, are traits that need to be used in the public good. I hope you will continue to seek public office in the future. NC needs people like you to represent us.*

Other replies were reassuring in their more personal relevance. Some who had not been active in the campaign and who were not in my camp ideologically took this opportunity to reach out and compliment my efforts. A few responses from leaders of special interest groups were validation that I had earned their respect through my grassroots undertaking. Their interest in my future plans to run for office revealed that I was still someone to be reckoned with. Finally, within the party structure there was a recognition by some that more could have been done for my campaign and a call to action to make sure that all candidates recruited by the party would be well supported.

Given time and reflection, no regrets on my part, but some lessons learned.

# Section 4 – Conclusion: Post Mortem

## Elections Have Consequences

Legislatively, elections have consequences! In his first term one of the main pieces of legislation Neal Hunt introduced was "In Defense of Marriage Act" to make sure that marriage was between a man and a woman. In May of 2012, after redistricting had turned our legislature Republican for the first time in 40 years, he got his way with the passage of an amendment to the NC Constitution making it so. So the notion of Neal Hunt espoused by many in the Democratic leadership and the editorial board of the *News and Observer* as being "not so bad for a Republican," proved to be an illusion.

There was a chance with this election cycle that I could have become the representative in place of Neal Hunt with a more robust embrace by the Democratic leadership at the beginning of the race. I came close to winning. In the subsequent election cycles for this seat, no other grassroots candidate has come closer to victory. Furthermore, even the recent candidate who was well funded and able to financially match the Republican opponent, is not called Senator. It is hard not to wonder if whether something as simple as the seal of approval from the party could have tipped the scales to a win.

## Unintended Consequences

### *Live a More Public Life*

Most folks expect that life will change when you "toss your hat into the ring" but there are things of which you might not be aware. Your life is lived in a fishbowl for a time. As a candidate, ever mindful of how my actions might be perceived, I found myself much more cautious in responding to questions and in voicing my opinions unless asked. One of the positive factors in living like this was that I became a much safer driver - no road rage for me! I also was more careful with my use of humor. In the past, I found that people were not always aware that I was joking with some of my responses. I didn't stop communicating in this manner but tried to be more thoughtful about how my answers might be interpreted. In this regard, I was especially mindful of my email messages. The rule of thumb I used was to ask myself how I would feel if I read the message as a headline on the front page of the *News and Observer*.

If elected, it is understood that your life will become even more public, with privacy possibly becoming a thing of the past. But, what is also true is that your life still changes even if not elected by the sheer act of having been in the public arena for a short time. You don't have the office title but "it ain't over when it's (the election's) over." After having introduced yourself constantly to everyone leading up to the election, you discover that many people feel they know you. Your anonymity is gone.

## *Become a Graduate of the School of Politics*

Being a candidate is an education that you can't pay for - the curriculum is ever changing, requiring strength in multi-tasking. You likely have identified the issues that are important to you and you gain further insight into the passions of your fellow voters. You learn the nuts and bolts of structuring a campaign that fits you personally. Your literal familiarity with the lay of the land in your district grows significantly as does your knowledge of the people within, both those who may vote for you and those who may become more active and volunteer for you. In handling fundraising events, financial reports, and communications linked to your campaign, you develop an awareness of the intricacies behind campaigning. Consistent throughout your education is the strong concentration in the psychological sciences. You are given the opportunity to understand the people behind the issues and at the door, the consultants advising on finances and how to win, the party establishment, and your own campaign team. And throughout the process, your ethics are continually tested. Be aware that everything in your campaign has your name on it and everyone who works on your campaign (your team) is your representative. You will need a strong moral compass to stand up to the "consultants" who try to tell you that up is down. If you don't want to be bought and paid for, don't be. Don't be afraid to challenge the current wisdom and follow your own gut instinct. At the end of the day, I graduated without wearing orange, unlike a number of other political players that were my colleagues who ended up serving time in prison (e.g. former NC Commissioner of Agriculture, Meg Scott Phipps, and former

Speaker of the House, Jim Black). Furthermore, my curriculum didn't lead to being indicted and paying heavy fines, as did my former opponent's, Senator John Carrington.

## *Identified as a Political Expert*

Another outcome of running for office is that you become the resident expert on your political experience. Other candidates seek you out to gain your knowledge about connecting with voters in your district. I have shared many a lunch with hopeful candidates for Mayor, City Council, NC House and Senate who were looking for my thoughts on campaigning in North Raleigh. In addition, high school students and academics have sought me out post-election to participate in surveys about running for office. Less specific to my personal campaign, people recognize me as someone involved in politics and I have become their go-to person for all questions political. I am constantly asked, "what's going on…" with local, state, and federal issues. Just recently, 10 years after running for office, I was asked by a repairman "weren't you in politics?" after which he wanted my views on the presidential candidates and the recent passage of NC-HB2 known by many as the "bathroom bill," one aspect of which requires people to use the bathroom of the sex noted on their birth certificate as opposed to how a person self-identifies. I am even asked to weigh in on who someone should vote for, which I find most troubling and usually respond by redirecting to who I am voting for and why as opposed to who they should vote for. On a more gratifying level, I have been able to help friends connect to the relevant people in local and state government when they have had a problem and didn't know how to navigate the system.

## *Effects on the Family*

Your family is impacted. When I made the decision to run for state office in 1999 my boys were all in college, which was a consideration. My nuclear family was non-political but has become more interested as time has passed. Nonetheless, they all helped in some way. In 2006, all my sons were working in the area so having the same last name became an object of interest to many of their business contacts who were more politically inclined. This circumstance led to interesting dinner table conversations. During one of my election cycles I was running for the State

Senate and Erskine Bowles was a candidate for the US Senate. Folks in my district had the opportunity to vote for two Bowles! Despite his deep Carolina ties and state wide, as well as national, political connections, Erskine, was less well known by my youngest son, Matt. Over one Sunday dinner he asked me "Are we related to 'Ernsky' Bowles? The fellows at work want to know!" By the end of that election cycle they had all become more knowledgeable about the political scene. They were helpful along with their friends in some door-to-door canvassing and Hal was most helpful in all things having to do with shaping and publishing our message. An upside to being a candidate for public office was that all of my sons voted for me the first time they had the right to vote

Being the candidates' spouse can be more difficult than being the candidate - just ask Bill Clinton! Harry was working for one of the foremost commercial development companies in the Triangle at the time. A key issue for my campaign was unprecedented growth and its impact on the environment and education. This industry is often filled with good ole' boys whose attitudes are more aligned with the "can't you keep your wife in line"? mentality. I know without knowing that there were concerns. I was never the darling of this group nor seen as a pro development candidate. I was open to all possibilities about growth and who should pay for the growth and was willing to question the special interests that lobby the legislature on behalf of the industry. As a result, I never earned the endorsement of the realtors or the homebuilders.

Harry took my losses more to heart than I did. He was aggravated with the citizens of Wake County for not electing me. Having been so involved on a personal level, his awareness was heightened regarding the socially conservative stances being taken by the local and state Republican party. After the election he changed his registration to Unaffiliated.

## *Effects on Friendships*

In the words of a great country western song by Rascal Flatts, "You Find Out Who Your Friends Are." My relationships with friends were tested. I discovered that a few I had thought were closer relationships were more acquaintances. Some I suspect did not vote for me but were interested in the campaign and wished me well. Others promised me their vote but were not comfortable participating more actively in my campaign. Then there were some who dropped everything, as in the song, and came to my assistance, resulting in closer, strengthened friendships.

# The Numbers:

There are many ways to measure success. We focused on many factors to determine how well our campaign was doing. Our fundraisers were not just about the money we raised, but were also seen as measuring how many people were becoming engaged in a more intimate level with the campaign and how others might hear of my candidacy because their friends had attended and spoke of it.

### *Voter Turnout*

Returning to the strategic outlook of numbers predicted by my campaign manager, Dan:

Predicted Turnout: 38.5% of 126,776 voters (48,809) requiring 24,405 voters to win

Actual Turnout: 44% of 126,776 voters (56,267) requiring 28,134 voters to win

So, the reality was I exceeded our hoped for number of 24,405 by capturing 25,277 votes. Unfortunately, with the higher voter turnout, which surpassed even the high end (41%) of our calculations, it was not enough coming to just 45% of the votes cast.

### *Precinct Strategy Evaluated - Was This the Right Approach?*

Reviewing the voter turnout in terms of the go-to precincts we had identified as part of our strategy and in terms of the campaign activity focused on those and other precincts, you can appreciate areas of success and challenge (see the Table below). With our nine 1$^{st}$ Tier precincts, we were successful in 6, either winning outright or tying in one. In the remaining 3 precincts we were close, needing only 15, 21, and 34 voters to have switched from my opponent to me in their voting choice to have won or tied.

We were less successful in our ten 2$^{nd}$ Tier precincts, winning only 3 of the 10 precincts, but coming quite close in all but one other – most would have required fewer than 50 voters switching from my opponent to me, and in one case just a change with one voter would have tied the race.

In the 3$^{rd}$ Tier, we won 2 of the 9 precincts and needed fewer than a 50 person vote switch to me from my opponent in 5 of the others. In addition, there were 11 precincts not targeted in our strategy but given some focus in the campaign due to voter interest and volunteer presence. Not surprisingly, we did not win any of these less favorable areas but notably we came within a 50 person switch to victory for 4 of them.

Given that these were the precincts that we were most hopeful of winning, we felt fairly good about our showing.

| Voter Turnout & Campaign Activity for "Go To" Precincts for November 2006 | | | |
|---|---|---|---|
| 1$^{st}$ Priority | | | |
| Precinct | Vote Outcome: GB v NH | | Campaign Activity |
| 07-04 | WIN | 759 v 554 | * Canvassed door-to-door (first area: May 4, 6, 16, 17, 19, 22, 23 & Jun 2)<br>* 5 Campaign Committee members<br>* Precinct Point Person<br>* IAC Member<br>* Covered polls on election day |
| 08-06 | WIN | 314 v 208 | * Covered on election day |
| 01-43 | WIN | 390 v 280 | * Canvassed door-to-door (June 2, 5, 6, 7, & Sep 15)<br>* Katherine Morgan Meet &Greet (Oct 10)<br>* 1 Campaign Committee member<br>* Precinct Point Person<br>* Covered polls on election day |
| 01-51 | TIE | 280 v 280 | * Canvassed door-to-door (Aug 25, Sep 13, 15 & 20)<br>* Covered polls on election day |
| 07-09 | | 424 v 454 | * Literature drop (Oct 16 &19)<br>* Covered polls on election day |
| 07-12 | | 385 v 426 | * Canvassed door-to-door with Dems (Oct 7)<br>* Covered polls on election day |

| | | | |
|---|---|---|---|
| 07-13 | WIN | 325 v 264 | * Literature drop (Oct 21) |
| 13-05 | WIN | 107 v 94 | |
| 01-15 | | 288 v 356 | * Canvass door-to-door (Jun 21&22)<br>* Literature drop (Jun 8, 9 &13)<br>* Precinct Point Person<br>* Covered polls on election day |
| 2nd Priority | | | |
| Precinct | | Vote Outcome:<br>GB v NH | Campaign Activity |
| 01-29<br>(split district) | | 181 v 322 | * Literature drop (Oct 30)<br>* Covered polls on election day |
| 01-30 | | 327 v 382 | * Canvassed door-to-door (Jun 28, 29, 30, Jul 3, 5, 7, 10, 11, 30 & Oct 13)<br>* Dellinger Meet the Mayor Event (Jul 18)<br>* 2 Campaign Committee Members<br>* Precinct Point Person<br>* Covered polls on election day |
| 01-39 | WIN | 466 v 355 | * Canvassed door-to-door (Sep 25, 27, 30, Oct 2 & 13)<br>* Covered polls on election day |
| 01-44 | WIN | 623 v 511 | * Canvassed door-to-door (Aug 17, 18, 24, 30, Sep 7, 8, & 20)<br>* Covered polls on election day<br>* Precinct Point Person |
| 01-45 | | 364 v 375 | * Canvassed door-to-door (Sep 27)<br>* Literature drop (Nov 5) |
| 19-07<br>(split district) | WIN | 255 v 245 | * Meet and Greet (Aug 20) |
| 07-02 | | 234 v 331 | |
| 07-03 | | 318 v 369 | * Canvassed door-to-door (Oct 23)<br>* Lit drop (Oct 24, 25 & 26)<br>* 1 Campaign Committee Member<br>* Precinct Point Person<br>* Covered polls on election day |
| 07-05 | | 366 v 368 | |
| 07-07 | | 668 v 689 | * Canvass door-to-door (Jul 20, 21, 24, 26, 31 & Oct 7)<br>* Make Lemonade Event (Aug 3)<br>* Precinct Point Person<br>* 1 Campaign Committee Member<br>* IAC Member<br>* Covered polls on election day |

| | 3rd Priority | | |
|---|---|---|---|
| Precinct | Vote Outcome: GB v NH | | Campaign Activity |
| 08-01 | | 723 v 787 | * Campaign Committee Member |
| 08-02 | | 671 v 770 | |
| 08-09 | WIN | 352 v 316 | |
| 13-02 | | 289 v 401 | |
| 01-17 | | 237 v 245 | * Canvassed (Jul 3, 5, 6, 7, 10, 18 & Oct 13)<br>* 2 Campaign Committee Members<br>* Precinct Point Person<br>* IAC member<br>* Covered polls on election day |
| 01-18 | | 444 v 519 | * Canvassing (Jul 12 & 13) |
| 01-36 | | 321 v 516 | |
| 01-37 | WIN | 514 v 423 | * Canvassed door-to-door (Sep 22, 29, 30, Oct 3, 9, 10, 12, 13 & 20) |
| 13-06 | | 428 v 447 | |
| Other Precincts Covered | | | |
| Precinct | Vote Outcome: GB v NH | | Campaign Activity |
| 01-11 | | 294 v 849 | * Canvassed door-to-door (Jul 21, Aug 4, 8 & 11)<br>* Precinct Point Person |
| 01-42 | | 425 v 797 | * Canvassed door-to-door (Sep 8)<br>* Campaign Committee member<br>* Precinct Point Person |
| 01-47 | | 375 v 564 | * Campaign Committee Members<br>* IAC member |
| 02-01 (My precinct) | | 646 v 748 | * My precinct and neighborhood<br>* Pre-Independence Day invitation drop (Jun 15, 19, & 21)<br>* Pre-Independence Day Ice Cream Social Event (Jul 27th)<br>* Strong Women's Tea Event (Sep 10)<br>* Goodberry's event (Oct 1)<br>* 5 Campaign Committee Members<br>* Precinct Point Person |
| 02-02 | | 679 v 1065 | * Canvassed door-to-door (Jul 12)<br>* 5 Campaign Committee Members<br>* Precinct Point Person |
| 02-03 | | 457 v 879 | * Coachman's Trail Meet & Greet with Rodger Koopman (Oct 11) |

| | | | |
|---|---|---|---|
| 02-05 | | 202 v 281 | * Pre-Independence Day invitation drop (Jun 19)<br>* 3 Campaign Committee Members<br>* Precinct Point Person |
| 07-06 | | 610 v 725 | * Canvassed door-to-door Jul 24, 26, Jul 20, 21 & 31<br>* Precinct Point Person |
| 07-11 | | 250 v 298 | * Precinct Organized Ice Cream Social (Jun 25)<br>* Dieter-Maradei Meet & Greet (Aug 29)<br>* Campaign Committee Member<br>* Precinct Point Person |
| 08-04 | | 366 v 460 | * Desert and Dancing (May 24)<br>* Rodham Meet & Greet with Rodger Koopman (Jul 9)<br>* Campaign Kickoff with David Price (Aug 8)<br>* 4 Campaign Committee Members<br>* Precinct Point Person |
| 19-12 | | 283 v 380 | * Canvassed door-to-door (Aug 9, 11, 15)<br>* Oakforest Event (Aug 20) |

## *People Raising*

A huge sense of accomplishment in my election came from the large numbers of people I engaged in my campaign. From a starting point of roughly 200 contact names in my database in mid-April, I grew the contact database to 3,282 people by Election Day. Of this number, 1,101 members (1/3$^{rd}$) had been engaged enough to give me their email addresses and receive campaign updates. Reflecting that I was able to state at my September 7$^{th}$ campaign meeting that we had 50 days of canvassing under our belts, tackling 15 precincts and knocking on approximately 3,900 doors, I appreciate the success this demonstrates in terms of my goal to run a grassroots campaign. The following Table summarizes the growth in the numbers associated with engaging voters in the political process:

| Engagement of People in the Political Process |||||
|---|---|---|---|---|
| Timing in the Campaign | Number of Contacts in Database | Email Addresses for Contacts | Doors Knocked/Lit Drops | Events Attended* |
| Apr 17 | 200 | Approx. 130 | Started in May | 0 |
| Jun 13 | 1300 | 360 | Approx.1500** | 5 |
| Jul 12 | 1700 | 475 | 1850-1900 | 11 |
| Jul 27 | 2000 | 520 | 2450-2500 | 14 |
| Sep 7 | 3000 | 720 | 3900 | 27 |
| Oct 18 | 3224 | 1057 | Over 5000 | 43 |
| Nov 8 | 3282 | 1101 | Approx. 7000 | 45 |

\* Events for Gerry, Community Events, Forums and Democratic Party Events
\*\* Based on our average of 100 doors per day and 15 days of canvassing 4 precincts

## *Funds Raised & Expenses*

In reflecting on the campaign's success, a huge area of disappointment was in the financial realm (see Table below). As I have indicated previously, I just didn't receive the same amount as in past campaigns. I don't feel there was less enthusiasm in supporting me, rather, this difference may be attributed to a shorter campaign cycle. With just 8 months versus 19 months to ask supporters for contributions, there was less opportunity for repeated solicitations. Also, I was reluctant to ask the same people for additional funds. With 20/20 hindsight, I would have "gone to the well" more frequently and hopefully been able to finance some TV spots.

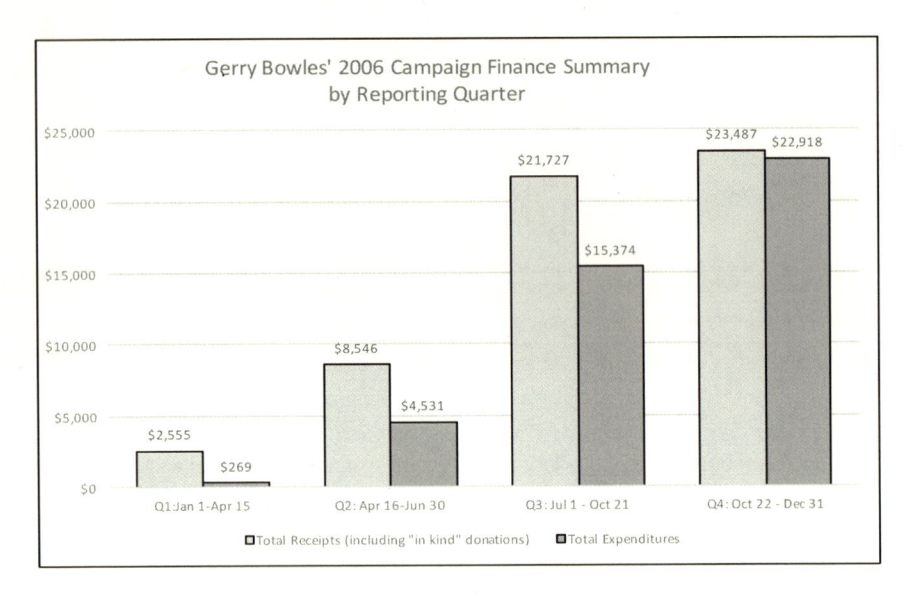

**Gerry Bowles' 2006 Campaign Finance Summary by Reporting Quarter**

| Quarter | Total Receipts (including "in kind" donations) | Total Expenditures |
|---|---|---|
| Q1: Jan 1 - Apr 15 | $2,555 | $269 |
| Q2: Apr 16 - Jun 30 | $8,546 | $4,531 |
| Q3: Jul 1 - Oct 21 | $21,727 | $15,374 |
| Q4: Oct 22 - Dec 31 | $23,487 | $22,918 |

In terms of expenses, on the whole I ran a tight ship. One area that didn't pan out was tied to my campaign message on transportation linked to "no tolls." I had spent time and money on this issue that did not seem to catch fire with *my* voters. The campaign had 2 websites; gerrybowles06.com and www.stop540toll.com. The second site was a vehicle for getting the message out that I was opposing this action on toll roads but a good amount of the traffic seemed to be from other parts of the country and world (as far as Australia) and less locally. Those who were local, were not my voters but lived in the immediately affected areas. I had also spent money on "no toll" stickers for cars but few were used in our district and I still have many in my possession even after sending dozens around the world. In lieu of this decision I would have directed these funds to the more traditional "Gerry Bowles for Senate" bumper stickers.

While the Table above with my campaign finance summary shows that I received more funds than I spent, in reality I had to pay for outstanding expenses. The discrepancy comes from having to include a monetary amount for "in kind" contributions. Sadly, I could not pay my vendors with brownies. Some candidates hold post-election fund raisers to pay off their outstanding campaign debt. I didn't feel comfortable doing so. I made a decision to spend more, thinking the funds would be there and I didn't feel right in asking others to pay for my miscalculation.

In comparing my quarterly financial reports to Neal Hunt's, the David and Goliath aspect of our budgets is obvious (see the Table below). Just call me David. From the beginning, the contrast was stark. The State Board of Elections reported that on December 30$^{th}$, 2005 my opponent lent his campaign $100,000, likely to ward off any primary opposition. By contrast, I lent my campaign 1/100$^{th}$ of that at $1,000. In addition, the grassroots nature of our contributions can be seen in my receiving 246 contributions from individuals versus my opponent's receiving just 123 such contributions. Furthermore, while I received $1,400 from Political Action Committees, my opponent received $9,300, almost seven times as much.

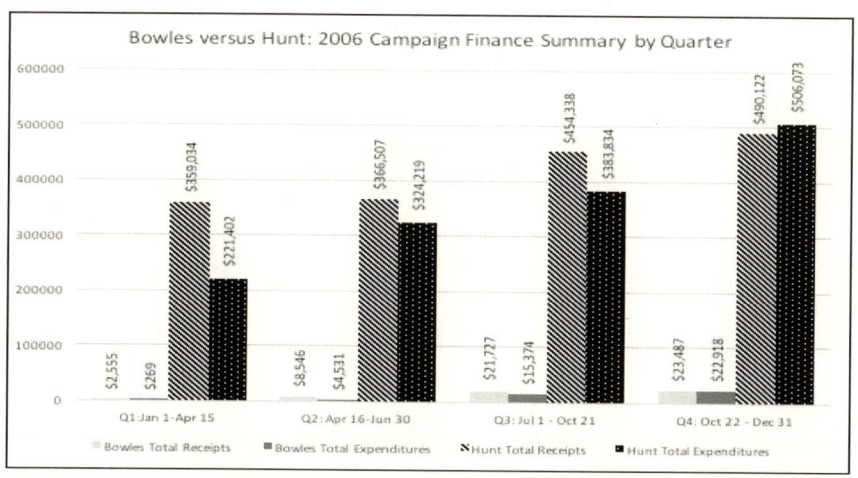

**Bowles versus Hunt: 2006 Campaign Finance Summary by Quarter**

| Quarter | Bowles Total Receipts | Bowles Total Expenditures | Hunt Total Receipts | Hunt Total Expenditures |
|---|---|---|---|---|
| Q1: Jan 1 - Apr 15 | $2,555 | $269 | $359,034 | $221,402 |
| Q2: Apr 16 - Jun 30 | $8,546 | $4,531 | $366,507 | $324,219 |
| Q3: Jul 1 - Oct 21 | $21,727 | $15,374 | $454,338 | $383,834 |
| Q4: Oct 22 - Dec 31 | $23,487 | $22,918 | $490,122 | $506,073 |

Finally, it is interesting to compare the vote split over the subsequent years for NC Senate District 15 versus the budgets at play (see Table below). Mine was presumably the 2$^{nd}$ smallest budget (unclear what Mintz's and Deegan's final numbers were) and likely had the fewest expenditures after Malone. For all of that, I got a greater percentage of the vote than 2012's Hutchinson who had close to 6 times the receipts as me. The Democrat that came closest to winning had a budget of over one million dollars (almost 46 times greater than mine). Money alone has not seemed to lead to a win. Achieving the vote split I did with financially so little in relation to my opponent and other Democratic candidates, I feel affirmed in my belief that a grassroots campaign stood as a sound way to make inroads with voters in my district.

| Election Year | Democratic Candidate for NC Senate District 15 | % of vote for candidate | % of vote for opponent[1] | Receipts as of 4th Quarter | Expenditures as of 4th Quarter |
|---|---|---|---|---|---|
| 2006 | Gerry Bowles | 45.10 | 54.90 | $23,487 | $22,918 |
| 2008[2] | Chris Mintz | 42.89 | 52.83 | $19,159 [3] | $11,582 [4] |
| 2010 | Charles Malone | 39.45 | 60.55 | $7,690 | $7,690 |
| 2012[5] | Sig Hutchinson | 44.18 | 54.9 | $136,664 | $135,073 |
| 2014 | Tom Bradshaw | 49.57 | 50.43 | $1,074,288 | $1,071,120 |
| 2016[6] | Laurel Deegan-Fricke | 45.69 | 50.01 | unavailable[7] | unavailable[8] |

[1] Neal Hunt was the Republican winning candidate from 2006-2012; John Alexander has been the Republican representative from 2014 until now.

[2]&[6] 2008 and 2016 had a percentage of the vote going to the Libertarian candidate.

[3] & [4] No campaign finance reports listed by the NC State Board of Elections for Chris Mintz in 2008 for the third or fourth quarters - amounts provided are from second quarter report.

[5] First election year after the Republican led redistricting process following the 2010 US Census – in 2016 the state legislative district maps were cited for illegal racial gerrymandering.

[7] & [8] The data has not yet been summarized on the State Board of Elections website.

## What Next?

After the election, I took time to celebrate the holidays with my family. In the New Year, I was ready to reflect on the campaign and figure where best to direct my energies. The loss of community working together toward a goal hit me particularly hard with this defeat. I felt cynical about party establishments and yet reluctant to speak about it lest it be seen as sour grapes. I felt I needed to disengage from the political scene for a time and be more selective in where I spent my days. Never having lost my passion for engaging people in the process, I decided to move forward in writing about my campaign experiences in the hope of their being a blueprint of sorts for others interested in undertaking a grassroots approach to running for office. I had in mind from the start to write a book and would say often to folks that I would be writing about some of the things that amazed me along the way. With this ongoing idea, I had documented much anticipating that I would share my journey. With luck, one of my partners on the campaign trail, Andrea, was able to join me in this new undertaking. Meeting regularly over the following year provided structure, focus, and a new goal. Two heads were indeed better than one in recalling and recapturing the campaign highlights in our first rough draft.

In 2008, two years after my campaign, Barrack Obama gave me the spark and opportunity to return to the doors. I campaigned in 5 states on his behalf and was fortunate to be present for his acceptance speech at the Democratic National Convention in Colorado.

Andrea and I never dreamed this journey would last longer than the campaign, now stretching to a decade, but life happens, as it did in the campaign itself. Babies were born, sons were married, trips were taken, parents died, Obama was elected twice and I welcomed grandchildren, gaining the happy title of Gigi.